IN DEFIANCE OF THE LAW

IN DEFIANCE OF THE LAW

❖ ❖ ❖

The Standing-Army Controversy,

The Two Constitutions, and the Coming

of the American Revolution

❖ ❖ ❖

by John Phillip Reid

The University of North Carolina Press
Chapel Hill

For All The Finnegans
of Madbury Road

© 1981 The University of North Carolina Press
All rights reserved
Manufactured in the United States of America
ISBN 0-8078-1449-0
Library of Congress Catalog Card Number 80-14002

Library of Congress Cataloging in Publication Data

Reid, John Phillip.
In defiance of the law.

(Studies in legal history)
Includes Index.
1. Standing army. 2. United States. Army—
History—18th century. 3. Great Britain. Army—
History—18th century. 4. United States—Constitu-
tional history. 5. Great Britain—Constitutional
history. I. Title. II. Series.
UA25.R44 343.73'015 80-14002
ISBN 0-8078-1449-0

CONTENTS

CONTENTS

CONTENTS

CONTENTS

IN DEFIANCE OF THE LAW

WE BEG LEAVE to present our most dutiful Thanks to your Majesty, for having taken such steps as You judged necessary for supporting the Constitution, and for repressing that Spirit of Faction and Disobedience, Which, in the chief Town of one of your Majesty's Colonies, appears to have proceeded even to Acts of Violence, in direct Defiance of all legal Authority.—Address of the House of Commons, 8 November 1768

YOUR GENERALS then reaped laurels abundantly, and transmitted them to you in the triumphant assurance, that *they were in full possession of the town.* Such was their phrase for *quartering troops there in defiance of law*, and making a hostile parade in the midst of peace.—Junius Americanus to the earl of Hillsborough, 12 October 1769

WE YET ENTERTAIN the Hopes that the Military Power so grievious to the People, will soon be removed from the Province, to Stations where it may better answer the Design for which it was originally rais'd. Till then, we have nothing to expect but that Tyranny and Confusion will still prevail, in Defiance of the Laws of the Land, and the just and constitutional Authority of Government.—Massachusetts Bay House of Representatives to Lieutenant Governor Thomas Hutchinson, 23 April 1770

❖ 1 ❖

A TOWN LESS FREE:

INTRODUCTION

A dimension is missing from our histories of the American Revolution: the dimension of law. The reason is not that the importance of law has been unacknowledged, but that its role often has been unrecognized, its principles frequently misapplied, and its significance generally undeveloped. Historians admit that the Revolution had something to do with law, yet, when they write of law during the revolutionary era, they assume that law meant what it does today—that it was the command of the sovereign. They do not discuss law as defined in the 1760s; they do not speak of it as John Adams or Lord Mansfield spoke of it. According to most accounts, the controversy, starting with the Stamp Act and continuing to the Declaration of Independence, was a debate turning largely on constitutional issues. When historians discuss those issues, however, they write as if the participants were arguing about a single constitution. They do not notice that the imperial government premised its claims on the eighteenth-century British constitution of parliamentary supremacy, while American whigs defended colonial rights by appealing to the seventeenth-century English constitution of customary restraints on arbitrary power.

The double mistake leads historians into a triple error. Thinking more like lawyers than historians, they define eighteenth-century law with twentieth-century exactitude. Knowing the American Revolution occurred during the eighteenth century, they overlook the possibility that colonial whigs found their constitutional arguments in the seventeenth-century law of Sir Edward Coke, John Hampden, and John Pym. One result has been that the constitutional theory of American whigs has never been accorded the credit it deserves.

To measure the dimensions that are missing, no topic is more revealing than the standing-army controversy. Although writers have noted its importance to the prerevolutionary debate,[1] the fact that it was a legal argument turning on correct interpretations of two different sets of constitutional variables has not been given its due. The British defended the constitutionality of their standing army on the grounds it was sanctioned by Parliament. American whigs replied that a standing army in the colonies was unconstitutional because Parliament alone could not give it constitutional sanction. A modern assumption would be that one of these interpretations of the constitution had to be in error. This would be a mistake. Twentieth-century constitutional certitude must not be imposed on eighteenth-century constitutional issues. The obviously constitutional may have been less obvious than has been realized.

There are other dimensions that the standing-army controversy, when studied from the perspective of law, adds to our knowledge of the American Revolution. One is the degree to which eighteenth-century Americans thought seventeenth-century English thoughts. Hostility to standing armies by colonial whigs was not an isolated phenomenon conjured by radical spokesmen to harass British imperial policy. It was an intellectual legacy of seventeenth-century English constitutionalism from which the defenders of American opposition to military intervention in government inherited not only the substance of their arguments, but also much of their vocabulary.

Another dimension is provided by nonconstitutional, or positive, law. Rules regulating the military's role as a police force deserve more attention than they have received. Historians have noted that the British army was sent to North America in the 1760s and 1770s to enforce imperial law, and have assumed it was empowered to act as imperialists are known to act. Histo-

1. See especially 1 Bailyn, *Pamphlets*, at 41–43, 44, 71–74.

rians have also emphasized that no colonial whig was arrested, no houses occupied, and no towns placed under martial law, and have written of British "forbearance."[2] The story that is told, therefore, reveals less than half the tale. Ignoring law has meant overlooking the historical fact that the imperial army, because of legal principles originating in the standing-army controversy, had no role to play; as a police force it was constitutionally impotent.

The evidence presented in this book deals not only with jurisprudential ideas, but also with a manner of arguing and a manner of thinking. There are words and sentences needing more attention than has been realized. All too often, later generations have dismissed as political propaganda statements that people in the eighteenth century evaluated as pronouncement of legal or constitutional principles.

A difference between the twentieth century and the prerevolutionary era is that today the tendency is to be more careless with words, labeling as "political" things the eighteenth century knew were "legal." The standing-army controversy might be better understood today if the constitutional nature of the argument were kept in sight. The "Controversy about a Standing Army," the Reverend Samuel Johnson explained in 1697, "is a dispute betwixt Legions and Laws,"[3] and American whigs agreed. When they protested against the British army that was stationed in their seaports during peacetime, they were appealing, not to a political theory of what should be, but to a customary constitution that ordained the legally permissible. "A military Force," the Massachusetts House of Representatives protested, "if posted among the People, without their express Consent, is itself, one of the greatest Grievances, and threatens the total subversion of a free Constitution: Much more, if

2. *In a Defiant Stance*, at 169–73.
3. Johnson, *Works*, at 321.

❖ 5 ❖

designed to execute a system of corrupt and arbitrary Power, and even to exterminate the Liberties of the Country."[4] The reason, a whig told a Boston newspaper, was that it was "universally allow'd by the supporters of English Liberty, that the keeping up standing Armies, to enforce upon British Subjects, Laws, made by a British Parliament, is entirely subversive of their Rights and just Claims."[5]

It would not do to put these words in an American context only. Better to relate them to their origins: to the constitutional disputes that shaped legal attitudes in the mother country. Consider the argument of Philip Yorke when, as the earl of Hardwicke, he addressed the House of Lords nine years before the prerevolutionary controversy between Great Britain and her American colonies commenced.

> What do the Commons do in every Mutiny Bill, which they annually send up to your lordships? They constantly insert the same preamble, and repeat the recitals. "That a standing army in time of peace; execution of martial law in a time of peace, are against law."
>
> These points are as known established law, and declared by as expressed acts of parliament still in force, as the power of the crown over the militia; and yet are always repeated by way of continual claim, even in Bills, which import no repeal, nor colour of repeal, but proceed on the contrary supposition. And I hope the Commons will always continue to adhere to this practice. It is right in such fundamental points.[6]

It is the speaker that gives this statement significance. Many of Yorke's countrymen made the same point in clearer language.

4. *Gazette and Post-Boy*, 30 April 1770, at 1, col. 2.

5. *Post*, 10 September 1770, at 4, col. 1.

6. Speech of Lord Chancellor Hardwicke, Lords Debates of 24 May 1756, 15 *Parliamentary History*, at 727–28n; [Hardwicke,] *Two Speeches*, at 42–43.

He is quoted because of who he was. Admitted as a barrister at the Middle Temple, he had been a bencher of Lincoln's Inn, solicitor general of England, privy councillor, chief justice of the king's bench, and at the time he spoke was lord chancellor, which placed him at the head of the English bar. He was, therefore, one of the most prominent common lawyers of the century, and what he said bears close attention. Yorke not only agreed with the Massachusetts House and the writer to the Boston newspaper that standing armies were unconstitutional. He insisted that Parliament when enacting the annual Mutiny Bill—the statute that made the unconstitutional legal—should continue to reiterate its unconstitutionality.

If the notion of the legal unconstitutionality of the Mutiny Act seems strange today, it is because of the assumption that what was "constitutional" and "legal" in the eighteenth century can be equated with the modern definitions of "constitution" and "law." The idea did not puzzle people in the eighteenth-century. It was not a legalism known only to lawyers. The army, a pamphleteer wrote the commander in chief of the armed forces in Great Britain, "by the Letter of our Constitution . . . undoubtedly is, a temporary and occasional Establishment" that was "by a kind of political Necessity, rendered permanent and engrafted as it were on the Being of the State."[7] The writer of a military tract in 1761 was even more explicit. "A standing army," Campbell Dalrymple conceded, "is universally known to be contrary to law in this kingdom; however, the continuance of it from year to year, is, unfortunately for the advocates against it, as great a proof of the necessity of having it, as of its being unconstitutional."[8]

Claiming the unconstitutional had, by necessity, been made constitutional, Dalrymple was suggesting that an old constitutional debate had ended. He was wrong. It would not only

7. Anon., *Letter to Granby*, at 20.
8. Dalrymple, *Military Essay*, at 153.

continue to be a factor in British politics, but it was also about to cross the Atlantic and become a major grievance for American whigs. Indeed, the colonial argument would echo what was being said in London, and would also resurrect much seventeenth-century rhetoric, in part because colonial whigs, like the lawyers who had opposed Charles I and James II, defined "law" as an entity existing separate from power, an immutable apparatus of customs that could not be altered by mere government command. Oliver Saint-John, solicitor general of England, had that concept of law in mind when, during the first great constitutional confrontation of the year 1641, he told the Lords why the Commons had attainted the earl of Strafford for advising the king to enforce his will by military might. "The Law said, he should not thus proceed in subversion of it," Saint-John explained, "he saith, he will, and will enforce obedience by the Army."[9] The next year, the English Civil War commenced, and it became an historical truism during the eighteenth century that the cause was Parliament's fear that Charles I would attempt to rule as Strafford had advised. The Parliament, a writer explained in 1710, was "doubtless very apprehensive of the Danger that threaten'd the Constitution from this Encrease of Power on the Crown side, and therefore endeavoured to have the Militia settled by Act of Parliament in such a way that it might not be made use of to destroy the People's Liberties; and the King's utterly refusing to consent to this, seems to be the principal point that occasion'd that fatal War between him and his Parliament."[10]

The eighteenth-century result of this seventeenth-century heritage was as much a matter of political rhetoric as of constitutional law. All during the time that military necessity was eroding the constitutional prohibition against professional soldiers,

9. Saint-John, *Argument of Law*, at 20.
10. [Clement,] *Faults on Both Sides*, at 5.

❖ 8 ❖

adherents of limited government continued to resist. To claim
that William III needed a standing army for foreign wars, a
writer argued, was "odious language from the mouth of a Whig,
with whom it should be a maxim never to be departed from, not
to trust the Crown with any such overbalance of power as can
enable it to endanger the liberties of the nation."[11] From that
premise—that unchecked power could not safely be vested in
government—two other principles followed that formed a constitutional creed espoused by political theorists fearful of power.
The first was that use of soldiers as police endangered constitutional liberty. As the influental *Cato* contended, "What is got by
Soldiers, must be maintained by Soldiers."[12] The second was
that laws needing military enforcement were not properly "law"
and should not be enforced. One quotation should be enough to
outline the theory, especially because it comes from a period
before the British government made a practice of using troops to
police civilians. Following the Rising of '45, London undertook
to destroy the power of the Scottish clans by altering the governance of the Highlands. The cure was more dangerous than the
disease, ten dissenting lords protested, because

> such an Alteration of Government may necessitate the
> Introduction of a military Force. A fatal Symptom. When it
> can even be mention'd in a *British* Parliament, that a Mea-
> sure avowedly ineffectual for the Safety of Government,
> and evidently unnecessary for the publick Utility, must,
> probably, be carried into Execution by military Force,
> which, if allowed, and not exerted, must produce an Influ-
> ence of the most pernicious Kind; if exerted, establishes
> a military Government of the most dangerous Nature,
> because marked under the former Civil Government, a

11. [Clement,] *Faults on Both Sides*, quoted in Holmes and Speck, *Divided
Society*, at 102–3.
12. Thomas Gordon, Letter 25, 15 April 1721, "Cato's Letters," at 71.

Practice tending, in either Case, totally to subvert the Constitution of this Country, and to which, therefore, we can never consent.[13]

It was this constitutional history, producing these constitutional misgivings, that explains why the decision of the British ministry in 1768 to station troops in what London regarded as the "rebellious" town of Boston cannot be evaluated in an American context only. Few actions during the prerevolutionary era were more fraught with constitutional innovations. From the perspective of American whigs, the occupation of one of their towns violated two tenets of the current British constitution. First, it compounded an earlier illegality, the creation of an American establishment[14] following the French and Indian War. Second, should soldiers be employed to police colonial civilian

13. Protest of 21 May 1747, 2 *Lords' Protests*, at 238–39; 2 *Protests of the Lords*, at 51.

14. The word establishment is used in this book as eighteenth-century speakers used it. For example, Governor George Johnstone told the Commons: "No man is less desirous of augmenting a military establishment than myself. I foresee that the liberties of this country must, in the end, fall a sacrifice to that power which has annihilated the rights of mankind in other states. Between the danger from abroad, and the danger from those who are to defend us, according to the present establishments of *Europe*, the situation is very nice." Speech of Johnstone, Commons Debates of 16 December 1774, 1 *American Archives*, at 1480. The word was not precisely used, sometimes referring to the military organization, sometimes to its size, and sometimes to its aspects of permanency. Establishment also referred to a purpose for which taxes were raised or to a fund in the public treasury or a purpose for which taxes were expended. Thus the town of Boston protested a scheme to pay Massachusetts judicial salaries out of the royal treasury by arguing: "Such an Establishment is contrary not only to the plain and obvious sense of the Charter of this Province, but also some of the fundamental Principles of the Common Law." The same petition also contended that "the establishment" was "pregnant with such fatal Evils as that the most distant thoughts of its taking effect fills their minds with dread and horror." Petition of the Town of Boston to Governor Thomas Hutchinson, 30 October 1770, 18 *Town Records*, at 91.

political activities, American constitutional rights could not only be radically altered, they could also be rendered substantively different from those enjoyed by fellow British subjects living in England, Scotland, and Wales. These apprehensions were not American constitutional apprehensions alone. They were British constitutional apprehensions, the residue for colonial whigs of a shared English constitutional history.[15]

Two quotations from the other side of the Atlantic emphasize that opposition to standing armies was not a constitutional grievance concocted by American whig politicians. It was a fear central to English constitutionalism, a constitutional standard vital to the preservation of British liberty. The first may have been written by no less a British minister than George Grenville, the man responsible for the "ill-considered attempts . . . to establish a permanent force of some ten thousand English soldiers in America, and to raise money by parliamentary taxation."[16] Not only is there some truth in saying that Grenville "produced the American revolution,"[17] but, as head of the king's ministry, he had also used the navy to enforce Great Britain's customs laws in North America, a precedent for ordering the army to police Boston. Yet, in the year British regulars were sent to Massachusetts Bay, he was credited by contemporaries with restating the constitutional demurrer against employing troops in the governance of civilians. "[T]o encrease the military standing force of this country, in time of peace, under any pretence," a pamphlet attributed to Grenville argued, "must always be a suspicious, and some time or other a fatal measure, and that it matters not whether the military power of the crown be increased in Ireland or in Great Britain."[18]

15. Acherley, *Britannic Constitution*, at 57.
16. G. F. Russell Barker, "George Grenville," 23 *Dictionary of National Biography* 113, 116 (1890).
17. Ibid.
18. [Grenville,] *Letter to Grafton*, at 23–24.

❖ 11 ❖

Second are the words of Sir Charles Bingham, which are
worthy of attention as much as for where he wrote as what he
said. They were published neither in the American colonies nor
Great Britain, but in Ireland. If any subject of George III was
likely to think that standing armies were constitutional in peacetime, it would have been an Irish Protestant like Bingham, who
conceded some regulars were necessary "to protect our Gover-
nours from Mobs, Parade at the [Dublin] Castle, to quell sudden
insurrections, and to keep up the Dignity of the Magistrate."[19]
An Irish baronet who knew his religion needed military force to
maintain its ascendancy, Bingham remained English enough to
worry about the constitutional risk. Although Ireland might
have to have a standing army, it should be strictly limited.
"More than this Number," he warned, "may be dangerous to
our Liberties, and might occasion worse Evils than those we
wish to prevent."[20]

Any Number of Royal Troops, in a Country where the
People are unarmed, is alarming to the Liberties of the
People, for whatever Purpose they are instituted, however
cloathed, armed or lodged, they may easily be made the
Instruments of destroying a Free Constitution; being sepa-
rated from the rest of their Fellow Citizens, having other
Customs, and subject to other Laws, they imagine they
have separate Interests, and as they draw their only Subsistence, in some Shape, from Oppression, they may become
the Tools of Tyranny.[21]

If these constitutional ideals were held by a Protestant living
in the relative insecurity of county Mayo during 1767, it is no
wonder that American whigs were constitutionally aroused the
next year when British forces took up stations of occupation in

19. [Bingham,] *Essay on Militia in Ireland*, at 17.
20. Ibid.
21. Ibid., at 18–19.

what for 140 years had been the free town of Boston. By the most fundamental principles of the constitution they professed to cherish, it had become a town less free.

❖ 2 ❖

IN EXECUTION OF THE LAWS:

THE BRITISH INNOVATION

Two regiments of British regulars landed in the capital town of the Massachusetts Bay Colony on the first day of October 1768. Details of why they came or where they encamped are of less concern than that they were not opposed. That fact no longer seems surprising to scholars of the American Revolution. They do not expect to encounter bloodshed when reading of the prerevolutionary era. Colonial whigs resisted by law, not by force. British military officers of the time, however, had anticipated a violent reception. When the disembarkation proved peaceful, they could not credit whig assertions that there never had been much likelihood of armed resistance. "I am in possession of the town," the commanding officer of the army regiments wrote the commodore of British naval units in North America, "and therefore nothing can be apprehended; had we not arrived so critically, the worst that could be apprehended must have happened."[1] The officer's assessment of what might have been does not need to be questioned. His words are striking enough. When he said "I am in possession of the town," he was privately stating what was the most public of whig worries.

There were different ways for imperialists to state their inten-

---

1. Lieutenant Colonel William Dalrymple, quoted in letter from Commodore Samuel Hood to George Grenville, 15 October 1768, 4 *Grenville Papers*, at 376.

tions. The king sent troops to Boston, General Thomas Gage explained, "to protect his loyal subjects in their persons and properties, and to assist the civil magistrates in the execution of the laws."[2] A London newspaper was more blunt. Sufficient forces had been ordered to Boston, it reported, to "intimidate those people to comply with the laws enacted in England."[3] One explanation was as objectionable to American whigs as the other.

"All business is at a stand here," James Otis wrote a London merchant from Boston, "little going on besides military musters reviews and other parading of the Red Coats, sent here, the Lord I believe only knows for what."[4] Almost everyone else, on both sides of the Atlantic, knew "for what." Moreover, they knew Lord Hillsborough had dared initiate a measure from which all his predecessors had shrunk.[5] Troops were in Massachusetts "to support the earl of H[illsboroug]h's measures," *Junius* charged.[6] Those measures, *Junius Americanus* agreed, sought to abolish "the whole system of civil liberty in the Colonies, by *rendering the military power in* Boston, *supreme and uncontrolable.*"[7] The point was stated even more emphatically by a committee of the town. The soldiers, it insisted, were "forced upon us contrary to our inclination—contrary to the spirit of Magna Charta—contrary to the very letter of the Bill of Rights, . . . and without the

2. Letter from General Thomas Gage to Certain Members of the Massachusetts Council, 28 October 1768, *Chronicle*, 31 October 1768, at 524, col. 2; *Annual Register, 1768*, at 253.

3. Quoted in *Chronicle*, 17 October 1768, at 401, col. 3.

4. Letter from James Otis to Arthur Jones, 20 November 1768, 43 *Massachusetts Historical Society Proceedings* 493 (1910). See also Labaree, *Patriots and Partisans*, at 24.

5. Christie and Labaree, *Empire*, at 122.

6. 39 *Gentleman's Magazine* (1769), at 67.

7. Letter to Lord Hillsborough, 16 February 1770, [Lee,] *Junius Americanus*, at 22.

desire of the civil magistrates, to aid whom was the pretense for sending the troops hither."[8]

The fact was, whigs knew, Hillsborough had established in America the very program his colleagues in the cabinet were criticized for following at home. He had reacted to a situation of political discontent by seeking a military solution. "Instead of *preventing* complaints by removing the causes," Benjamin Franklin explained, "it has been thought best that Soldiers should be sent to *silence* them."[9] Put even more strongly, Lord Hillsborough sent troops "to create rather than appease disorders."[10] Before concluding that this statement is hyperbole, consider that, in an official report, the Massachusetts council would speak harsher words of Thomas Hutchinson, the lieutenant governor of the province and chief justice of the superior court. "So far as his Excellency has been instrumental in procuring regiments to be sent hither," it charged, "he has been instrumental in effecting a measure which has been productive of great confusion and bloodshed."[11]

❖ 3 ❖

IN A REBELLIOUS SPIRIT:

ARGUMENTS OF FACT

The Massachusetts council did not speak idly. The charge leveled against Thomas Hutchinson was one of the most serious in the

8. *Short Narrative*, at 8.

9. *London Chronicle*, 8 November 1770, reprinted in *Franklin's Letters to the Press*, at 217.

10. Anon., *Letter to Hillsborough*, at 35.

11. Report of the Executive Council, 24 June 1773, *Gazette and Post-Boy*, 28 June 1773, at 2, col. 2.

whig criminal code. Tales told to London, it was believed, were responsible for much of the growing animosity between the American colonies and Great Britain.

For Massachusetts whigs, the case was proven. It was evident from the London press, which reported that the temper and conduct of the colonies was becoming "every day more licentious,"[1] or published exaggerated reports such as that Bostonians "threatened to pull down the Custom house,"[2] a rumor without foundation in fact. Worse, was the discovery that such stories were believed in the highest circles of the imperial government, and were the basis upon which current policy was being formulated.

The people of Massachusetts Bay, King George III asserted in a speech from the throne, were guilty of "acts of Violence, and of resistance to the execution of the Law." He was explaining why soldiers had been sent to Boston. It was because that town "appears, by late Advices, to be in a state of Disobedience to all law and government; and has proceeded to measures subversive of the Constitution, and attended with circumstances that manifest a disposition to throw off their dependance on *Great-Britain*."[3] The same "Advices" had been laid before Parliament, and, from what Americans could tell, were believed by members of both Houses. Replying to the king, the Lords pledged to "support Your Majesty in such further Measures as may be found necessary to maintain the Civil Magistrates in a due Execution of the Laws within Your Province of Massachusets-Bay,"[4] and the Commons praised the government "for having taken such Steps as You judged necessary for supporting the Constitution, and for repressing that Spirit of Faction and Disobedience, which, in the chief Town of one of Your Majesty's

1. *Annual Register, 1768*, at 71*.
2. 38 *Gentleman's Magazine* (1768), at 245.
3. *Post* (Supplement), 16 January 1769, at 1, col. 1.
4. *Gazette and Post-Boy*, 17 April 1769, at 2, col. 1.

Colonies, appears to have proceded even to Acts of Violence, in direct Defiance of all legal Authority."[5]

Boston, the House of Lords voted, "has for some time past been in a state of great disorder and confusion, and . . . the peace of the said town has at several times been disturbed by riots and tumults of a dangerous nature, in which the officers of his Majesty's revenue there have been obstructed, by acts of violence, in the execution of the laws, and their lives endangered." Confronted by such facts, the legal mind of imperial Britain excogitated an imperial solution. Under the circumstances, the Lords resolved, "the preservation of the public peace, and the due execution of the laws, became impracticable, without the aid of a military force to support and protect the civil magistrates, and the officers of his Majesty's revenue."[6]

Comment by American whigs took a peculiar slant. Many seemed less upset by the troops than the "Advices" bringing them to Boston. Someone, *Junius Americanus* wrote, "brought upon the good people of that town their S[overeig]n's displeasure, and the heavy censure of both Houses of P[arliamen]t, with a formidable armament both by sea and land."[7] The "good people" themselves resolved in town meeting that they had "been grossly misrepresented to our Sovereign,"[8] and a committee of the town wrote Thomas Pownall, a former governor of Massachusetts Bay, that "wicked and designing men" intrigued "to bring us into a state of bondage and ruin, in direct repugnance to those rights which belong to us as men, and as British subjects."[9]

5. *Gazette and Post-Boy*, 23 January 1769, at 1, col. 2.

6. Resolutions of the House of Lords, 15 December 1768, 16 *Parliamentary History*, at 478.

7. *Post*, 15 October 1770, at 1, col. 1.

8. Boston Town Meeting, 4 October 1769, *Gazette and Post-Boy*, 9 October 1769, at 2, col. 2.

9. Report of the Committee of the Town of Boston, transmitted to Governor Pownal[l], in 40 *Gentleman's Magazine* (1770), at 146.

Reports depicting rebelliousness in Boston had been sent to London at least since the Stamp Act crisis.[10] Ever since hearing of them, Boston whigs had realized the town could "be punish'd with Troops to keep us in Order."[11] They knew who was "guilty." It was Governor Francis Bernard and "a few interested Persons,"[12] chiefly the commissioners of the American customs who had first arrived in Massachusetts Bay in November 1767, and almost immediately began petitioning London for military assistance.[13]

As official correspondence became available, whigs documented their case. Newspapers added extra pages for letters written by the governor and others,[14] and books were even published,[15] "to persuade the People," Bernard said, "that Troops would not have been sent here if they had not been misrepresented; and all charges of Misrepresentation are naturally applied to the Gov'r."[16] The charge was not only made, it was made frequently[17] and successfully, because it contained enough substance in fact to be convincing. Bernard, the customs commis-

10. Thus, in 1766 the pastor of Boston's first church protested that "friends at home" had "received injurious representations" of colonial conditions that were not manifested by "a spirit to raise needless disturbances." Chauncy, A Discourse on "the good News," at 25.

11. Post-Boy, 27 April 1767, at 3, col. 2.

12. Message from the House of Representatives to Governor Francis Bernard, Post, 17 July 1769, at 2, col. 1.

13. Morgan, Birth, at 39.

14. For example, Boston Gazette, 31 July 1769.

15. For example, Bernard and Gage, Letters; Hutchinson, Letters.

16. Letter from Governor Francis Bernard to Lord Hillsborough, quoted in Walett, "Bowdoin," at 324.

17. Answer from the House of Representatives to Governor Francis Bernard, 15 July 1769, Speeches, at 185; Resolves of the House of Representatives, 8 July 1769, Gazette and Post-Boy, 10 July 1769, at 2, cols. 1–2; Resolution of the House of Representatives, Post-Boy, 3 July 1769, at 1, col. 1; Letter to Lord Hillsborough, 12 October 1769, [Lee,] Junius Americanus, at 15; Letter to Sir Francis Bernard, 19 December 1769, [Lee,] Junius Americanus, at 42; 38 Gentleman's

sioners, and other revenue officials wanted military support. Whether or not they misrepresented facts to obtain it is a different matter. The answer depends not only on the evidence, but also on how the word "misrepresentation" is defined.

Bernard had had to overcome a constitutional obstacle. He wanted troops in Boston, but under the imperial constitution could not obtain them on his sole authority, at least not for purposes of policing the non-Indian, civilian population. Before making a request, he needed the advice and consent of the executive council, which, because it was controlled by the whigs, he had no hope of obtaining. The governor's task, therefore, was to persuade London to order troops to Boston without a formal request from the Massachusetts government. As a result, the "Advices" he and others sent the ministry may have misled historians. They have generally been interpreted as factual, explaining events and revealing motivations. They, instead, should be used with the caution accorded arguments of forensic facts. Bernard and his fellow imperial officials were not reporting a political situation. Advocates in a litigation, they were seeking to persuade the British government to alter the imperial constitution by changing or suspending the requirement that, for purposes of police enforcement, soldiers could not be sent to colonies settled by the English, unless formally requested by proper authorities in that colony.[18]

The event deserves to be understood in proper perspective. A "litigation" was truly being conducted by imperialists on one side, and Boston whigs on the other. As in a common-law courtroom before judge and jury, facts were manipulated to sustain a

---

Magazine (1768), at 511; *Military Massacre* (no pagination); *Short Narrative*, at 7; *Appeal to the World*, at 21–22.

18. The substance of this paragraph, as well as an evaluation of the probativeness of the "forensic" evidence, is dealt with in a full-length study, *In a Rebellious Spirit*.

case. They may even have been created, as when following a customs riot, the commissioners fled Boston and announced it was unsafe for them to return. By merely staying out of town, they created a fact probatory on the issue of whether or not troops were needed to protect imperial officials.[19] To whig dismay, they were successful. Asked why he had been ordered to Boston, Gage later replied that the commissioners had been "forced" to flee. That fact and "other outrages" "was the cause of sending out General [Alexander] Mackay, with two regiments, and supposed to have been done to show a resolution in Government to protect the crown officers."[20]

Better than their imperial opponents, such as Gage, the whigs of Massachusetts Bay understood what was occurring. Appreciating the forensic nature of Bernard's evidence, they spent as much effort questioning its probateness as its accuracy. When one of the governor's letters to Hillsborough was published, it revealed Bernard reporting "Intelligence brought to him of the Conversation of 'private Companies,'" in one of which "it was resolved to surprize and take the Castle."[21] Even were they to admit that these conversations had in fact occurred ("which was by no Means the Case"), the town of Boston, whigs pointed out, was "not accountable for what one of his Excellency's Spies might have overheard in a 'private Company.'"[22] The example may seem extreme, but was not. It was fairly typical of the probative quality of Bernard's evidence.[23] He was also a master at inferring the worst. If there were no supporting facts, inference could do as well. A typical example is the following sentence from a letter the governor sent to Hillsborough. "For my part," Bernard wrote, "when I consider the defenceless state

19. Ibid.
20. 4 *Collections of the Massachusetts Historical Society*, at 370 (1858).
21. *Appeal to the World*, at 25.
22. Ibid.
23. For a fuller discussion and other examples, see *In a Rebellious Spirit*.

of this town, I cannot think they will be so mad as to attempt to defend it against the King's Forces: but the lengths they have gone already are scarce short of madness."[24]

The whigs countered with forensic evidence of their own, often as questionable, charging that the imperialists wrought up "trifling incidents,"[25] that were elevated into stories of mobs by "the Contrivance of some, who wanted a better Foundation to support the Representations they had already made, or were disposed to make, of the disorderly State which the Inhabitants of the Province in general, and particularly of the Town of Boston, were in."[26] It was in fact, British officials who "contrived and executed plans for executing disturbances and tumults, which otherwise would probably never have existed."[27]

There is no need to furnish more examples. The creation, manipulation, and argument of facts by both sides are detailed in a separate book.[28] The major concern here is that Massachusetts whigs believed their conduct had been misrepresented to London by Bernard and other imperial officials; that there was a basis of truth supporting that belief;[29] and that the "Advices," whether factually accurate or deliberate misrepresentations, had

24. Letter from Governor Francis Bernard to Lord Hillsborough, 18 June 1768, Bernard and Gage, *Letters*, at 37.

25. Letter from the Massachusetts Convention to Dennys DeBerdt, 27 September 1768, 1 Adams, *Writings*, at 244. See also *Boston Gazette*, 15 January 1770, at 1, col. 2.

26. [Prescott,] *Calm Consideration*, at 21.

27. *Short Narrative*, at 7.

28. *In a Rebellious Spirit*.

29. For other evidence substantiating the charge of "misrepresentation," see Letter from John Temple to George Grenville, 7 November 1768, 4 *Grenville Papers*, at 397; Letter from Commodore Samuel Hood to George Grenville, 15 October 1768, 2 Higgins, *Bernard*, at 169; Dickerson, *Acts*, at 209–10; Morgan, *Birth*, at 39. The best evidence may be the fact that, when the army arrived, its commander reported "not the smallest Intention of any Revolt." Letter from Colonel Alexander Mackay to General Thomas Gage, 5 July 1769, quoted in Waters, *Otis Family*, at 174. See also 38 *Gentleman's Magazine* (1768), at 512;

been successful. It was said in London, for example, that the commissioners of the customs, after experiencing "extraordinary acts of outrage," fled Boston "for the security of their lives,"[30] and that the "people" had "actually declared, that the commissioners shall never again come ashore."[31] None of these assertions was completely accurate, and some were unquestionably wrong. Yet they, like every other item reported to London, were believed. When ordering the first troops to Boston, Hillsborough sent General Gage copies of letters from the governor and the commissioners, which indicated he regarded them as evidence of reality, not arguments of probabilities. The letters, Gage was told, "will evince to you, how *necessary* it is become, that such Measures should be taken as will *strengthen the Hands of Government* in the Province of Massachusetts Bay."[32]

There were appendixes attached to tales of "misrepresentations" driving American whigs ever further from the mother country. Whether believed or not, the charge that troops would not be in Boston but for fictions told London furnished Massachusetts officials with a weak but not disloyal excuse to refrain from cooperating with the military. Because the "mistake" would soon be discovered and the troops recalled, there was no need to bother billeting the soldiers or housing the officers.[33] More significantly, two new counts were added to America's bill of constitutional grievances. First was the charge that if troops had been brought to Boston by misrepresentations, the

---

Journal of the Times, 30 September 1768, at 1, col. 2; and *Post*, 3 October 1768, at 3, col. 2.

30. *Annual Register, 1768*, at 71*.

31. "Extract of a Letter from Boston, in New England, dated 20th," *Annual Register, 1768*, at [141].

32. Letter from Lord Hillsborough to General Thomas Gage, 8 June 1768, *Boston Gazette*, 11 December 1769, at 2, col. 1.

33. Answer of the Council to Governor Francis Bernard, 5 October 1768, *Bowdoin Papers*, at 110–11.

town was convicted not only unjustly but without trial. Evidence of criminal conduct had been offered by one side, without providing Bostonians an opportunity to defend themselves.[34] Second, they were not treated equally with fellow subjects in Great Britain. Both Edinburgh in Scotland and London in England experienced crowds more vicious and destructive than any in the colonies. Yet the innocent citizens of neither city had been punished for what a mobbish few had done.[35]

The belief of misrepresentations, moreover, drove a further wedge between the colonists and the men London sent over to rule them. When General Gage, following Bernard's lead, told Hillsborough that "there was very little Government in Boston," the town could accuse him of "great Injustice"[36] and the House of Representatives spoke of "rashly and impertinently" meddling "in the civil affairs of this province, which are altogether out of his department."[37] More threatening to imperial authority was the erosion of Governor Bernard's effectiveness. His selfportrait of a defenseless imperial sentry standing watch in a mobbish town was redrawn by whig legal terminology into a picture of a machinating public "enemy." Resolved, the people of Boston voted, "that every such Person, who shall solicite or promote the importation of Troops at this time, is an Enemy to this Town and Province, and a disturber of the peace and good order of both."[38] Resolved, the House of Representatives echoed, that "whoever has represented to his Majesty's ministers, that the people of this colony, in general, or the town of Boston, in particular, were in such a state of disobedience and

34. Petition of the Town of Boston to the King, *Post-Boy*, 24 July 1769, at 2, col. 2.

35. Anon., *To Committee of the London Merchants*, at 27.

36. Resolves of the Town of Boston, 4 October 1769, *Post*, 30 October 1769, at 1, col. 2.

37. Resolves of the House of Representatives, 29 June 1769, *Speeches*, at 178.

38. Instructions of Boston, 17 June 1768, *Town Records*, at 259.

disorder, as to require a fleet and army to be sent here, to aid the civil magistrate, is an avowed enemy to this colony, and to the nation in general; and has, by such misrepresentation, endeavored to destroy the liberty of the subject here."[39]

These resolves must not be dismissed as mere rhetoric. They helped lay the foundation in whig law justifying later resistance to imperial authorities. It was those authorities, after all, who, by introducing troops into the governance of Massachusetts Bay, had implied that the American colonies were bound in "Allegiance and Duty to the best of Sovereigns, only by the Band of Terror and the Force of Arms."[40]

❖ 4 ❖

A COMMON ENEMY:

THE BRITISH COMPARISON

While we think American we also must think English. The colonists, after all, were subjects of the British crown, governed by constitutional principles largely English in origin. Sharing a common legal tradition and constitutional history, the rhetoric of one was the rhetoric of the other. It would be unwise to call an American statement extreme before checking its heritage. What some historians too easily dismiss as colonial dissimulating could be of pure English vintage. An unprepared reader may be startled coming across resolves passed by the Massachusetts lower house which stated that whoever misrepresented the people of the province and of Boston was "an avowed Enemy to the Colony, and to the Nation in general; and has by such

39. Resolves of the House of Representatives, 29 June 1769, *Speeches*, at 178.
40. Petition of the Town of Boston to the King, *Post-Boy*, 24 July 1769, at 2, col. 2.

Misrepresentations endeavoured to destroy the Liberty of the Subject."[1] There would be less surprise should the reader understand the extent to which eighteenth-century New England thought seventeenth-century English thoughts. The Massachusetts resolves belonged to an honorable constitutional tradition. Consider, as an example, how they echoed the whig divine Samuel Johnson. "Any man," he had asserted in 1697, "who suggests a pretence to the King for a Standing Army, *ought to be abhor'd by every* Englishman, *by every Man that loves Liberty and his Country*: for the reason and force of the Abhorrence does not lie in the difference of suggestions to the King, but in the Guards and Troops which are thereby rais'd; for it is that ruin our *Liberty and Country*, and therefore give but a bad character to any body that is for them."[2]

The point being stressed is not the often-noted British comparison to American whig legal theory.[3] More deserving of attention is that comparison's historical respectability and constitutional legitimacy.[4] Words are of concern not only because ideas determined action, but also because they reveal how American arguments were rooted in English precedents. Because Governor Bernard and the customs commissioners "were the procuring cause of troops being sent hither," a Boston town committee asserted, "they must therefore be the remote and a blameable cause of all the disturbances and bloodshed that have taken place in

1. Resolves of the House of Representatives, 8 July 1769, *Gazette and Post-Boy*, 10 July 1769, at 2, cols. 1–2.

2. Johnson, *Works*, at 324.

3. For example, Maier, *Resistance*, at 194–95.

4. Words, of course, changed to the degree institutions did. During the prerevolutionary era, Parliament posed the danger to American freedom, not the king. Earlier, Parliament was weaker than the crown. "Consider," a member warned the Commons in 1628, "how many parliaments have been unhappy by misrepresentations which are the bane of parliaments." Speech of Sir Thomas Wentworth, 24 March 1628, 2 *Commons Debates, 1628*, at 85.

consequence of that measure."[5] Before concluding the argument
farfetched, consider that no less a seventeenth-century common
lawyer than Edward Hyde, earl of Clarendon, believed that
criminal causation fit the context. Although a Stuart royalist, he
thought those misrepresenting facts to the crown legally responsible for any consequences. "[I]f those who mislead kings, or
obey them in unjust resolutions," Clarendon reasoned, "were to
be exempt all kingdoms and governments must be dissolved."[6]

During two centuries and on both sides of the Atlantic,
Englishmen strove for accountable government. Officials had to
be made responsible for their policies, and blame fixed on the
blameworthy. When John Wilkes, speaking to the Court of
Common Council in London's Guildhall, said that George III's
recent answer to a petition was an affront to the people, a
contemporary corrected him. Wilkes, he pointed out "should
never ascribe so obnoxious a measure to the King, but to those
Ministers who sought our ruin, . . . and from the first moment
of their power had constantly and sedulously endeavoured to
create dissentions between the King and his people."[7]

The constitutional theory was explained by the Massachusetts
House of Representatives. "The law and reason teaches," it
wrote the colony's London agent, "that 'the King can do no
wrong;' and that neither the King nor Parliament are inclined
but to justice, equity and truth. But the law does not presume,
that the King may not be deceived, nor that his Parliament may
not be misinformed. If therefore any thing is wrong, it must be
imputed to those causes."[8] Sir Edward Coke, history's greatest
common lawyer, had explained the doctrine more simply when
he noted that the king "deals with other men's hands and sees

5. *Short Narrative*, at 8.
6. Quoted in [Bollan,] *Continued Corruption*, at 44.
7. *Annual Register, 1770*, at [132].
8. *Extract of Letter to De Berdt*, at 5.

with other men's eyes."[9] It was this constitutional reality that explained the doctrine that kings did no wrong, which, in fact, meant that other persons, generally ministers, were accountable for constitutional offenses. "They were," someone wrote the year troops arrived in Boston, "supposed to have capacity in every respect to their offices, and, as they might lay these down if they received commands detrimental to the welfare, or contrary to the laws of the land, so whatever they delivered in the King's name, they delivered at their own peril; and thus, according to the maxims, the minister did the wrong and nothing was imputed to the throne."[10] Put another way, ministers committing constitutional mischief could not hide behind that throne.[11]

These legal premises were clear, and so were conclusions flowing from them. Resistance to ministerial tyranny was not only a civic responsibility, it was also an act of loyalty to the house of Hanover. "[I]t would be disrespectable to the c[row]n," a writer argued in 1764, "to fall into the notion, which so much prevails, that opposition to the mandates of the present motley group of ministers, has been, and is to be considered, *in some places*, as an insult to the [king] himself; a doctrine distructive to our liberties and constitution, yet much in vogue with certain degenerate hirelings."[12]

What strikes some historians as constitutional paranoia, sounded a call to constitutional barricades for radicals, libertarians, and commonwealthmen in contemporary Britain. Why else did so much of London's political and constitutional language sound as shrill as any voiced in whig Boston. The lord mayor, aldermen, and commons of London remonstrated against the

9. Speech of Sir Edward Coke, 22 March 1628, 2 *Commons Debates, 1628*, at 64.

10. "Philonomos," *Liberty of the Subject*, at 21.

11. *Common Sense*, 2 April 1737, at 68.

12. 34 *Gentleman's Magazine* (1764), at 224.

king's "evil counsellors."[13] The freeholders of the county of Surrey warned George III of past "Calamities" caused by "the pernicious counsels of wicked and corrupt ministers."[14] And, as defiant as any American whigs of the 1760s, London's livery spoke of government by "military force." "[B]y a fatal application of this maxim," it was charged, the ministry "have wantonly and wickedly sacrificed the lives of many of your majesty's innocent subjects, and have prostituted your majesty's sacred name and authority, to justify, applaud, and recommend their own illegal and bloody actions."[15]

Historians who dismiss Boston's objections to Governor Bernard and the army as political propaganda, intended to stir up the masses but not revealing motivations, would do well to consider the constitutional issues of eighteenth-century Great Britain. The danger of having soldiers available for police work, as they were in Massachusetts, the earl of Winchelsea had warned in 1733, was that they "made ministers of state more daring than otherwise they durst venture to be, both in contriving and executing Schemes and projects that were grievous and burthensome to the people; schemes that never could enter into the heads of any but those who were drunk with an excess of power."[16] By the 1770s a school of constitutional thought depicted these same ministers, with or without the support of troops, as the most menacing threat then existing toward British liberty. There was, a pamphleteer asserted, "a spirit of discon-

13. Humble Remonstrance of the Lord Mayor, Aldermen, and Commons of London to the King, 40 *Gentleman's Magazine* (1770), at 218; Humble Address, Remonstrance, and Petition of the Lord Mayor, Aldermen, and Commons of London to the King, 21 November 1770, 40 *Gentleman's Magazine*, at 523.

14. Humble Address, Petition, and Remonstrance of the Freeholders of the County of Surry, 13 June 1770, 40 *Gentleman's Magazine* (1770), at 277*.

15. The Humble Petition of the Livery of the City of London to the King, 39 *Gentleman's Magazine* (1769), at 329.

16. Debate in the Lords, 6 March 1733, 8 *Parliamentary History*, at 1236.

nection, of distrust, and of treachery, amongst public men."[17] No accusation seemed unreasonable. "[T]he troops of George the III," John Hancock charged, "have cross'd the wide atlantick, not to engage an enemy, but to assist a band of TRAITORS in trampling on the rights and liberties of his most loyal subjects in America."[18] Again, what appears extreme in the singularity of the American context becomes almost commonplace when shifted across the Atlantic. Compare what Hancock said about George III to what the same king was personally told by some English subjects. His advisers, the free burgesses of Newcastle claimed, were "incapable and mercenary" men, "who, under the specious Title of Ministers, are collusively transferring from one to the other, the exclusive Right of sporting with their Country, [and whom] we have every Calamity to dread both at Home and Abroad, as well from their want of Experience as from their Want of Integrity."[19]

Even the American whigs' most seemingly paranoiac state-ment—that Bernard and others instigated the very riots of which they complained—was matched in contemporary Britain, when Colonel Isaac Barré iterated their charge. Some legislation, he maintained, was introduced "in order to inflame the colonies, and drive them to extremity."[20] More to the point, for it had no reference to America, the lord mayor of London warned the livery that "your enemies seek to drive you to riot, disorder, and confusion."[21] He was referring to the king's ministers. Some

17. *Observations on the late State of the Nation* (1769), quoted in 40 *Monthly Review* (1769), at 143.

18. *Massacre Orations*, at 45.

19. Humble Address, Remonstrance, and Petition of the Free Burgesses of the Town and County of Newcastle to the King, 40 *Gentleman's Magazine* (1770), at 234.

20. Debate in the Commons, 9 January 1770, 16 *Parliamentary History*, at 708.

21. Speech delivered by the Right Hon. the Lord Mayor, at the last meeting of the Livery at Guildhall, 40 *Gentleman's Magazine* (1770), at 167.

citizens of Middlesex were more explicit. "Mobs and riots," they charged, were "hired and raised by the M[inistr]y, in order to justify and recommend their own illegal proceedings, and to prejudice your majesty's mind by false insinuations against the loyalty of your majesty's subjects."[22] This was what Boston whigs said Bernard and the customs commissioners had done.

Finally, the parallel becomes complete when it is realized that the reasons assigned as motivations for the misrepresentations were similar on both sides of the Atlantic. In Massachusetts, it was charged that imperialist slanderers acted on a plan "to raise their own fortunes, and advance themselves to posts of honor and profit, not only to the destruction of the charter and constitution of this province, but at the expense of the rights and liberties of the American colonies." For that end "the said persons have been some of the chief instruments in the introduction of a military force into the province."[23] Should the sincerity of the fear be doubted, one measure of its genuineness should be the extent to which it was expressed in the English-speaking world. The ministry, it was said in London in 1769, was guilty of "[w]icked attempts to encrease and establish a standing army, by endeavouring to vest in the crown an unlimited power over the militia; which, should they succeed, must sooner or later, subvert the constitution, by augmenting the power of administration in proportion to their delinquency."[24]

The fear should not be mistaken. Military power alone was not on the mind of British and American whigs. More worrisome was arbitrary use of that power by an executive unaccountable to anyone. Catharine Macaulay drew the picture when warning of government hidden from public scrutiny and manipulated behind a maze of double cabinets. One of these two

22. Middlesex Petition, 39 *Gentleman's Magazine* (1769), at 290.
23. Resolves of the House of Representatives, 16 June 1773, *Speeches*, at 407.
24. Middlesex Petition, 39 *Gentleman's Magazine* (1769), at 290.

cabinets, she said, was an exterior cabinet, visible to view, in which the appointed minister did the bidding of a second, internal cabinet, consisting of "a cabal of favorites," responsible to no one, not even to Parliament.[25] She was saying more than that current fears were reminiscent of seventeenth-century constitutionalism. Should her warnings prove valid, it was possible, even likely, that the eighteenth century's most cherished political truism, the balanced constitution, would prove to be an inadequate instrument for the preservation of liberty.

It would be well to hesitate before reacting. These fears may seem farfetched, arguing from extremes of conspiracy to extremes of tyranny, conjuring constitutional perils no ministers could have accomplished and to which probably none aspired.[26] But, to those experiencing apprehension, the possibility may not have seemed as remote as might be thought. After all, the ministry ruled Ireland by executive decree and military force.[27]

What is true is that British people sharing these fears were a minority, or at least a minority of those franchised to vote for members of Parliament. But they were articulate, and belonged to a legitimate English constitutional tradition opposed to "arbitrary" power.[28] In America, that constitutional tradition commanded the allegiance of a majority of the population. And, though its motivation was the retention of local autonomy, its origins were in seventeenth-century England. The guiding principles were English, not American. Now, with troops in Boston, the colonists could agree with a writer in London that they shared with their fellow subjects in Great Britain a common enemy, the king's ministers. "The same oppressors under which we groan, are their oppressors," he wrote of America six months

25. Book review, 40 *Gentleman's Magazine* (1770), at 222.
26. Christie and Labaree, *Empire*, at 276.
27. *In a Defiant Stance.*
28. See "In Legitimate Stirps."

after the soldiers had landed; "the same freedom which is the object of our generous pursuit, is the sole object of theirs."[29]

❖ 5 ❖

A LAW WE HAVE LOST:

THE TWO CONSTITUTIONS

It does not do to tell but half a tale. To say that the constitutional fear was a seventeenth-century fear, implies that, by 1768, it was an archaism. From the perspective of the British ministry and the parliamentary majority, it was: they thought of that fear in terms of the eighteenth-century constitution and the sovereignty of a supreme Parliament, to which the military was unswervingly loyal. So too, have most historians of the American Revolution, and that has been their undoing.

The words of those participating in the prerevolutionary debate deserve more attention than they usually receive. The question should be not only what they mean, but also whether they express what was a new or old idea. When Thomas Jefferson reflected on the British policy of garrisoning troops in a colony without consent of the local assembly, he employed a phraseology that might not be expected today. "To render these proceedings still more criminal against our laws," he said, "instead of subjecting the military to the civil power, his majesty has expressly made the civil subordinate to the military."[1] Scholars familiar with colonial history may say Jefferson wrote nonsense. Perhaps so, but before agreeing it should be asked how well today's legal mind understands Jefferson. One answer is that he cannot be understood without appreciating how much

29. 38 *London Magazine* (1769), at 205.
1. Jefferson, *Summary View*, at 134.

he was expressing a seventeenth-century constitutional anxiety. A century earlier, during the reign of Charles II, a member of Parliament had not used the word "criminal," but his thought had been similiar to what Jefferson meant. "If any man," he said, "is so hardy as to advise the King to govern by a standing army, he would subvert law."[2]

It was no accident that the words of the eighteenth-century Thomas Jefferson echoed those of a seventeenth-century member of Parliament. Both men were interpreting the same constitution. For too long it has been assumed that "constitution" in the eighteenth century meant what it means today. In fact, the definition was not only different, but its impreciseness may be beyond our comprehension. Unlike lawyers today, participants in the prerevolutionary controversy knew there were shadows about the term "constitution" that made definition more a matter of personal usage than of judicial certainty. It did not trouble them, as it would us, that "constitution" was a word more used than understood.[3]

It is not relevant to the theme of this book to define the meaning of "constitution." The concern here is that there were at least two conceptions of the British constitution, one the interpretation accepted by a majority of Parliament, the other accepted by a majority of Americans.[4] The parliamentary version was summed up by a ministerial writer who said, "The legislature is another name for the Constitution of the state; and,

2. Omond, *The Army*, at 19.

3. "Q. What is the constitution of England? A. It is not true like wit, 'a thing much talked of, not to be defined;'—but is like many other matters, a thing much talked of, and little understood." 35 *London Magazine* (1766), at 266. "There is scarce a word in the English language so frequently used, and so little understood as the word Constitution." 32 *Monthly Review* (1765), at 59. "This poor word *Constitution* has been more abused than any in the English language. Many have attempted to explain it; few have been satisfactory on the subject." 28 *Monthly Review* (1763), at 490.

4. McIlwain, *Revolution*, at 5.

in fact, the State itself."[5] The American version was the same as that defended in 1718 by thirty members of the House of Lords who were protesting the size of the military establishment. So many troops, they warned, could "endanger our constitution, which hath never yet been entirely subverted but by a standing army."[6] The ministerial writer was describing the constitution of parliamentary supremacy. The dissentient lords were adhering to the constitution of customary restraints.

Dogmatic assumptions must be avoided. The constitutional argument of American whigs was not, as sometimes asserted,[7] a new departure. It did not look ahead to a future that ought to be, but back to what the constitution had once been. If at times the American argument seems ambiguous, it must not be dismissed by recalling that there was no ambiguity in Great Britain. There was much more than historians generally realize. It is known today that the British constitution of 1768 was whatever Parliament said it was.[8] A fact overlooked is that people then did not have our certitude. Consider only Lord Camden. There were few better lawyers in the kingdom. He was chief justice of one of the central common-law courts and about to become lord chancellor, a post placing him at the head of the English bar. If anyone knew the British constitution, Camden did, yet he warned Parliament that there were steps, including taxing the American colonies, it could not take legally.[9] Obviously, Camden had not been told that the constitution was the will of the supreme legislature. Instead, he agreed with the Massachusetts

5. [Macpherson,] *Rights of Great Britain*, at 3. For discussion, see Wood, *Creation*, at 261.

6. Protest of 24 February 1718, 1 *Protests of the Lords*, at 241.

7. 1 Bailyn, *Pamphlets*, at 45; Hinkhouse, *Preliminaries*, at 81.

8. Robson, *American Revolution*, at 21; Waters, *Otis Family*, at 134; Ewing, "The Constitution," at 632.

9. Speech of Lord Camden, Lords Debate of 10 February 1766, 16 *Parliamentary History*, at 168 [hereafter cited as Lord Camden Speech].

House of Representatives, when it told him that the constitution was "fixed," meaning that Parliament was the constitution's creature, not its creator.[10] Camden put the same idea in the form of a question. "When did the House of Commons first begin?," he asked, and answered, "it began with the constitution, it grew up with the constitution."[11]

Something clearly is amiss. Camden's jurisprudential theory, according to the generally accepted historical interpretation of the eighteenth-century constitution, belonged to the seventeenth century or to American whigs, not to an English lawyer living in the reign of George III. More Cokean than Lockean, more common law than natural law, it postulated limits by questioning the origins of power. If this is puzzling today, it should not be. All that is necessary is acknowledgment that the constitutional case of eighteenth-century American whigs was based on the same constitution that seventeenth-century English whigs and their predecessors had made law against Charles I and James II. Because the legal theory came from the seventeenth century, it could, even in the eighteenth-century colonies, be argued by seventeenth-century constitutional analogies. "The late unhappy *Stamp Act* made here to operate in America," a British writer told his countrymen, "was certainly as unconstitutional a measure as king James II's dispensing power."[12]

To a degree, the two constitutional traditions were not incompatible. The assertion that the Stamp Act was unconstitu-

10. Letter from the Massachusetts House of Representatives to Lord Camden, 29 January 1768, *Post-Boy*, 4 April 1768, at 1, col. 1; Letter from the Massachusetts House of Representatives to Henry Seymour Conway, 13 February 1768, *Post-Boy*, 28 March 1768, at 2, col. 1. A contemporary Irishman argued: "The King, Lords, and Commons, are *not* the constitution, they are only the *creatures* of the constitution." [Sheridan,] *Observations on the Doctrine*, at 18.

11. Lord Camden Speech, at 179.

12. 38 *Gentleman's Magazine* (1768), at 356. In the same constitutional context, an American could ask, "Was not King Charles try'd and condem'd for breaking through the sacred rights of the people." [Allen,] *The American Alarm*, at 26.

tional did not have to mean it was illegal. It was possible to accept the new constitution of parliamentary supremacy while clinging to the old constitution of fixed restraints. What Parliament enacted was lawful because that body alone declared the law, but, if it went beyond the limits of the constitution, then what it enacted was also unconstitutional. The idea was less an anomaly than a consequence of contemporary jurisprudence. The British constitution had changed, and lawyers were not quite aware what had happened.

It can only be guessed, yet there is little doubt that most imperialist and tory lawyers approved Lord Hillsborough's decision to land troops in Boston—at least if they agreed New Englanders were rebellious and needed a show of force. Those same men, however, though believing force a legal foundation for maintaining or restoring law and order, would not have thought it inconsistent to deny that force was a necessary underpinning of legal authority. They might, in other words, have been reluctant to acknowledge that elements dividing their meaning of law from that of American whigs were the concepts of will and command.

Alterations had been occurring in British government generally unrecognized, by most educated people. Contrary to the taught traditions of English constitutionalism,[13] "will and pleasure" were becoming legitimate tests of lawfulness through the doctrine of parliamentary sovereignty. Very few contemporary observers, not even Sir William Blackstone or Lord Mansfield, were prepared to consider the implications and that a vocabulary inherited from an earlier constitutional era dominated the prerevolutionary controversy. An exception to the rule, indicating how the debate would terminate when political reality caught up with legal rhetoric, was a writer who answered the charge that Americans were not represented in the House of Commons by

13. "In Legitimate Stirps," at 461–93.

quoting a 1554 petition to Queen Mary in which Parliament purported to represent "the whole bodie of the realme of England." That declaration, he concluded, settled any dispute, and "the speculative opinions of modern politicians, and of the ablest writers on government, who reason from what they think the constitution ought to be, and who conjure up a representation of their own, must give way to this authority, which declares in the Journals of Parliament *what the constitution is*."[14]

For many common lawyers, the realization that power was now its own legitimacy was too wrenching a departure from English constitutional traditions to be acknowledged without reservations, and they vacillated, pulled on one side by the values of the old constitution, on the other by the realities of the new. A writer could assert that Parliament was sovereign, with complete absolute power to make law, and yet should "avoid exercising that power contrary to the fundemental [*sic*] principles of the constitution." Put another way, although sovereign power, by the very nature of sovereignty, cannot be restrained, it should be. In the context of the prerevolutionary controversy, the argument could be made that Parliament should have avoided "an unconstitutional Taxation of America, or in other words, should not have attempted to tax them [the colonists], without a previous or concurrent Act of Parliamens [*sic*], to make the same constitutional, by granting them the constitutional liberty of petitioning for, and having granted, the benefit of a reasonable representation."[15]

The pull between the two constitutional traditions created a constitutional tension that colored the legal abstractions of the prerevolutionary era. There was a manner of arguing constitutional principles allowing one to state contradictions as if they were reconcilable. Most frequently, absolute power was expressed in terms of restraints placing limits on that power. As we

14. Anon., *A Speech Never Intended*, at 19–20.
15. *Amor Patriae*, 2 March 1766, [Crowley,] *Letters*, at 14.

have seen, Parliament might be called supreme, yet not be so supreme it could exercise "power contrary to the fundemental [*sic*] principles of the constitution." In a similar vein, "an unconstitutional Taxation of America," such as the Stamp Act, could be made less unconstitutional by granting colonists a "constitutional liberty," or even made constitutional by extending the constitutional right of representation to the people being taxed.

A constitutional argument that took place contemporarily with the military occupation of Boston illustrates the constitutional tension from an American source. In 1769 the lower house of the New York Assembly passed a resolution excluding certain judges from membership. The purpose was to bar Robert R. Livingston, a justice of the supreme court. When he was elected despite the resolution, the house refused to let him take the seat. In his protest, Livingston was faced with the reality of sovereign power, yet could not bring himself to acknowledge its full implications. "[W]hatever a Legislature may do," he admitted, "Judges can have no Right to alter, but must be guided by the Laws."[16] The house, he also conceded, had exclusive jurisdiction over questions of members' qualifications and no appeal lay from its decision. "But does it follow," Livingston asked the assemblymen, "that you are at Liberty to determine contrary to Law? Far from us, from every one of us, be so dangerous a Thought. So far is this from being the Case, that it lays the House under the strongest Obligation to determine according to Law."[17]

Livingston may not have recognized the inconsistency that grabs our attention: that the legislature was both "Omnipotent" and "bounded" by law.[18] Like many of his contemporaries, he tried to answer eighteenth-century constitutional problems by

16. Livingston, *Address to the House*, at 2.
17. Ibid.
18. Ibid.

using seventeenth-century concepts. More likely than not, he thought it not unreasonable to acknowledge the principle of the new jurisprudence that legislative authority might "exercise an arbitrary uncontroulable Power,"[19] yet still argue from the old jurisprudence that "law" was an entity existing independently of power. Although the lower house had "arbitrary uncontroulable Power," it could, when exercising that power—making what is today called "law"—violate law.

One other example should be considered: how writers, during the 1760s, could discuss limitations on what they said was unlimited legislative power. Catharine Macaulay admitted that the execution of Thomas Wentworth, earl of Strafford, had been "constitutionally unjustified," yet she justified his execution. "The attacks of Charles I on the constitution," she explained, "rendered acts of power necessary expedients to reinstate the people in their long-lost privileges, and give to violated laws their due authority; not to mention that combination of circumstances which rendered the death of Strafford absolutely necessary to the safety of reviving liberty." She was saying that power is not law, yet, with necessity, power legally can violate law. A critic of Macaulay showed how the two constitutional traditions could twist into a single argument that today seems illogical. He did so by equating Parliament with both power and law, but, instead of concluding that Parliament was invincible, said there was something it legally could not do.

> We deny that any circumstances can be of so particular and urgent a nature, as to render it necessary for the *legislative* power to exceed the strict letter of the law. Indeed, there is an inaccuracy in saying that the *legislative* power can exceed the law, since whatever the *legislature* establishes *is* the law, and it is in the *judicial* and *executive* branches only that it can properly be exceeded. But, not to cavil about pro-

19. "Citizen," *Observations on Livingston's Address*, at 3.

priety of expression, we are bold to insist that all the three powers together, cannot legally or equitably declare a law *ex post facto*.[20]

It must not be thought that what is being said is that whigs and tories (or even that American whigs on one side and imperialist lawyers on the other) defined the word "constitution" differently. The jurisprudential premise that law rested on authority other than command—on custom, precedent, community consensus, reason, or consent, for example—had been the original English canon. Contrary to nineteenth-century legal folklore, it had lingered as a part of legal theory for many years after the Glorious Revolution of 1688. Later dogma would hold that the revolution had been the occasion when "law" assumed its current definition and, with the king in Parliament sovereign, the constitution forever changed. Perhaps so, but contemporaries were not aware of what was occurring. The proceedings by which James II was declared to have abandoned the nation, and by which the throne was bestowed upon William III, were, Samuel Johnson maintained, "according to the *English* Constitution, and prescrib'd by it."[21] William had come to England "to restore the Constitution,"[22] not to promulgate a new one.

Before the Glorious Revolution, there were some distinguished lawyers who expressed doubts that unalterable customary law could restrain the supreme legislature.[23] After the revolution, by contrast, it was just as fashionable to question whether the supreme legislature could alter vested constitutional rights. Parliament might be supreme, John Toland wrote in 1701, "yet it neither has, nor ought to have an arbitrary Power over the Lives, Liberties, or Fortunes of the Subjects; and,

20. 32 *Monthly Review* (1765), at 273.
21. Johnson, *Works*, at 271.
22. Ibid., at 257.
23. For example, [John Somers,] *A Brief History of the Succession* (ca. 1682), at 17.

shou'd they manifestly appear to aim at such an execrable Design, the whole People may justly call them to an Account."[24] For Toland, therefore, the seventeenth-century English constitution still existed, just as it would exist forty-seven years later for young Samuel Adams. In no other constitution, Adams wrote in 1748,

> is the power of the governors and the rights of the governed more nicely adjusted, or the power which is necessary in the very nature of government to be intrusted in the hands of some, by wiser checks prevented from growing exorbitant. This Constitution has indeed passed through various amendations, but the principal parts of it are of very ancient standing, and have continued through the several successions of kings to this day; having never been in any great degree attacked by any, but they have lost their lives or their crowns in the attempt.[25]

By 1764, when the prerevolutionary controversy commenced, the majority of British lawyers would no longer define "constitution" as Toland and Adams had. What American whigs were saying would have been clearer to them had they at least spotted its archaistic roots. "'Tis hoped," James Otis wrote that year, "it will not be considered as a new doctrine that even the authority of the Parliament of *Great Britain* is circumscribed by certain bounds which if exceeded their acts become those of mere *power* without *right*, and consequently void."[26] It was not a new doctrine. What was new was that the theory of law distinguishing between "power" and "right" no longer was dominant in London, and in that reality—that the legal mind of the colonies

24. Toland, *Anglia Libera*, at 4.
25. 1 William V. Wells, *The Life and Public Services of Samuel Adams* (Boston, 1865), at 21.
26. Otis, "Substance," at 476.

❖ 41 ❖

was not communicating with that of the mother country—lay seeds of misunderstanding and potential conflict.

Scholars today must not be more dogmatic than were people of that time. When encountering eighteenth-century British theorists speaking of parliamentary supremacy, it is too easily assumed they mean the nineteenth-century constitution. The danger is an anachronistic interpretation of a parcel of concepts that already were archaic. The prerevolutionary Parliament was —like the Parliament of today—supreme and beyond legal restraint, but not yet so supreme that everyone thought it and the constitution were one. Certainly not *Junius*, whose popularity indicates people believed they understood what he was saying, whether or not they agreed with him. "[L]et me exhort and conjure You," he wrote in 1772, "never to suffer an invasion of Your political constitution, however minute the instance may appear, to pass by without a determined, persevering resistance. One precedent creates another. They soon accumulate, and constitute law. What yesterday was fact, to-day is doctrine."[27] After the Battle of Lexington, some members of the House of Lords sounded the same warning when Parliament indicated readiness to subdue the colonies by military force. "We have," they protested, "beheld with sorrow and indignation, session after session, and notwithstanding repeated warnings of danger, attempts made to deprive some millions of British subjects of their trade, their laws, [and] their constitution."[28] A few months earlier, the Massachusetts lawyer Josiah Quincy had applied the same principle to the standing-army controversy.

At first even the highest courtiers would argue—that a standing army, in time of peace, was never attempted. Soon after the court speakers urged for continuance of a numer-

27. 1 "Junius," *Junius*, at iv.
28. Protest of 26 October 1775, 2 *Protests of the Lords*, at 160.

ous army for one year longer. At the end of several years after, the gentlemen throw aside the mask, and boldly declare such a number of troops must always be kept up. In short, the army must be continued till it becomes part of the constitution.[29]

Quincy's theory was not unique. "It is," a London reviewer wrote in 1767, "a very pleasing, and not unprofitable speculation, to observe with what vigour many abuses and alterations of the constitution, were opposed in their infancy, and their fatal consequences clearly manifested, which are now tamely acquiesced in, and become, as it were, a part of the political system."[30] The words to be marked are "abuses" and "alterations." One using them thought the constitution "fixed," not whatever Parliament said it was. If not fixed, it neither could have been abused nor altered by Parliament.

Although the concepts remained traditional, an innovation was creeping in. Historical dynamics was entering the legal conscious. Lawyers were realizing not only that "alterations" could occur, but also that they could become "part of the constitution." As recently as 1754, John Perceval, member of the British Commons, and earl of Egmont on the Irish establishment, denied that the constitution could change.

> I shall readily grant, that almost every administration has in some respects acted contrary to our constitution; but a breach of our constitution is not surely to be called an alteration of our constitution; for if it were, I am afraid, it could not be justly said, that we have had a fixed constitution since the Revolution any more than before, as ministers have since frequently acted contrary to our constitution. . . . What was the cause of the Revolution? Was it not because

29. Quincy, *Observations with Thoughts*, at 438.
30. 37 *Monthly Review* (1767), at 357.

the prince then upon the throne had acted contrary to, and was endeavouring to subvert our constitution. How could this be true if we had then no constitution?[31]

Egmont was speaking from a seventeenth-century constitutional tradition. By the prerevolutionary era, even John Wilkes's *North Briton* would complain not only that laws were unconstitutional, but also that a "most grievous system of laws have, in a good measure, repealed the most favourite law of our constitution, which has ever been considered as the birth-right of an Englishman, and the sacred paladium of liberty; I mean trial by jury."[32] Reluctantly, perhaps unknowingly, opponents of the contemporary British ministry were conceding that the legal force determining the meaning of the constitution was command, rather than custom, right, reason, consent, or community consensus.

Placed in a time perspective longer than the prerevolutionary era, what was occurring was that seventeenth-century legal absolutes were evolving into nineteenth-century constitutional relevants. Two statements, 135 years apart, indicate the thrust of constitutional change. When Parliament in 1721 refused to revoke authority granted the government for fighting the plague, dissentient lords complained "of our great confidence in his Majesty's wisdom and goodness, when we trust him with such powers, unknown to the constitution."[33] In 1856, when warning that an unprecedented act of prerogative could become a precedent if not voided, Lord Brougham reminded the House of Lords that "[t]hings might be legal yet unconstitutional."[34]

31. Speech of the earl of Egmont, Commons Debates of 14 November 1754, 15 *Parliamentary History*, at 365–66.

32. *North Briton*, No. 43, at 149.

33. Protest of 13 December 1721, 1 *Protests of the Lords*, at 267.

34. The Wensleydale Peerage, 5 *House of Lords*, at 958, 956, 10 *English Reports* 1181, 1186 (1856).

Brougham's jurisprudential riddle is puzzling only to modern Americans. Their error is to interpret the eighteenth-century British constitution through the perspective of America's nineteenth-century constitutionalism and the judiciary's usurpation of the power of judicial review. For a law to be unconstitutional in the 1760s, did not mean it was illegal or void. John Adams gave as clear examples of legal unconstitutionalities as did any participant in the prerevolutionary debate. "If the king," he wrote, "should suffer no parliament to sit for twelve years, by reason of continual prorogations, this would be an unconstitutional exercise of prerogative. If the commons should grant no supplies for twelve years, this would be an unconstitutional exertion of their privilege. Yet the king has power legally to do one, and the commons to do the other."[35]

The notion of the legal unconstitutional statute will be encountered many times in the following chapters. Its most famous and far-reaching manifestation bears directly on the topic of this book, for it was the Mutiny Act, a parliamentary statute that made licit the professional military establishment. One or two instances of this constitutional erraticism are worthy of consideration at this point. "[T]he keeping up of a numberous Standing Army in time of peace," a member of the Commons asserted in 1739, "by authority of parliament, is not contrary to law; but I will aver, that it is contrary to, and inconsistent with our constitution."[36] "[T]he raising or keeping up a Standing Army within the kingdom, in time of peace," another member had said the year before, "is inconsistent with our constitution; for though a law agreed to by Kings, Lords, and Commons,

35. 3 *The Works of John Adams, Second President of The United States* 556 (Charles Francis Adams, ed., 1851).

36. Speech of Mr. Shippen, Commons Debates of 14 February 1739, 10 *Parliamentary History*, at 1343.

cannot be said to be against law, yet it may be, and may properly be said to be, inconsistent with our constitution."[37]

Again the concept of power has been encountered. Kings, Lords, and Commons had the legal power to act, but that power alone did not make the action constitutional. Constitutionality was a consideration separate from legality. A gray area was whether such actions could be resisted legitimately. For some nonlawyers the answer was easy,[38] but others knew it was a matter of how much power the government exerted to enforce an unconstitutional law. The colonists, a clergyman asserted, probably would have resisted attempts to collect revenue under the "unconstitutional" Stamp Act "unless they had been obliged to it by superior power."[39]

Seventeenth-century English constitutionalism was lusty in eighteenth-century New England. Law had not been command then, and it was not now. "[T]he Conqueror himself," John Pym said in 1628, "though he conquered the kingdom, he conquered not the law."[40] Law remained something independent of power. Edward Hyde, earl of Clarendon, made the same point when writing of Charles I's efforts to collect "shipmoney" by prerogative taxation. Englishmen, he asserted, "heard this demanded in a court of law as a right, and found it by sworn judges of the law adjudged so, upon such grounds and reasons as every stander-by was able to swear was not law."[41]

37. Speech of Lord Polwarth, Commons Debates of 3 February 1738, ibid., at 456. The justification, stated in 1766, for the unconstitutional law was necessity. Other European kingdoms maintained standing armies. "Great Britain therefore is obliged to keep, tho' contrary to the genius of its constitution, a large body of regular troops in constant pay." Anon., *Justice and Necessity of Taxing*, at 10.

38. For example, Christopher Gadsden. [Drayton, et al.,] *The Letters*, at 217–18.

39. Chauncy, *A Discourse on "the good News,"* at 20. See also Emerson, *Sermon of Thanksgiving*, at 13.

40. Speech of John Pym, 25 March 1628, 2 *Commons Debates, 1628*, at 106.

41. Quoted in Hill, *The Century of Revolution*, at 55–56. This statement by

Clarendon seems to have thought every "stander-by" knew
what was not law. He might have been less confident if asked
how many knew what was law. What law was in seventeenth-
century England is today a harder question to answer than what
it was not. It certainly was not command, or will, or as Clarendon makes clear, necessarily what judges declared it to be. But
how did people know that what the judges declared was not
"law"? The answer is found in the fact that the doctrine promulgated in that decision, the shipmoney case, was not ancient, it
was not immemorial. For law to be "law," at least in the sense it
was immutable or "right," not an exercise of mere power, it had
to date back beyond the reach of historical memory.[42]

It was "right" not "power" that Americans meant when they
said the standing army in peacetime was illegal as well as
unconstitutional. The British said it was only unconstitutional.
The dilemma of the two constitutional traditions might not have
been resolved, but the heat of discussion might have been
tempered had the British realized that the Americans were
appealing to a constitution for which Englishmen had once
fought and died. One year after Lord Hillsborough's soldiers
disembarked at Boston, an unknown Massachusetts whig protested the illegality of the new constitutionalism of command
and power in place of the constitutionalism of consent and right.

The constitution which I hold myself bound in conscience,
duty and allegiance to maintain, frees me from obedience to
the edicts of any one or more absolute despots; let them

Clarendon was used and quoted by a number of prerevolutionary writers. [Lee,]
Junius Americanus, at 74; John J. Zubly, *An Humble Enquiry into the Nature of the
Dependency of the American Colonies upon the Parliament of Great-Britain, and the
Right of Parliament to lay Taxes on the said Colonies* 1 (1769). See also, Charles
Carroll, "First Citizen," reprinted in *Maryland and the Empire, 1773: The Antilon-
First Citizen Letters* 82–83 (Peter S. Onuf, ed., Baltimore, 1974).
42. Nenner, *Colour of Law*, at 14–16; Pocock, *Ancient Constitution*, at 30–55.

pretend divine right, virtual representative right, ministerial representative right, or what right they please, underived from the free consent of the people, the alone natural source of all legislative and executive right whatsoever.[43]

British lawyers might have known how better to deal with such ideas had they recognized their origins. Statements of this sort were not original. Law by the "right" of consent, custom, or consensus, rather than the "power" of coercive force, was the constitutionalism to which they still were emotionally attached. What the unknown writer said in Boston in 1769 only restated thoughts expressed in 1675 by Anthony Ashley Cooper, earl of Shaftesbury. He was one of the first Englishmen to feel the tension between the two constitutions.[44] He knew government existed to administer justice, but it also could command, and there was one source of command—military command—that he would not accept, either as legal or as constitutional.

> The King governing and administrating Justice by His House of Lords, and advising with both His Houses of Parliament in all important matters, is the Government I own, am born under, and am obliged to. If ever there should happen in future ages (which God forbid) a King governing by an Army without His Parliament, 'tis a government I own not, am not obliged to, nor was born under.[45]

The unknown Boston writer of 1769 and the earl of Shaftesbury spoke of the same constitution. The differences between them were those of two centuries and two continents. The British nobleman feared the king would attempt to govern by an army without consent of Parliament. The American feared

43. "Providus," in *Post*, 2 October 1769, at 2, col. 2.
44. B[etty] Behrens, "Whig Theory," 7 *Cambridge Historical Journal* 42, 67 (1941).
45. Shaftesbury and Buckingham, *Two Speeches*, at 10.

Parliament, not the king. When the earl of Hillsborough was allowed to order troops to Boston, Parliament provided colonists a striking indication that it might seek to govern by an army without consent of local assemblies.

In time, a second difference could prove as perilous as the first. When Shaftesbury spoke in 1675, everyone understood what he meant. In 1768 many would not have understood that the American not only was threatening to resist, he was saying he had a legal right to resist.

❖ 6 ❖

AN IMPENDING BLOW:

THE AMERICAN ESTABLISHMENT

Few of those fateful decisions precipitating the prerevolutionary crisis were more casually made than the creation of an American military establishment. The ministry decided it without public discussion and without parliamentary challenge.[1] Indeed, most observers had expected that, following the end of the French and Indian War, the imperial army would be withdrawn from the colonies. Although the same number of regiments and naval stations as had existed before the war were to be continued in the British Isles, soldiers assigned to duty in North America were to be increased greatly.[2] Indicative of the vagueness of the decision, the colonial public never knew how large the forces were that they might expect. The figures they were given ranged from 5,000 to 13,000 men, exclusive of provincial militia.[3] At the time

1. Thomas, *British Politics*, at 101; Christie and Labaree, *Empire*, at 30.

2. Knollenberg, *Origin*, at 34; Robson, *American Revolution*, at 48.

3. *Boston Gazette* (Supplement), 20 April 1767, at 2, col. 1; *Gazette and News-Letter*, 4 April 1765, at 3, col. 1; [Whately,] *Considerations on Trade*, at 5.

of Boston's occupation in 1768, William Bollan estimated that, before the war, Britain and France combined "did not both maintain one fourth part of the troops stationed there since the whole was reduced to his majesty's obedience."[4]

The policy of creating an American military establishment was not only made at the highest circles of imperial government without publicity or public discussion, but it was also made without consulting colonial governments about the number, composition, or distribution of the troops.[5] The ministers, however, realized that garrisoning such large forces in America drastically departed from imperial custom, and must have suspected that most colonials would, to use Samuel Adams's words, "look upon [the innovation] as entirely needless at present for their Protection, & as dangerous at all times to Virtue & Liberty."[6]

To say the troops were "needless" was to speak a whiggish thought. "[T]hey are of no Use, but a Burthen to the Colonies," pamphlet writer Nicholas Ray agreed, pointing out that the Americans did not have "an Enemy worth Notice within 3000 Miles of them."[7] One writer suggested that should another war begin, the colonies would invade the French West Indies, not the French invade the colonies.[8] Not so, the other side replied, for "the colonies may be conquered by our enemies in one campaign."[9] Although strong when united, they were weakened by dissensions, jealousies, and bickering, so that troops had to be maintained in North America by the mother country for their "safeguard."[10]

4. [Bollan,] *Continued Corruption*, at 75. He meant foot soldiers. [Bollan,] *Free Britons Memorial*, at 28.

5. Knollenberg, *Origin*, at 12–13.

6. Letter from Samuel Adams to Dennys De Berdt, 16 December 1766, 1 Adams, *Writings*, at 112.

7. Ray, *Importance of the Colonies*, at 15.

8. "Ignotus," *Thoughts on Trade*, at 25.

9. Anon., *Justice and Necessity of Taxing*, at 11.

10. Ibid., at 17. See Headlam, "Imperial Reconstruction," at 636–39.

The differences in perspectives are startling. George Grenville, the man who proposed the stamp tax to pay for the troops, not only argued they were needed to protect Americans, but also that Americans would reap economic benefits from the security they provided. That security, he reasoned, "will greatly promote the Settlement of the new Colonies; for Planters will value Property there much higher, and be more sollicitous to acquire it."[11] William Bollan, by way of contrast, could not understand why Parliament should impose customs duties on colonial trade to pay for soldiers when Americans had been able to defend themselves at times of greater danger. "For now that Louisiana, Cape Breton, and Canada, are all reduced to the obedience of, and possessed by the crown of England; now that there is not a French subject left on that continent, it is thought necessary to keep fifteen battalions of regular troops in the colonies, and for the support of them those grievous duties are imposed."[12]

Ironically, the very fact the French had been defeated furnished one argument why troops should be left in North America: the extent of the newly conquered territories required "a proportional Addition of Forces for their Security and Defence."[13] In both former French colonies to the north and Spanish to the south, "the Allegiance of the Inhabitants cannot be relied on" and the military was needed to hold them in "Subjection."[14] Making the problem even more serious, the "new Subjects (about an Hundred Thousand Persons) are all Roman Catholicks, entusiastick, bigotted, and superstitious, in Proportion to their Ignorance."[15] Twentieth-century historians as well as

11. [Grenville,] *The Regulations*, at 22.

12. [Bollan,] *Mutual Interest Considered*, at 10; Ray, *Importance of the Colonies*, at 15.

13. Anon., *Letter to Charles Townshend*, at 18. See also Christie and Labaree, *Empire*, at 30.

14. [Whately,] *Considerations on Trade*, at 51–52.

15. Anon., *Letter to Charles Townsend*, at 18. In the same vein, see Letter from

eighteenth-century imperialists have found merit in the contention that the security of Nova Scotia, Canada, and the Floridas required that the British government maintain a considerable military force in America.[16] Even if true, however, it was no reason for garrisoning New York, Boston, Charles Town, or any of the other communities of the older colonies settled more than a century before by English citizens and populated mainly by their descendants.

The same objection was raised to what was unquestionably the soundest reason for stationing British regulars on the continent: the regulation of Indian affairs. Their assignment was not to defend the frontier from the Indians. As Bollan contended, "the colonies were able and did defend themselves hundted [sic] years since against the Indians, and are they now, all of a sudden, become unable, with the addition of several hundred thousand men."[17] The service the army could have performed would have been to protect Indians from colonials.[18] It was necessary to keep squatters off tribal lands, regulate the fur trade, and police interracial intercourse,[19] but whether British regulars were needed for the job is another matter. Historians contending that colonials were temperamentally unsuited for the discipline of frontier garrison duty,[20] fail to realize that Americans would perform the task after independence. Also overlooked is the fact that the British did not do the job. By 1768, less than five years after creation of the American military establishment, the imperial government returned trade regulation to colonial jurisdic-

---

the House of Representatives to Dennis De Berdt, 11 January 1768, *Boston Gazette*, 4 April 1768, at 2, col. 1; 28 *Monthly Review* (1763), at 316.

16. Shy, *Toward Lexington*, at 62.

17. [Bollan,] *Mutual Interest Considered*, at 11; Ray, *Importance of the Colonies*, at 15.

18. Christie and Labaree, *Empire*, at 30–31.

19. Shy, *Toward Lexington*, at 82.

20. Gipson, "Revolution as Aftermath," at 95–96.

tion.[21] To save costs, frontier outposts were abandoned and all regulars within the old English colonies were stationed along the coast, far from the western Indian nations.[22]

There is no need enumerating more objections. Specific decisions were less significant than the manner in which they were made. Ministers in faraway London were formulating basic policy choices such as to abandon the frontier and garrison the seaports. That fact raised the first of four constitutional objections colonial whigs postulated against the American military establishment. Expressed in its most extreme form, incorporating not only local autonomy but popular control, the constitutional objection was stated by Samuel Adams shortly after the first regiments marched up from the long wharf to the common. A standing army, he explained,

> is an army rais'd, and kept within the community, to defend it against any sudden attacks.—If it be ask'd who is to judge, when the community is in danger of such attacks? one would naturally answer, The community itself: For who can be more proper judges of it than they, for whose safety alone, and at whose expence alone, they are kept and maintain'd. The people, while they enjoy the blessings of freedom, and the security of their property, are generally early enough in their apprehension of common danger; especially when it is so threatening as to require the military aid: And their judgment of the necessity or expediency of a standing army, is generally, at least as *honest*, as that of their superiors.[23]

Five years later, a more concise Thomas Jefferson recognized

21. Wright, *Freedom*, at 73–74; Humphries, "Lord Shelburne," at 262–65.

22. *Boston Gazette*, 26 December 1768, reprinted in 1 Adams, *Writings*, at 274; 38 *Gentleman's Magazine* (1768), at 511.

23. *Boston Gazette*, 26 December 1768, reprinted in 1 Adams, *Writings*, at 272–73.

the same constitutional truism. "Every state," he asserted, "must judge for itself the number of armed men which they may safely trust among them, of whom they are to consist, and under what restrictions they are to be laid."[24]

This charge—that the creation of an American military establishment controlled by London violated colonial rights of local autonomy—was the weakest constitutional grievance raised by the whigs. It was less persuasive because it was not as well understood in London by either British whig or tory than were the other three: a standing army in time of peace is unconstitutional; the maintenance of an American military establishment by the mother country amounted to unconstitutional taxation; and employment of regular soldiers to police civilians was unconstitutional. These three grievances were familiar in the colonies because they were rooted in English constitutional history and part and parcel of the current British constitution. The grievance of local autonomy arose from a peculiar American perspective of how authority was distributed throughout the empire.

Not many British leaders were willing to consider the American perspective. Thomas Pownall, former governor of Massachusetts, was one of the few. "When," he told the Commons in 1770 of Americans, "they see a military power established within the jurisdiction of their government—neither depending for its establishment on the will of the community, nor exercising its powers by command derived from the supreme authority of that jurisdiction, they think this military body foreign to their community, and brought upon them by force of external power."[25] Pownall's listeners had less trouble sympathizing than comprehending. Members of Parliament and crown lawyers could understand that American whigs were demanding local

24. Jefferson, *Summary View*, at 134.

25. Speech of Thomas Pownall, Commons Debates of 8 May 1770, 16 *Parliamentary History*, at 987.

autonomy without recognizing any legal basis to the demand. From the British perspective, the colonies were equated constitutionally with Cornwall or Scotland. English counties had nothing to say about how troops were raised, employed, or garrisoned. American colonies stood on the same constitutional footing. It was for Parliament and its agents, not a colonial assembly, to say how military men were to be housed, punished, and commanded.[26]

Many Americans, who were at the other extreme of the political spectrum, were unable to tolerate the imperial perspective. Of these, one of the most interesting is Eliphalet Dyer of Windham, Connecticut, who had the advantage of viewing matters from the dual background of a legal education and extensive military experience. A leading lawyer, he had taken part in the Crown Point operation and commanded a regiment in the 1758 expedition against Canada.[27] If any man could have balanced the legal rights of the colonies against the defensive needs of imperial unity, it might have been Dyer, yet he was so disturbed by the constitutional implications, he considered no other issue. In London on legal business representing the Susquehannah Company when the American military establishment first became public knowledge, Dyer wrote as if it were the beginning of a new program of parliamentary legislation or ministerial fiat that could force Americans to take up arms in defense of existing rights. Grenville, he reported, had introduced a bill levying customs duties on the colonies to defray the expense of their military security. "But," Dyer asked, "may it not be concluded that those Regiments destined for America, for the support of which those Methods [of taxation] are taking, are not primarily for our Defence (as they are undesired by us) but

26. Report of the Privy Council Committee [1756], reprinted in Ritcheson, "Introduction," at 30.

27. H. W. Howard Knott, "Eliphalet Dyer," 5 *Dictionary of American Biography* 581 (1930).

rather as a standing Army, to be as a Rod and Check over the Colonies, to enforce those Injunctions which are to be laid upon us, and at the same Time to oblige us to be at the Expence of their Support." Dyer then answered his own question. "If the Colonies," he continued, "do not now unite, and use their most vigorous Endeavours in all proper Ways, to avert this impending Blow, they may for the future, bid Farewell to Freedom and Liberty, burn their Charters, and make the best of Thraldom and Slavery."[28]

❖ 7 ❖

A MEDITATED BLOW:

THE IRISH ESTABLISHMENT

Dyer was not speculating. He was not a political theorist postulating extreme hypotheses in order to construct a model for ideal conduct. He was a lawyer arguing from the precedent of past and present legal reality. Like many other Americans, he was surely skeptical of George Grenville's claim that a large military establishment must be kept in the colonies following peace with France.[1] Historians of the imperial school have agreed that Great Britain needed troops in North America to defend her subjects,[2] but Americans had reason to doubt the claim when the new military establishment offered no commissions for colonial officers, not even those who had served with distinction in the French and Indian War,[3] and retained none of the units trained in scout-

28. Letter from Eliphalet Dyer, 1 March 1764, quoted in Knollenberg, *Origin*, at 172.

1. [Grenville,] *The Regulations*, at 56.

2. Gipson, "Revolution as Aftermath," at 96.

3. Knollenberg, *Origin*, at 12–13.

ing or foraging peculiar to Indian warfare.[4] For such observers, it was obvious that, whatever the purpose of the American establishment, it was not for the benefit of the colonies.

For whose benefit then? The American suspicion that London had sent over a police force is a likely answer. Another just as possible is that the ministry created the American military establishment, not to police the colonies, but to solve a domestic political problem. Following the great victories over France and Spain, the cost of supporting the British military establishment became enormous, as much as £300,000 higher than during the previous peace.[5] To placate fears of Parliament, the government had to keep as low as possible the number of soldiers stationed in the home islands and supported by British taxpayers.[6]

Expenditure was not the only consideration. Counter political factors pressured the ministry to maintain a much larger military establishment than before the war, perhaps as many as seventy regiments.[7] As during the aftermath of every long, costly struggle, the question of how to take care of the veterans was acute, though in eighteenth-century Great Britain the political problem was not quite what we would expect. There was little dispute about the enlisted men. Very few of those forming contemporary public opinion thought about what one writer called "those intrepid fellows, to whose bravery we are chiefly indebted for all our triumphs." He was almost alone worrying about them, and his concern was not only for their welfare, but also for the community should circumstances make them desperate. "They are," the writer warned, "suffered to roam abroad to the terror of their fellow subjects, and to commit acts of violence and rapine in the broad face of day, as if there was no

4. Ibid., at 89.
5. [Whately,] *Considerations on Trade*, at 35–36, 51.
6. Omond, *The Army*, at 49.
7. Anon., *Letter to Charles Townshend*, at 23.

civil government in Britain, but all was anarchy and uproar."[8] Most British whigs and tories thought that possibility was a matter for the police, not the taxpayers. They agreed with John Toland, an ardent opponent of standing armies, whose pamphlets were still read by radical whigs. "I cannot determin[e]," he wrote in 1698, "whether it would occasion more Indignation or Mirth to hear a Man contending, that because the Souldiers defended our Liberty at the public Charge for nine Years against the *French*, we can do no less than become their Slaves for ever."[9]

First impressions must not mislead. Social concern was not lacking in eighteenth-century Britain. It was, however, limited to deserving groups that the twentieth century no longer thinks deserving. Even more pertinent, they were not thought deserving in colonial America. In London, different values prevailed, values that would help drive the colonies further from the mother country. The British government, able to ignore their enlisted men, could not ignore their officers. They, after all, belonged to the class for whom eighteenth-century government functioned, and in the economy peculiar to the British aristocracy their case was meritorious. Officers as much as privates had been losers when the ministry disbanded sixteen regiments previously maintained on the British establishment. "They are," one of them protested, "to support their Poverty with Dignity: They are to starve like Gentlemen."[10] An alternative to dismissing these officers was to place them on half pay,[11] a condition one Boston newspaper described with some exaggeration as "scanty Subsistence."[12]

Today, the choice between discharge from service and accept-

8. [Ruffhead,] *Considerations*, at 6.
9. [Toland,] *Militia Reform'd*, at 15–16.
10. Anon., *Letter to Charles Townshend*, at 23.
11. Anon., *Letter Relating to Mutiny*, at 16–24.
12. *Gazette and News-Letter* (Supplement), 4 April 1765, at 2, col. 2 (quoting a London journal).

ing half pay would seem to be a decision about employment. From the perspective of the eighteenth century, it was cruelty to gentlemen. "Many of them," it was pointed out, "had purchased their Commissions;—Many had no other Means of Subsistence, except their Pay;—and All in general must be supposed to be influenced by the laudable Ambition of rising in that Profession, which they had chosen in their Youth; . . .—All hopes of which must have been cut off by their being reduced to half Pay."[13]

There was a third alternative. Officers who could no longer be supported by the reduced British establishment were, it was suggested, "to continue in, and to be paid by, *Ireland* and *America*."[14] Put more bluntly, one reason regiments were to be kept in North America after the French had been driven from the continent, and why London wanted an American military establishment, was to "afford full pay to a greater number of officers."[15] In fact, the argument contained a self-expanding logic. All half-pay officers, it was pointed out, continued on the British establishment and, therefore, had to be "maintained by *Great-Britain* alone." Better for everyone to support them "in full Pay," by shifting their units to either the Irish or American establishment.[16] This would relieve British taxpayers of expense and half-pay officers of pecuniary distress.

In 1768, the year British troops were sent to Boston, the Irish military establishment, as American whig leaders knew, consisted of "a greater Number, by six Regiments, than was ever before kept up in this Kingdom, in Times of Peace."[17] The impressive figure is the cost to Irish taxpayers, not the size of the Irish army. There were fewer men than would be expected, because money was spent on officers, not troops. The policy—

13. Anon., *Reasons for an Augmentation*, at 8.
14. Anon., *Letter to Charles Townshend*, at 16.
15. Anon., *Letter to Hillsborough*, at 24.
16. Anon., *Letter to Charles Townshend*, at 21.
17. Lucas, *An Address to Dublin*, at 5.

made in London, not Dublin—was "to preserve as many Officers as possible, and to reduce the Number of the private Men."[18]

It is worth dwelling on some of those numbers. An infantry company on the British establishment consisted of forty-seven or forty-eight men; on the Irish it had but twenty-eight, "with the same number of Officers as in *England,* that is, one Captain, one Lieutenant, one Ensign, two Sergeants, two Corporals." Moreover, "four of these twenty-eight, will be found but nominal or non-effective Men, whose Pay is destined to other purposes." In the cavalry, the ratio was less, for there were six officers to twenty privates, and four of those privates were nominal. The average in the dragoons was seven officers to twenty privates, four of whom were "nominal onely, Warrant-men, whose Pay is destined to other Purposes; while the Hautboy is a Non-entity, whose Pay and Cloathing make some of the many Perquisites of the Colonels."[19] Where a British regiment generally had 500 members, a regiment of foot on the Irish establishment in 1768, "when compleat," did "not consist of above 328 Men."[20] An example is the Twenty-ninth Foot, one of those ordered to Boston that year. In 1763, while assigned to garrison duty in Ireland and paid on the Irish establishment, each company had twenty-seven privates. In 1765, when the regiment was sent to Halifax and placed on the British establishment, there were forty-seven privates in each company.[21]

Unfortunately, American whigs made few comments about the Irish comparison. Their specific words, when reacting to what was reported from Ireland, could have provided a measure of their disenchantment with imperial authority. Surely they felt forebodings on reading how the Irish establishment supported

18. Anon., *Reasons for an Augmentation,* at 9.
19. Lucas, *An Address to Dublin,* at 3.
20. Anon., *Reasons for an Augmentation,* at 7.
21. Everard, *The 29th Foot,* at 56.

2,940 commissioned and noncommissioned officers "to command only 9060 private men!"[22] Americans did not have to be told what was meant when London's *Monthly Review* (in an article reprinted by the *Boston Gazette*) commented that "[t]he conclusions to be drawn from this deficiency are sufficiently obvious."[23] English and Scots might say the deficiency "arose from Motives of the very best Kind, Policy and Justice."[24] Irishmen and Americans could not.

From the colonial perspective, manipulation of the Irish military establishment smacked too much of the English legal mind. Because the group benefited was of the right type, the method did not matter. Causes could be aided by money raised for other purposes as long as they were good. A related manipulation occurred in the Mutiny Act, which regulated military affairs in Great Britain. According to one section, the king "in Compassion to the distressed Condition of several Widows of Officers of the Army, who have lost their Lives in the Service of the late War," had ordered that "a number of fictitious Names" be entered on the muster roles of all companies, "in order to raise and settle a Fund for the Maintenance of such Widows."[25] This fund, of course, was for the widows of officers, not "private Men."

Our contemporary prejudices create both surprise and unsurprise: surprise that there were defenders of the Irish establishment, unsurprise because they were not troubled that it benefited only officers. After all, one wrote, release from service was no "Hardship on the private Men." "[T]hey cou'd easily turn themselves to more lucrative Employments than that of a common Soldier, and most of them were well pleased to obtain their

22. 38 *Monthly Review* (1768), at 503. See also Lucas, *An Address to Dublin*, at 6.

23. 38 *Monthly Review* (1768), at 503; *Boston Gazette*, 26 September 1768, at 1, cols. 1–2.

24. Anon., *Reasons for an Augmentation*, at 7.

25. Section 14, Mutiny Act (29 George II), reprinted in 2 Neville, *New-Jersey Acts*, at Appendixes 8–9.

Discharge."[26] Ironically, these enlisted men were more likely to be Irish than were the officers. Even so, defenders of the system were not lost for arguments why Irish taxpayers should support unemployed English officers while leaving Irish enlisted men to shift for themselves. Evidence comes not only from government supporters, but also from an antiadministration writer who conceded that "[a]n overproportion of officers to men upon the establishment," made sense "for a country which has concluded a peace hollow and unlikely to be permanent."[27]

From the Irish point of view, matters were not so simple. The Irish were paying for what was "the most expensive and burdensome, though the least efficacious Establishment in Europe."[28] Dr. Charles Lucas, member for Dublin in the Irish Parliament and a "commonwealthman"[29] well known to Boston whigs,[30] charged that the officers whom the system was designed to support gave little service in return. His description of the twelve generals on the Irish establishment reminds readers of the other bane of Irish society, absentee landlords. The officers were so often in Great Britain the king appointed a junior officer, a native of Ireland, "to act as Major-General" so tasks requiring officers of that rank could be performed.[31] A critic could easily have described the Irish establishment as just one more count in the sorry indictment of British misrule of that unhappy nation.

The anonymous author of *The History of the Reign of George the Third* posed a relevant question. Why, he wondered, was Ireland, with such limited wealth and population, supporting in peacetime a military establishment only two thousand men fewer than that of Great Britain. The thoughts occurring to him

26. Anon., *Reasons for an Augmentation*, at 9.
27. Anon., *Budget Inscribed*, at 9.
28. Lucas, *An Address to Dublin*, at 3.
29. Robbins, *Commonwealthman*, at 143.
30. *Post*, 18 March 1771, at 3, col. 2; *Boston Gazette*, 25 March 1771, at 1, col. 3.
31. Lucas, *An Address to Dublin*, at 8.

were not the same as those occurring to Irishmen, but they might have occurred to Americans. "Is it," he asked of the Irish establishment, "the intention of the ministry to make the same use of it, that they made of the last troops sent out of this island? Are they meditating any new blow against North America, and the commerce of the empire?"[32]

❖ 8 ❖

IN A PRECARIOUS CONDITION:

THE IMPERIAL INCENTIVE

All in all, the Irish establishment could have been a model of what American whigs were determined to prevent. Many Bostonians at least knew Charles Lucas, the "Wilkes of Ireland," member of Parliament for Dublin, and the most vocal critic of the Irish military establishment. In 1771 "an elegant and pathetic letter from the famous Dr. Lucas in Dublin" was read to the annual Boston town meeting.[1] "In this letter the Doctor sympathizes with his American Fellow-Sufferers, and enumerates so many Instances of Military Barbarity, Insolence and unbounded Licentiousness, as demonstrates that Law is the Will of the Ministry for that Kingdom."[2]

Lucas's last sentence is especially important. It demonstrates the universality of constitutional principles in the English-speaking world. Writing of Ireland, he raised an issue to which close attention will be given later in this book in both its British and American contexts. It was the whig fear that law would become the will of the British ministry and its agents would be

32. Anon., *History of George III*, at 389.
1. *Boston Gazette*, 25 March 1771, at 1, col. 3.
2. *Post*, 18 March 1771, at 3, col. 2.

responsible to no one, not even the king.[3] A related code word was "influence," obtained by purchasing support with public funds. Whigs reading Lucas's pamphlets surely spotted parallels between the Irish establishment he described and other ways Irish government was manipulated, "extending ministerial Influence."[4] Just as the Irish army was used to provide income for English or Scottish officers rendering no service to Ireland, so the Irish civil list furnished pensions for crown and ministerial favorites who had not served Ireland but were British, generally English, often impoverished aristocracy, sometimes mere political hacks. In 1763, for example, a fire at Grosvenor Square killed the viscountess dowager Molesworth and two daughters. Three other daughters survived. "His Majesty," it was announced, "has been further pleased to settle a pension of 400 *l.* a year on each of them, upon the Irish establishment."[5] That was a year in which, it was claimed, pensions on the Irish establishment were "not much less than one half the whole circulating money in that kingdom."[6] Moreover, it was charged by a lawyer who documented his case, all Irish pensions were "clearly illegal."[7] If so, London's government again demonstrated insensitivity about illegalities concerning what contemporaries called "corruption." By 1770, a London-published pamphlet asserted, the Irish pension list was "drawn annually from the vitals of Ireland, and thrown into the ministerial *pool* to be sported for."[8]

Historians who are unable to credit the sincerity of American constitutional fears about British rule should ponder the meaning of Ireland. Irish law was not American law, but the example

3. "In Legitimate Stirps," at 486–93.
4. McAulay, *Legality of Pensions,* at 5.
5. 32 *London Magazine* (1763), at 276, 334.
6. 29 *Monthly Review* (1763), at 289.
7. Ibid., at 291–92. See particularly, McAulay, *Legality of Pensions,* at 5, 18–20.
8. Anon., *Thoughts English and Irish,* at 7.

of one posed warnings for the other.[9] The Irish military establishment indicated where the new American military establishment could lead. Many young, would-be officers in England, Scotland, and Wales were anxious for duty with an undermanned company garrisoned in Boston, New York, or Philadelphia. The same was true for the Irish civil list. The recently enacted Townshend duties[10] implied the threat that revenues raised in America might end up like that of Ireland, strengthening ministerial rule by awarding ministerial "tools." "[I]f we judge from what is past," a pamphlet of 1768 asked, "must we not suppose, that if a large revenue could be collected, it would on the first emergency be mortgaged, and forever alienated to those who are always ready for large premiums to supply the exigencies of the state; and from that time becoming the property of private persons, be no longer of any public utility?"[11] If one judged by Ireland, that would be the future of public revenue in America, reason enough for colonial whigs to keep on their constitutional guard and resist constitutional innovations in the imperial connection.

Troops maintained by Irish taxation did not serve only in Ireland. In 1765, for example, three regiments of foot "on the Irish Establishment" were sent to the colonies.[12] Not all the burden of American defense was shouldered by British taxpayers as often charged. Two of the four regiments ordered to Boston in 1768 came from Ireland, and a pamphlet published in Dublin that year asked "[w]hy shou'd this Kingdom contribute to the Defence of the Colonies of *America*, where she is not allowed to Trade but under such Restrictions as make it of little Value?"[13]

9. For discussion, see *In a Defiant Stance*.
10. 7 George III, cap. 46.
11. Anon., *Power and Grandeur*, at 19.
12. *Gazette and News-Letter* (Supplement), 6 June 1765, at 2, col. 1.
13. Anon., *Reasons for an Augmentation*, at 25.

Important to American whigs was the political reality that decisions were made in London, not Dublin, for the benefit of British, not Irish, taxpayers. Thomas Whately, one of the most prominent imperial subministers,[14] openly boasted of this fact. "The Garrisons of *Gibraltar* and *Minorca*," he wrote of the postwar army, "have been reduced from 3260 to 3116 Men on the *British* Establishment, the Difference being made up by *Irish* Regiments; in consequence of which Arrangement between 30000 and 40000 *l.* is annually saved to *Great Britain*."[15] It was saved, of course, by a London decision transferring the expense to the Irish establishment. After the American establishment was functioning, much could be charged to it besides the maintenance of over-officered regiments stationed in the colonies.[16]

British statesmen knew what was needed. "The forming an American fund to support the exigencies of government," Secretary of State Lord Shelburne wrote the commander in chief in the colonies, "in the same manner as is done in Ireland, is what is so highly reasonable that it must take place sooner or later."[17] From any point of view, therefore, the decision to create an American military establishment was as much a decision to impose taxes as to alter the constitution by maintaining a standing army in the colonies. British writers could justify the decision as one dictated by colonial defense needs, but from the American perspective London was promulgating a system of taxation.[18] Indeed, when it was first proposed to augment the army establishment in North America, Parliament was assured

14. Wickwire, *Subministers*, at 79.

15. [Whately,] *Considerations on Trade*, at 27.

16. In fact, Whately complained that the savings to Great Britain by putting increased cost of forces on the Irish establishment was lost when Britain decided to keep additional troops in America after peace with France. Ibid.

17. Letter from the earl of Shelburne to General Thomas Gage, 11 December 1766, quoted in Humphries, "Lord Shelburne," at 274.

18. Anon., *General Opposition*, at 36.

that after one year Americans would be paying all the costs.[19] The report that a regiment was to be raised in Great Britain (not in the colonies) for service "in each of the four provinces of New-York, New-England, Pennsylvania, and Massachusett's Bay," was accompanied by an announcement that its maintenance would "be entirely on the North American Establishment, and quite independent of the Pay of Great-Britain."[20]

Americans did not have to guess what the British government was up to; there were no secrets. Both of the first two attempts to raise revenue from the colonies, the Sugar Act[21] and the Stamp Act,[22] had been justified in Great Britain with the argument that Americans should pay for their own defense, even for troops posted among them by London.[23] Nor was the idea new. As early as 1739, two pamphlets proposed a colonial stamp tax to raise revenue for regiments defending British North America.[24] The argument was disarmingly simple. By assuming the colonies were "dependant on us for their security and protection," British imperialists could claim the right to regulate American trade and tax American subjects.[25]

This bit of legislative history lends substance to American complaints. The pleas of Bernard and the customs commissioners for the assignment of troops to Boston had, from the whig point of view, brought the argument full circle. By saying

19. Christie and Labaree, *Empire*, at 31.

20. *Gazette and News-Letter* (Supplement), 4 April 1765, at 2, col. 1.

21. 4 George III, cap. 15; Robson, *American Revolution*, at 54.

22. 5 George III, cap. 12; Robson, *American Revolution*, at 56–57.

23. Anon., *Justice and Necessity of Taxing*, at 10; Anon., *A Complaint against a Pamphlet*, at 19; Grenville, *The Regulations*, at 101; [Whately,] *Considerations on Trade*, at 71, 139; 16 *Parliamentary History*, at 34n; 33 *London Magazine* (1764), at 446, 555; *Gazette and News-Letter*, 13 June 1765, at 2, col. 2; Christie and Labaree, *Empire*, at 50, 82–83; Robson, *American Revolution*, at 16–17.

24. Anon., *Two Papers*, at 8–9, 14.

25. [Mildway,] *Laws and Policy*, at 85.

they needed soldiers to support the revenue service, they were saying soldiers were needed to collect a tax imposed to maintain soldiers.

When the Irish background is considered, it is easier to understand why creation of an American military establishment was opposed. Not only would it be largely for the benefit of the English officer corps and British taxpayers, but who could say where it might lead in the future when it was realized that by 1769 half the forces supported by Irish taxes were "merely imaginary."[26] And, like Irish-paid soldiers garrisoning Gibraltar and Minorca, where would those supposedly defending the colonies be sent? The money from the Sugar and Stamp Acts already was promised for regiments in Canada, Pensacola, and Mobile,[27] provinces governed by Britain through military commanders, not elected assemblies, and held as conquered territories, from which the colonies anticipated few benefits.

The rub was not whether or not Americans needed British protection, but who decided they did, who decided how much defense was necessary and where, and who decided how the money was to be raised and from whom. The assumption in London was that all questions would be answered by the ministry or Parliament. "It was found *necessary*," Charles Lloyd argued in 1767,

> to maintain upwards of 10000 men for the defence of our *colonies*; an expence of between 3 and 400,000 *l. per ann.* great part of which was entirely new, was, on that account, to be incurred; it was *just* that the *colonies* which had profited so much by the war, whose interests, commerce and security had been the first objects of *the peace*; and of whose ability to bear at least some proportion of that new expence there neither was nor is any reason to doubt, should contribute

26. 38 *London Magazine* (1769), at 585.
27. Anon., *Necessity of Repealing the Stamp Act*, at 12.

(not to support or to defend Great Britain but) *about a third part of the expence* necessary for their own defence and protection.[28]

Such reasoning was behind passage of the Stamp Act, which precipitated the first crisis of the prerevolutionary era. It was precisely on the same argument—necessity of defense—that (as *Junius Americanus* pointed out) Charles I had justified prerogative taxation and imposition of "ship money," which fomented the English revolution of 1642.[29]

It was evident in the eighteenth century that the creation of the American military establishment was part and parcel of the Stamp Act controversy. It was a matter of taxation, though the two sides had difficulty concentrating on that issue. It was not as clear and direct as when the Sugar Act, the Stamp Act, or the Townshend duties were being debated. From the British perspective, it was a question of fairness. The mother country was paying nearly £500,000 a year for defense and asking rich America to contribute only £160,000.[30] From the colonial side, the matter was often viewed as a question of necessity: British troops were not needed for there was no danger[31] and "we are both able and willing to defend our own frontiers, without putting the government to the trouble of transporting troops for that purpose, at such an immense expense."[32]

Fairness and necessity were surface issues, easily debated, but of slight substance. More constitutional in the eighteenth century was taxation without representation. It was irrelevant that

28. [Lloyd,] *Conduct Examined*, at 7.

29. [Lee,] *Junius Americanus*, at 76–77.

30. 38 *Gentleman's Magazine* (1768), at 530.

31. Letter from the House of Representatives to Dennys de Berdt, 12 January 1768, 1 Adams, *Writings*, at 144–45.

32. [William Hicks,] "A CITIZEN," in *Pennsylvania Journal*, reprinted in *South Carolina Gazette*, 4 April 1768, at 2, col. 3. See also *Extract of a Letter to De Berdt*, at 8.

the soldiers were for American purposes when Americans were not asked but told to contribute.[33] A hundred and fifty years of customary constitutional practice were being swept away. As a Salem resident pointed out, the Massachusetts charter empowered the General Court to levy on the people "for our Service in the necessary Defence and Support of our Government." Creation of an American military establishment supported by local taxes imposed by the imperial government threatened the colonial constitution and the destruction of local government. "[C]an it," the Salem man asked, "be thought reasonable in itself, or safe for them, to have their Support, Preservation and Defence taken out of their own Hands, and intrusted in the Hands of Men who are a thousand Leagues distant from them?"[34]

James Otis might have said the same had he understood the constitutional perplexity. As usual, he missed the full implications, and, seeing but part of the problem, raised but part of the objection. Because Parliament was supreme in his constitutional theory, it could station troops in the colony as it pleased. But wiser policy would have left the method of support to each colony. "[T]o have the whole levied and collected without our consent," Otis thought, "is extraordinary. 'Tis allowed even to *tributaries* and those laid under *military* contribution to assess and collect the sums demanded."[35]

Although missing the constitutional issue, Otis did focus attention back on the Irish precedent. "The case of the provinces is certainly likely to be the hardest that can be instanced in story," he concluded. "Will it not equal anything but downright military execution? Was there ever a tribute imposed even on the conquered?"[36] The answer, as those better versed in imperial

33. "L.," *Letter to G[renville]*, at 40.
34. [Prescott,] *Calm Consideration*, at 17.
35. Otis, *Rights*, at 451.
36. Ibid.

constitutionalism knew, was irrelevant. The Irish model, which Governor Francis Bernard and other British officials sought to impose on the American colonies,[37] revealed that Otis's scheme would not have preserved American constitutional autonomy. In Ireland, that scheme was the constitution, and Ireland had no freedom of choice. "[N]ot one essential of independency of legislature" remained to the Irish House of Commons "except that of raising money."[38] The British ministry may not have understood the irony, but by combining the Stamp Act revenue with the American military establishment, it was placing the English-populated colonies of North America in a more constitutionally precarious condition than that of conquered Ireland.

❖ 9 ❖

IN A FREE COUNTRY:

THE AMERICAN SUSPICION

Some people in London were convinced that Americans were being taxed for their own defense. These persons believed that if colonial whigs were correct in asserting that troops were not necessary for their defense, then there would be no justification for taxation.[1] Americans seldom made this argument. They did not confuse British excuses with British motivations. Nor did the Irish model trouble them as much as might be thought. They were determined to resist parliamentary taxation no matter what

37. *In a Defiant Stance*, at 15–16.
38. 39 *London Magazine* (1770), at 208.
1. "[I]f regular troops are not necessary for the defence of that people, the whole system of levying taxes falls to the ground and there is no pretence for doing of it in violation of their charters." Second letter from a London Merchant to a Noble Lord, reprinted in *Gazette and News-Letter*, 2 January 1766, at 1, col. 2.

the parliamentary justification. Their fear was not that the British would establish the constitutionality of colonial taxation, but that they would attempt to enforce unconstitutional taxes with unconstitutional force. When contemplating the American establishment, colonial whigs suspected it might not be there for defense at all, that they could expect eventually that "a military power shall supersede their civil authority," and that the towns of the colonies would be "dragooned to an obedience to Laws, made, not only without, but against their Consent."[2]

The American suspicion was that the ministry planned to use the soldiers, supported by the American military establishment and American taxation, to enforce imperial law and collect imperial taxes. After all, as a London pamphlet stated in 1766, "If a standing force be necessary in these colonies, it must be for the purposes of the civil magistrate, *viz*. preserving peace, and executing justice."[3] "Broad hints have been given," the *Providence Gazette* noted before the Stamp Act crisis erupted, "that *standing forces* are to be sent amongst us, to humble us, and to enforce execution of such laws, as we must esteem grievances."[4]

Whether or not the Grenville ministry had intended the American military establishment to police the colonies is a question that cannot be answered. At best, it is doubtful. Resistance to taxation was not foreseen, and there was probably very little thought given to using the troops to suppress factions.[5] The fact is, however, that Americans suspected that was the intention, and they had several reasons for thinking so.

First of all, the idea was not new. As early as 1739, a London

2. Letter from the Town of Medford to the Town of Boston, 14 March 1770, *Boston Gazette* (Supplement), 19 March 1770, at 2, col. 1.

3. Anon., *Necessity of Repealing the Stamp Act*, at 12.

4. Quoted in *Boston Post-Boy*, 15 July 1765, at 2, col. 2.

5. For discussion, see Shy, *Toward Lexington*, at 82–83; Christie and Labaree, *Empire*, at 31; and Knollenberg, *Origin*, at 88–93.

pamphlet had stated several reasons why standing forces should be maintained in the colonies. One reason was that the army "would gradually, with Time, introduce amongst them a more just and favourable Opinion of their Dependency on a *British* Parliament, than what they generally have at present."[6] Later, in 1763, the point was made even more forcibly.

> It will be necessary, besides, to establish some new Systems of Police in all our different Colonies, that all may concur in bearing a Proportion of the general Expence of Government; and particularly, that they may be compelled *next Year*, however reluctantly, to maintain the Troops that are necessary for their Defence. For these Purposes, a very respectable Force is absolutely necessary.[7]

Secondly, some rather inabstinent statements were published in the British press that Americans could ignore only at a risk. "I take your word for it," one pamphlet told them in 1766,

> and believe you are as sober, temperate, upright, humane and virtuous, as the posterity of independents and anabaptists, presbyterians and quakers, convicts and felons, savages and negro-worshippers, can be; that you are as loyal subjects, as obedient to the laws, as zealous for the maintenance of order and good government, as your late actions evince you to be; and I affirm that you have much need of the gentlemen of the blade to polish and refine your manners, to inspire you with an honest frankness and openness of behaviour, to rub off the rust of puritanism and to make

6. Anon., *Two Papers*, at 21. Unpublished documents drafted for ministers also urged that the colonies be made "Subservient to the Interests of the Principal State." Abercromby, "Examination of the Acts," at 2.

7. Anon., *Letter to Charles Townshend*, at 19.

you ashamed of proposing in your assemblies, as you have
lately done, to pay off no more debts due to your original
native country.[8]

Another British writer would have stationed troops in America
on the questionable premise that the mainland colonies were
"jealous of their Mother-Country, and envious of each other's
Prosperity." His second argument was a bit stronger: that Ger-
mans in Pennsylvania were "wholly unacquainted with the laws
and Manners, and Language of this Country."[9] They needed
policing, a task some British writers knew would not be arduous
because Americans were militarily inept and could mount no
resistance. It would require no more than "ten thousand of our
Regular Troops, to drive all the Colonies before them."[10] For
colonial whigs, perhaps the most chilling argument was that
troops were necessary in the colonies for the same reasons they
were in Great Britain.

> Britain observes this policy within herself; is it not absurd
> to imagine she would not follow the same maxim with
> regard to her colonies? She keeps on foot a considerable
> body of forces to be prepared on every emergency, not only
> to oppose a public foe, but also to enforce the decisions of
> the civil magistrate.[11]

A third reason Americans had grounds to suspect the troops
were in the colonies to police civilians is that they had previously
been sent for that same purpose. It is no exaggeration to call the
administration of the Dominion of New England, under Governor Edmund Andros, a "garrison government."[12] He had two
companies of regular troops maintained "upon His Ma'ties

8. Anon., *Justice and Necessity of Taxing*, at 23–24.
9. Anon., *Letter to Charles Townshend*, at 18.
10. Anon., *General Opposition*, at 16.
11. Anon., *Justice and Necessity of Taxing*, at 17–18.
12. Webb, "Trials of Andros," at 42.

establishment in England,"[13] which he was specifically authorized by James II to employ as police.[14] Explaining why they had rebelled against Andros, Bostonians mentioned these soldiers "brought from Europe, to support what was to be imposed upon us, not without repeated Menaces that some hundreds more were intended for us."[15]

Fourth, there was the example of Ireland. "It is vain," a writer told the *London Gazetteer* of the Americans, "to pretend that Ireland affords us an example of a more obedient people, for we all know, that the Irish are kept in awe by a military power only."[16] It ought, therefore, "not to be mentioned as a rule for your conduct towards the colonies,"[17] yet it was. "Regular troops," former Governor Thomas Pownall insisted, "are in the same manner and degree necessary in North America, as in Britain or Ireland."[18] Because Pownall was considered to be a friend of the colonies, Americans could only hope that he did not mean in exactly the "same manner and degree." If so, it meant an end to customary colonial definitions of law. In Ireland, law was command, and the command came from the sword. "Protestant Gentlemen of *Ireland* . . . often sollicited the Government to build Barracks on their Estates," seeking "Soldiers as a Protection against the too formidable numbers of Roman Catholicks."[19] As one of the gentlemen explained during the year of Boston's occupation,

we owe our present Security, and the Preservation of our happy Constitution, chiefly, if not solely, to our Connexion

13. "Andros's Report of his Administration, 1690," in *Narratives of the Insurrections, 1675–1690*, at 229, 233.

14. Webb, "Trials of Andros," at 35n18.

15. "Declaration of the Gentlemen," at 177.

16. "Equity," in *London Gazetteer*, 3 September 1765, reprinted in *Post*, 2 December 1765, at 1, col. 2.

17. Anon., *Late Occurrences in North America*, at 5.

18. Pownall, *Administration*, at 99.

19. Anon., *Letter to Charles Townshend*, at 17.

with *Great-Britain*, and the Protection of taking her Forces into our Pay for our Defence. For there is no good Reason can be assign'd, except the foregoing, Why the Religion of the Majority is not in this Country, as well as in others the Religion of the State; as it would soon become, if once the Protection of *Great Britain* was withdrawn.[20]

Americans might not worry that British troops would impose Anglicanism, but they had to be concerned about what the word "law" had come to mean in Ireland. A hint of things imperialists might attempt had been given during the Stamp Act crisis. Today, we suspect London knew better than try to collect stamp taxes by force,[21] but we cannot be certain. Some ministers urged using troops,[22] and Americans had reasons to think regiments might be sent "to quicken the Execution,"[23] especially when reading of sloops being fitted out to carry the stamps to America and reports of naval units being ordered to stand by.[24] More alarming were stories that soldiers had been used in other colonies to enforce the Stamp Act. "The Stamps," a New York newspaper warned,

> are by a Military Power forced upon the Inhabitants of *Canada*, *Nova-Scotia*, and the new conquered Settlements in *America*, as also upon the Islands where a sufficent Military Force is maintain'd to enslave the Inhabitants, viz *Jamaica*, the *Grenadas*, *Barbados*, and *Antiqua*; and by the same Means

20. Anon., *Reasons for an Augmentation*, at 12. Charles Lucas, of course, insisted that law could be enforced in Ireland without military power. Lucas, *An Address to Dublin*, at 16.

21. For discussion, see Maier, *Resistance*, at 142–43.

22. Christie and Labaree, *Empire*, at 64.

23. "Piece lately Published in Philadelphia," *Gazette and News-Letter*, 6 December 1765, at 2, col. 2.

24. *Gazette and News-Letter*, 9 January 1766, at 2, col. 2, and 17 April 1766, at 1, col. 2.

it may be enforced upon all *America*, when the Military Power becomes superior to that of the united Colonies.[25]

According to stories out of Philadelphia, the stamp distributor in Halifax was "guarded by a party of soldiers night and day,"[26] and on Antigua stamped paper was "guarded by 100 men, and the inhabitants forced to accept them, though solely against their wills."[27] What matters is not whether these stories were true, but that they were printed. They caused Americans to worry that in some British colonies, as a "son of liberty" told the *Providence Gazette*, the inhabitants "were kept in awe by a military power." "Indeed," he wrote, "the military in Nova Scotia have nearly extinguished the civil government, and in Canada, all decisions are by guns and cutlery ware."[28]

If American whigs drew a false impression of British military activity during the Stamp Act crisis, it was an impression reenforced by rhetoric in the mother country complaining that Americans had defied the government and the government had backed down. "Sedition," the author of the Stamp Act complained, "never met with so little Resistance from Government."[29] Henry Seymour Conway, secretary of state in charge of the colonies, was criticized for not making Americans obey the law.[30] "The *right of Taxation* over the colonies," the Reverend James Scott wrote in a widely circulated article, "is a point

25. Quoted in *Boston Post-Boy*, 13 January 1766, at 3, col. 2; *Gazette and News-Letter* (Supplement), 16 January 1766, at 2, col. 2.

26. Philadelphia newspaper, quoted in *Gazette and News-Letter*, 2 January 1766, at 2, col. 1.

27. Philadelphia newspaper of 26 December 1765, quoted in *Gazette and News-Letter*, 9 January 1766, at 3, col. 1.

28. "A SON OF LIBERTY," in the *Providence Gazette* (Extraordinary), 12 March 1766, reprinted in *Boston Post-Boy*, 24 March 1766, at 1, col. 3.

29. [Whately,] *Considerations on Trade*, at 217.

30. [Lloyd,] *Conduct Examined*, at 29–50.

which none but a *republican leveller*, or the wildest visionary in politics would dare to dispute; and the necessity of *enforcing the tax*, after it has been violently and rebelliously withstood, is evident to every man, who has the credit and dignity of the British legislature at heart."[31]

The British complaint had two elements. To say the government should have enforced the Stamp Act was, first of all, to say it possessed the legal right to enforce it, probably with soldiers. About as worrisome was the second: that military power could have collected the stamp taxes. Troops in Ireland joined with those already in the colonies, one source theorized, "would have formed a body of near 5000 men, ready and able to have reduced the revolting provinces to obedience."[32]

Thus, Americans thought that the British government would attempt imposing imperial law upon the colonies by military force,[33] and so did many British citizens.[34] It was this suspicion that most troubled colonial whigs about British intentions. But to understand the American suspicion is not the same as understanding the American alarm. It must be asked not only what they thought the troops were sent to do, but what they thought the decision to use military force meant. It is the answer to this question that raised the constitutional issue. The introduction "and quartering standing armies in a free country in times of peace, without the consent of the people" was unconstitu-

31. "Anti-Sejanus," reprinted in 35 *London Magazine* (1766), at 73.

32. [Lloyd,] *Conduct Examined*, at 108–9.

33. Newspapers were filled with accounts of regiments being raised to garrison colonial towns, of soldiers held in readiness to embark upon the first notice of civil unrest, and of army officers making preparations to govern with military force. *South Carolina Gazette* (Postscript), 27 April 1767, at 2, col. 1, and 15 June 1767, at 2, col. 2; *Boston Gazette*, 12 September 1767, at 3, col. 3; *Boston Post-Boy*, 20 April 1767, at 2, col. 1; *Boston Chronicle*, 31 October 1768, at 523, col. 1, 7 November 1768, at 424, col. 2, and 17 November 1768, at 438, col. 3.

34. For example, [Erskine,] *Shall I Go to War?*, at 24–25.

tional.[35] "[T]o enforce obedience to acts of the British parliament," John Hancock said, was not the role of troops.[36] "Did his majesty possess such a right as this," Thomas Jefferson pointed out, "it might swallow up all our other rights whenever he should think proper. But his majesty has no right to land a single armed man on our shores."[37] Jefferson was referring to purpose. The purpose of landing soldiers, not the action of landing them, was unconstitutional. The soldiers disembarking at Boston during 1768, James Warren explained, were on an unconstitutional mission because they had been sent "evidently for the purpose of effecting *that,* which it was one principal design of the founders of the constitution to prevent (when they declared a standing army in a time of peace to be AGAINST LAW) namely, for the enforcement of obedience to Acts which, upon fair examination, appeared to be unjust and unconstitutional."[38] For the remainder of this book, the two questions posed will be: What did Warren mean, and was he correct in law?

❖ 10 ❖

A STANDING FEAR:

THE ORIGINS OF CONTROVERSY

The point in contention was a matter of law—not of politics, of argument, of negotiation, but of constitutional law. The American colonies were settled by the English, their inhabitants were subjects of the British crown, and they were entitled not only by

35. *The Boston Declaration,* quoted in Christie and Labaree, *Empire,* at 158.
36. John Hancock's Oration (1774), *Massacre Orations,* at 45.
37. Jefferson, "A Summary View," at 79–80.
38. James Warren's Oration (1772), *Massacre Orations,* at 22.

customary prescription to liberties and privileges established by the imperial and colonial constitutions, but also to all rights traditionally associated with the ancient English constitution.[1] Few of the rights were better known to the general public than the right to be free of standing armies.

In truth, the tradition might as accurately be termed a "fear" as a "right." "[A] Standing Army," the seventeenth-century Samuel Johnson wrote, "was always a name of dread and horror to an *English* Ear, and signify'd the worst sort of Invasion, being intestine, and already got within us."[2] "Their fear," Bernard Bailyn has explained, "was not simply of armies but of *standing armies*, a phrase that had distinctive connotations, derived, like so much of their political thought, from the seventeenth century."[3] For Americans, a Boston clergyman best defined a "standing army" as "a number of men paid by the public, to devote themselves wholly to the military profession; while the body of the people followed their peaceable employments, without paying any attention to the art of war."[4]

Few dogmas in the liturgy of whig historiography were so sacrosanct as the belief that, before the seventeenth century, standing armies had not been part of the English constitution. Aside from William the Conqueror (who used Normans to keep the English in subjection and English to coerce the Normans),[5] people were told, the rulers of England had never possessed sufficient military strength to execute internal policy with armed force. "Such an establishment," it was theorized, "was so repug-

1. "In Accordance with Usage"; "In an Inherited Way."
2. Johnson, *Works*, at 324.
3. 1 Bailyn, *Pamphlets*, at 41.
4. Howard, *Artillery-Election Sermon*, at 26.
5. "Copy of a Letter sent by a Committee of the Supporters of the Bill of Rights to the South Carolina Commons House of Assembly," *Annual Register, 1770*, at [225]. See also, St. Amand, *Historical Essay*, at lxviii.

nant to the genius of feudal policy, and so incompatible with the privileges and pretensions of the nobles, that during several centuries no monarch was either so bold, or so powerful as to venture on any step towards introducing it."[6] Sir Walter Raleigh had said much the same when pointing out that England's gentry "are the garrisons of good order throughout the realm."[7] The explanation might lie in the fact that Great Britain was an island and England's natural defense was the navy,[8] but what was ordained by nature became historical fact and historical fact was the source of constitutional custom. "If there were no other argument against it," an anonymous 1648 pamphlet said of England maintaining a standing army, "it is enough that it is a thing [that] was never used in this Kingdome."[9]

The anonymous pamphleteer spoke too late. His constitutional world was already crumbling. England maintained a standing army in Ireland[10] and the house of Stuart was on the throne. He, himself, believed that the Civil War had been caused by the dispute over the milita.[11] The king had hitherto appointed the officers.[12] When Parliament sought control, the English for the first time encountered the ultimate question of sovereignty.[13] Charles I claimed that "Kingly Power is but a shadow" without command of the militia,[14] and knew his refusal to relinquish it meant his death.[15] Had Charles retained command,

6. 38 *London Magazine* (1769), at 157.

7. Hill, *Century of Revolution*, at 28.

8. Ibid., at 15; Omond, *The Army*, at 5.

9. Anon., *Peaceable Militia*, at 2.

10. H. W. Koch, "Cromwell's Genius," in *Cromwell: A Profile*, ed. Ivan Roots (New York, 1973), at 20, 22.

11. Anon., *Peaceable Militia*, at 1.

12. Gardiner, *Two Stuarts*, at 130.

13. Schwoerer, "The Fittest Subject," at 66.

14. Ibid., at 45.

15. Wedgewood, *Trial*, at 20.

the parliamentary opposition maintained, he would employ "the Militia to the destruction of his people."[16] "[T]o what purpose," a writer asked in 1643, "do we strive for liberty & property, & laws to conform them? these are but imaginary things, if they have no hedg[e] to fence them. If the *Militia* be for the King, let us burne the Statutes we have already, and save a labour of making more."[17]

An even greater risk of standing armies than trusting that kings would obey the law was the army itself. "[T]hough no man ought to question His Majesties personall goodnesse," another writer warned in 1644, "yet no man can doubt, but that this Army, thus composed, when it hath mastered the Parliament, will also give Law to His Majesty, as the Roman Army did to the Emperours, after the conquest of the Empire: and then, the question is not, Whether we shall trust His Majesty? which no man will question; but whether we will subject our selves, with the most desired, and best deserving Parliament that ever was, to Papists and Delinquents?"[18]

The prophecy was fulfilled, but with an ironic twist that made the event even more ominous for eighteenth-century Americans. Dissenters not papists, parliamentary not royal troops, turned on their masters and with force altered the form of government. The army that defeated Charles I became disenchanted with the parliamentary leaders for whom it had fought. "A military force which themselves had raised, paid, new modelled, and in which they disposed of all commands, seeing plainly that they had

16. Anon., *Fundamentall Lawes*, at 11. The theory that Charles I would have used the army to suppress political opposition was repeated as historical fact by such prerevolutionary British historians as Catharine Macaulay, who was popular with American whigs. 29 *Monthly Review* (1763), at 418.

17. Anon., *Fundamentall Lawes*, at 12.

18. Anonymous, *Prerogative Anatomized: or, an Exact Examination of those Protestations and Professions whereby she hath attempted and indeavoured to preferre her self above the Parliament* (London, 1644), at 7–8.

given them the power to do all that they had done, undid it at once, and raised their General to supreme power, which he exercised in a manner before unknown to this island, and much beyond what had ever been effected by the most ambitious and absolute of our Kings."[19] As James Lovell told a Boston audience, "A less body of troops than is now maintained has, on a time, destroyed a King, and fought under a parliament with great success and glory; but upon a motion to disband them, they turned their masters out of doors, and fixed others in their stead."[20]

In fact, the army acted on two occasions. "The first under *Cromwell*, expell'd that Parliament under which they had fought successfully for many Years; afterwards under General *Monk* they destroy'd the Government they before set up" and restored to the throne Charles II.[21] More accurately, Monk used his army to suppress a second army seeking to proclaim another government. "The army in England has broken up the Parliament," he told his troops, then in Scotland. "I think it is the duty of my place to keep the military power in obedience to the civil. It is the duty of us all to defend the Parliament from which you receive your pay and commission."[22]

With Charles II, the old constitution was restored. Parliament declared that "the sole supream government, command and disposition of the militia, and of all forces by sea and land, and of all forts and places of strength, is, and by the laws of *England* ever was the undoubted right of his Majesty, and his royal predecessors, Kings and Queens of *England*; and that both, or

19. "Philonomos," *Liberty of the Subject*, at 40–41. Other pamphlets of the time contended that Parliament abrogated constitutional responsibility before the army proclaimed Cromwell. Anon., *Letter to Charles Townshend*, at 12; [Tindal,] *Present Disaffection*, at 23.
20. James Lovell's Oration (1771), *Massacre Orations*, at 9.
21. [Trenchard,] *An Argument Shewing*, at 28.
22. Omond, *The Army*, at 13.

either of the houses of parliament cannot, nor ought to pretend to the same."[23]

The standing army had been disbanded,[24] yet the constitutional fear remained. During Charles's reign, the earl of Shaftesbury warned that "neither our Ancestors, nor any other Country free like ours, whilst they preserv'd their Liberties, did ever suffer any *mercenary, or standing Guards to their Prince*, but took care that his safety should be in Them, as theirs was in him."[25] The first article of impeachment exhibited against the earl of Clarendon asserted he "hath designed a standing army to be raised, and to govern the kingdom thereby; advising the King . . . to govern by military power, and to maintain the same by free quarter and contribution."[26] This charge about standing armies seems to have bothered Clarendon more than any of the other sixteen levied against him. It was, he said, "the most unpopular and ungracious Reproach that any Man could lie under."[27]

The last Stuart king sought a new constitutional arrangement, partly, many constitutional theorists believed, because he thought he could depend on military support.[28] Following the Glorious Revolution, Scotland not only declared standing armies a constitutional grievance but, also, as a contemporary observed, "made the keeping them up an Article in the Forfeiture of the late King James."[29] In England, the throne was held abandoned not forfeited, yet among the constitutional violations the Bill of Rights levied against James was the accusation of "raising and

23. "An Act declaring the sole right of the militia to be in the King," 13 Charles II, cap. 6.
24. See 33 *London Magazine* (1764), at 66.
25. [Shaftesbury,] *Person of Quality*, at 16–17.
26. 1 Costin and Watson, *Documents*, at 155.
27. Schwoerer, *No Standing Armies*, at 93.
28. [Tindal,] *Present Disaffection*, at 14.
29. [Fletcher,] *Discourse of Government*, at 37.

keeping a standing army within this kingdom in time of peace, without consent of parliament, and quartering soldiers contrary to law."[30]

Perhaps the Bill of Rights inaccurately charged James II with violating the law,[31] but no matter. The constitution was forever changed by the sixth article, which provided "That the raising or keeping a standing army within the kingdom in time of peace, unless it be with consent of parliament, is against law."[32]

The crisis of the seventeenth-century constitution had been resolved. "The power of the monarchy had been broken in its most essential feature."[33] Yet the controversy had only just begun. "The Revolution," it was said four years before troops arrived in Boston, "by a most extraordinary concurrence of causes, established the very grievance which the principles of it had long sought to abolish; I mean, a formal standing-army."[34]

❖ 11 ❖

A HATEFUL NEED:

THE MUTINY ACT COMPROMISE

The constitutional world of prerevolutionary America owed much of its form and character to the Glorious Revolution. More had changed than merely constitutional command of the

30. "An act for declaring the rights and liberties of the subject," 1 William and Mary, session 2, cap. 2.

31. Schwoerer, *No Standing Armies*, at 151. On the other hand, see Trevelyan, *English Revolution*, at 94.

32. "An act . . . ," *supra*, note 30.

33. Schwoerer, *No Standing Armies*, at 189.

34. Anon., *Independency of Military Officers*, at 18.

army. Standing armies had become part of William III's government, which maintained seven thousand men in Great Britain and twelve thousand in Ireland.[1] Looking backward, writers of the 1760s saw in this fact the passing of feudalism and the emergence of a new constitution.[2] More pertinent to their politics, they also recognized that the constitutional controversy had not been resolved, it had only been compromised. William III had not received all the troops he had desired. Not even permitted to retain his Dutch guards, it was believed he seriously contemplated leaving England forever.[3]

It would not do to exaggerate the constitutional. True, as historian Christopher Hill maintains, a "lasting legacy of the Interregnum was a hatred of standing armies among men of property. Before 1640 they had feared that the monarchy might use an army to win independence of Parliament; after 1646 their own Army threatened to deprive them of the fruits of victory."[4] Still, the standing army was sometimes less the cause of controversy than a pawn in the constitutional struggle. An objection stated in 1634 to giving Charles I a standing army was more concerned with formulating an excuse for Parliament exercising independent authority than warning about constitutional dangers.[5] Dislike of methods employed for billeting soldiers, concern about the cost of a military establishment, and (in the case of James II) worry about the religion of commissioned officers were other reasons standing armies had been opposed.[6] With the

1. Anon., *Independency of Military Officers*, at 18–21.

2. 38 *London Magazine* (1769), at 157. It was possible to turn the argument around and contend that the standing army, because it was not basically different from an army raised by military tenure, was sanctioned by custom. Speech of Lord Hinton, Lords Debates of 9 March 1738, 10 *Parliamentary History*, at 524–25.

3. 38 *Monthly Review* (1768), at 466–67.

4. Hill, *Century of Revolution*, at 189.

5. [Herle,] *An Answer*, at 33–35.

6. Schwoerer, *No Standing Armies*, at 19–147.

triumph of Parliament and the Glorious Revolution, these issues became less important. What concerned people now was the power of the state and how power was exercised.

The contours of constitutional contention, delineating the controversy as it would be debated for the next hundred years, were formed during the period when William of Orange was demanding and obtaining the constitutional alteration giving England a standing army. The opposition was as vocal then as later. Its fears and arguments were concisely summed up by the Reverend Samuel Johnson. No king, he contended, could be trusted with a standing army, "nay, if he were an Angel, he were not fit for this Trust."[7] With memories of James II vivid on everyone's mind, the point might have been unanswerable had not James II been alive. The possibility of French and Irish armies rallying to his standard conjured for Englishmen nightmares more constitutionally frightening than the prospect of professional troops under William's command.[8] The point, therefore, could be answered, if not in terms of constitutional guarantees, at least as a matter of necessity. One of those to answer it was John Somers, the lord chancellor, who is of particular interest because he would be forced to surrender the great seal partly due to his support of William's standing-army policy. Writing the same year as Johnson, Somers insisted the issue was not whether England should maintain a standing army, but "whether considering the Circumstances that we and our Neighbours are now in, it may not be both prudent and necessary for us to keep up a reasonable Force from Year to Year. The State of Affairs both at Home and Abroad being every Year to be considered in Parliament, that so any such Force may be either encreased, lessened, or quite laid aside as they shall see cause."[9]

7. Johnson, *Works*, at 325.
8. Anon., *Reflections on the Short History*, at 8, 18–19.
9. [John Somers,] *A Letter Ballancing the Necessity of Keeping a Land-Force in*

Writing of the constitutional dilemma, Somers outlined both the constitutional reality and the constitutional solution. The reality was Louis XIV, poised across the English Channel with his own standing army.[10] The solution was Parliament. Under the new-modelled constitution, it controlled the kingdom's finances. Possessing power of voting and withholding money, potentially it controlled the military. In that fact lay the permanent solution, a constitutional compromise already codified much as Somers outlined it. The solution was the Mutiny Act, part of the revolutionary settlement of 1689. Legalizing the machinery of court-martial, it authorized the crown to define and punish military crimes beyond the compass of common law.[11] In its preamble, the statute promulgated what, in hindsight, became the constitutional solution, resisted down to the days of the American Revolution by men like Johnson, and accepted by such as Somers with more reluctance than generally admitted. The preamble for the first time codified that peculiarity of English jurisprudence, the legal unconstitutionality. To emphasize that what was now made legal remained unconstitutional, the act had a limited duration, renewed generally on a yearly basis, with each successive preamble repeating that, for another annual period, what was unconstitutional would be legal. In time, with usage, a new customary rule would develop that, by act of Parliament, what previously had been unconstitutional became both legal and constitutional. "Whereas," the preamble provided,

> the raising or keeping a Standing Army within this Kingdome in time of Peace unlesse it be with Consent of Parlyament is against Law And whereas it is judged necessary by Their Majestyes and this present Parliament that

---

Times of Peace: With the Dangers that may follow on it (London, 1697), at 3.

10. Omond, *The Army*, at 34.

11. Ibid., at 26–28.

dureing this time of Danger severall of the Forces which are now on foote should be continued and others raised for the Safety of the Kingdome for the Common Defence of the Protestant Religion and for the reducing of Ireland.[12]

The Mutiny Act made the standing army permanent by annual vote of Parliament. The crown received authority to grant commissions, convene courts-martial, and maintain general discipline. Parliament created that army, defined its size, and limited its duration. The standing army was made legal by the very statute declaring it unconstitutional. Although standing armies remained unconstitutional in legal theory, the standing army voted by Parliament from year to year was a legal military force.[13]

For adherents of parliamentary government, the constitutional settlement contained in the annual Mutiny Act removed the constitutional danger posed by standing armies. With Parliament the paymaster, there was no longer any need to worry, a writer in 1698 assured his fellow subjects, because "no Army will endeavour to abolish that Power which sees them duly paid; so that your *Freedom* and *English Constitution* is safe."[14]

The constitutional settlement of the Mutiny Act could be viewed in three ways. It was either a constitutional compromise, a total victory for Parliament that vested constitutional control over coercive power in the two Houses, or it was a meaningless statutory formula that did not alleviate the constitutional menace of a standing army. For Daniel Defoe, it was a constitutional compromise in which both sides in the seventeenth-century struggle for dominance gave up something to establish constitutional harmony. "The parliament," he believed, "will consent to no Force, but such as they shall judge safe and necessary; and the

---

12. 6 *Statutes of the Realme*, at 55; 1 William and Mary, cap. 5.
13. Samuel, *British Army*, at 198.
14. Anon., *An Argument*, at 11.

King shall insist on no other Army than the Parliament consents to; and while they agree to it, why should we be concern'd."[15] Matthew Tindal, on the other hand, regarded the settlement not as a compromise between crown and Parliament, but as a total victory for Parliament because the two Houses now had it "in their power to do with the Forces they raise and pay, as they think fit."[16] There were even some who thought that the settlement was not a constitutional innovation but constitutional continuity, and that the constitutional reservation stated in the Mutiny Act's preamble somehow safeguarded the constitution without changing it in any respect. As late as 1764, a pamphlet writer would argue that

> the British constitution, like a geometrical staircase, is so skilfully put together, that not the smallest member of it can be altered without the destruction of the whole. To its honour be it said, that though, ever since the Revolution, this nation never has been without a standing army, yet the unconstitutionality of that army is written upon the front of that very bill to which it owes its existence.[17]

These arguments were either naive or wishful, or they deliberately glossed over constitutional residua. Many problems remained that caused concern among a wide cross section of British subjects. Even for some who believed the constitutional balance had been tilted entirely in the direction of Parliament, constitutional dangers still remained. One fear shared by many was voiced in 1738 by the earl of Chesterfield. "[W]e are," he warned the House of Lords, "like to have a perpetual army palmed upon us, under colour of an annual Bill. An army kept up by a perpetual law, would be as much an army kept up by consent of

15. [Defoe,] *A Brief Reply to the History*, at 22.
16. [Tindal,] *Present Disaffection*, at 21.
17. Anon., *Independency of Military Officers*, at 2–3.

parliament, as an army perpetually kept up by an annual Bill. I can see no difference between the one and the other: they are both equally dangerous to our constitution."[18] Lord Hinton, in reply, provided what would become the standard answer. It was, of course, that the constitution under which Stuart kings threatened arbitrary government was a thing of the past. "Whilst recourse must be annually had to parliament for a new law for keeping up our army, it will always be in the power of parliament to dissolve that army, by refusing their authority for keeping it up."[19]

Hinton stated the more optimistic constitutional theory. According to it, Parliament could "refuse the King even the necessary power of military discipline,"[20] a rather naive wish to the more constitutionally pessimistic who found no safety in annual bills. Once a standing army existed, it was argued, the monarch could enforce the royalist doctrine that crown proclamations had the force of law and, by proclamation, continue the Mutiny Act and all taxes.[21] Retention of power to grant or refuse money was not enough, Andrew Fletcher had contended in 1698, at least not when "a Standing Mercenary Army is kept up in time of Peace: For he that is arm'd, is always Master of the Purse of him that is unarm'd."[22]

The answer was not constitutional, it was necessity. It was a fact of life by 1766 that all the kingdoms of Europe maintained standing armies. This obliged not only Great Britain but also

18. Speech of the earl of Chesterfield, Lords Debates of 9 May 1738, 10 *Parliamentary History*, at 512.

19. Speech of Lord Hinton, Lords Debates of 9 March 1738, ibid., at 526. Interestingly, Virginia's Richard Bland said much the same at the start of the prerevolutionary controversy. Rossiter, *Six Characters*, at 201.

20. De Lolme, *Constitution*, at 57.

21. Speech of Lord Noel Somerset, Commons Debate of 3 February 1738, in 7 *London Magazine* (1738), at 261.

22. [Fletcher,] *Discourse of Government*, at 8.

America to do the same, though "contrary to the genius" of the constitution.[23] The unconstitutional had to be tolerated even by the worrisome. Men who might have been among the alarmists a hundred years earlier became resigned, though many, like Joseph Danvers, could never be reconciled. "I hate a standing Army as I hate the devil," he told the House of Commons in 1738, "but, hateful as it is, I do not know how we could live without it."[24]

❖ 12 ❖

A MORAL DISTEMPER:

THE ENGLISH LEGACY

Even before the standing army had been legitimatized into a legal unconstitutionality, the controversy had become chimerical. Opposition to permanent, mercenary forces, by ignoring the exigencies of contemporary warfare and failing to appreciate the significance of parliamentary control of taxation, was politically unrealistic at least as early as 1690.[1] Yet it remained a constitutional imperative. For about half a century, the government's annual motion to renew the Military Act met "with a strenuous and annual opposition."[2] The obvious must be restated. Opponents of standing armies forced Parliament each year to reconsider and resolve not questions of finance or political theory, but of fundamental organic law. Issues decided—how large a force

23. Anon., *Justice and Necessity of Taxing*, at 10.
24. Speech of Joseph Danvers, Commons Debates of 3 February 1738, 10 *Parliamentary History*, at 449.
1. Robbins, *Commonwealthman*, at 103.
2. 37 *Monthly Review* (1767), at 360.

to authorize and how much money to appropriate[3]—were uncomplicated, and debate would have been insignificant had not the opposition continually challenged the constitutionality of standing armies. During the early decades of the eighteenth century, this topic was said to be the one most frequently raised in Parliament.[4] It was, dissentient lords protested in 1730, "a Subject of such Importance, that we think hardly any Thing of more Moment can fall under our Considerations."[5]

If the realities of the day made the controversy militarily outdated, it remained for many years constitutionally viable. More vital for the purposes of this volume, the postulates of the debate eventually degenerated into a series of forensic formulae that employed premises from the seventeenth-century constitution of customary restraints to check executive power exercised under the eighteenth-century constitution of parliamentary supremacy. For people of the time, pleading an anachronistic constitution was not important, for they did not realize what was occurring. It is, however, important for us because Americans of the 1760s would rely on the same constitution to oppose British imperial innovations.

In seeking the antecedents of American contentions, we should first turn to generalities. It may be said that, in a broad sense, eighteenth-century British parliamentary opposition to standing armies repeated a seventeenth-century English constitutional concern: fear of power. "I am against the continuance of a standing Army," Lord Cavendish had said in 1678, "for it is easier with it, than without it, to change the Government."[6]

3. Anon., *Some Thoughts on the Land Forces*, at 7.

4. Speech of William Shippen, Commons Debates of 3 February 1738, 10 *Parliamentary History*, at 383.

5. Protest of 16 March 1729/30, *2 Lords' Protests*, at 62.

6. Speech of Lord Cavendish, Commons Debates of 4 November 1678, 6 *Grey's Debates*, at 141.

"[W]hat Security," Andrew Fletcher asked, "can the Nation have, that these Standing Forces shall not at some time or other be made use of to suppress the Liberties of the People."[7] "It is impossible," John Trenchard answered, "to consider of a STANDING FORCE which shall be sufficient to oppose a Foreign Power, without considering it at the same time sufficient to suppress the Subject at home."[8] They meant, Lord Bathurst explained, that "if the Army be sufficient for protecting the people, they must be sufficient for subduing and enslaving the people, as soon as their superiors shall give them the word of command."[9]

For many years during the eighteenth century, it was both a political and a constitutional certainty that once power existed command would issue. Josiah Quincy of Massachusetts was less definite than most when delineating the constitutional theory. "The army of the present king of Great Britain," he pointed out, "is larger than that with which Alexander subdued the East, or Caesar conquered Gaul. . . . Surely the liberties of England, if not held at will, are holden by a very precarious tenure."[10] After all, "he that is armed is always master of him that is unarmed."[11] Therefore, the seventeenth-century divine Samuel Johnson warned, "they who are for a Standing Army, endeavour to alter the Government all at once; and make it absolute and arbitrary, whether the King will or no, and tho he have no

7. [Fletcher,] *Militias and Standing Armies*, at 15.

8. [Trenchard,] *A Letter from the Author*, at 3.

9. Speech of Lord Bathurst, Lords Debates of 9 March 1739, 10 *Parliamentary History*, at 543. Or, as Isaac Barré, defender of American rights during the prerevolutionary era, put it, "if troops were once suffered to consider themselves as the executive power, they would soon become the legislative." Speech of Barré, Commons Debates of 8 May 1770, 16 *Parliamentary History*, at 1000. For a colonial statement of the fear, see Howard, *Artillery-Election Sermon*, at 27.

10. Quincy, *Observations with Thoughts*, at 427.

11. Andrew Fletcher, *A Discourse on Government with Relation to Militia's* (1698), quoted in Omond, *The Army*, at 40.

mind to it."[12] One reason, according to William Shippen, was psychological: "the very Name and Terror of it, would (without oppression) awe and subdue the Spirits of the People, extinguish their Love of Liberty, and beget a mean and abject acquiescence in Slavery."[13] Indeed, sufficient military force could convert psychological apprehension, especially when accompanied by constitutional acquiescence, into constitutional reality. "For if he [the king] have a Standing Army, he can enslave the Nation if he will, and then they are slaves already. For to depend upon Will and Pleasure is the lowest degree of Slavery."[14]

It was neither unrealistic nor an exaggeration to expect the worse. David Hume, for example, described the maintenance of a standing army as "a mortal distemper in the British government, of which at last, it must inevitably perish"[15] because, as a New Hampshire correspondent explained, "Standing armies have ever proved destructive to the Liberties of a People, and where they are suffered, neither Life nor Property are secure."[16] Conclusions that to us would be mere possibilities could, to the eighteenth-century legal mind, be certainties.[17] "It is a sure Rule in State Policy," an anonymous pamphleteer expounded as early as 1648, "to presume that *whatsoever is in the Power of another to do*, for the subversion of a State, *will one time or other be done accordingly*: Now it is apparent, where there is one constant Army

---

12. Johnson, *Works*, at 322.

13. *Three Speeches against Continuing the Army* (1718), quoted in Omond, *The Army*, at 42.

14. Johnson, *Works*, at 322.

15. Quoted in Noble, *Some Strictures*, at 30.

16. *New Hampshire Gazette*, 23 March 1770, quoted in *Post*, 2 April 1770, at 4, col. 1.

17. "I would fain know, if there be any other way of making a Prince Absolute, than by allowing him a Standing Army: if by it all Princes have not been made Absolute; if without it, any." [Fletcher,] *Discourse of Government*, at 39. See also "Cato," *Discourse of Standing Armies*, at 19.

kept on foot, there being no visible enemy to encounter (like water when it leaves running, and stands,) it wil[l] corrupt."[18]

As time went on the degree of certainty increased, becoming just about absolute a hundred years and more after the just-quoted pamphlet was published. By then whigs had generally deduced from history that (as the town of Boston asserted) "Standing Armies have forever made shipwrecks of free States."[19] Samuel Adams, lamenting that most governments were arbitrary, agreed with *Cato* that the reason was standing armies.[20] " 'Tis certain," *Cato* had argued in 1722, "that all Parts of *Europe* which are enslaved, have been by Armies, and 'tis absolutely impossible, that any Nation which keeps them amongst themselves, can long preserve their Liberties."[21] This political conclusion impressed the eighteenth-century legal mind more than it impresses us. Then it was a constitutional truism, not mere speculation, demonstrable by a rather sciolistic, yet surprisingly convincing, survey of history. "Look into all the nations of the world, ancient and modern, who have lossed their liberty," Charles Lucas urged his readers the year troops landed in Boston, and "you will find none of them were completely enslaved till they raised a standing army, superior in strength to the civil power."[22] England during the era of Charles I was only one example. Every educated English-speaking person of the eighteenth century knew a stock list of ancient states that had lost their liberties to standing armies: Athens,[23] Carthage,[24] and,

18. Anon., *Peaceable Militia*, at 3.

19. Instructions of the Town of Boston, 5 May 1773, *Gazette and Post-Boy*, 10 May 1773, at 1, col. 2.

20. "Vindex," in *Boston Gazette*, 26 December 1768, reprinted in 1 Adams, *Writings*, at 273.

21. "Cato," *Discourse of Standing Armies*, at 25. See also [Fletcher,] *Militias and Standing Armies*, at 4–11.

22. Lucas, *An Address to Dublin*, at 30.

23. James Lovell's Oration (1771), *Massacre Orations*, at 9.

24. [Trenchard,] *Short History*, at 1.

most notably, Rome.[25] More recently, there had been Denmark, a classic case of a nation losing its liberty to a standing army, held up as a warning by Robert Molesworth[26] in a book praised today for its influence,[27] but so ineptly written it is doubtful that many people read it.[28] American whigs did not have to master every detail to know what lesson to draw, just as they drew the lessons when, at the very time Great Britain was seeking to form a military establishment in the colonies, a French army subdued the island of Corsica and a standing army overturned the Parliament of Sweden.[29] "The spirit of tyranny," Boston's *Post-Boy* would observe in 1774, "seems, at this juncture, to have taken possession of the hearts of all the Princes in Europe."[30] Whether invading the lands of other peoples or subjugating their own citizens, their instrument for "tyranny" was a standing army.

There were speakers and writers who denied armies were responsible for Denmark[31] or other places losing their liberties[32] or that standing armies endangered constitutional government.[33] Their facts were as strong, but their arguments less emotional and familiar than those condemning standing armies. It was the other side that made the impression, for it stated an undeniable law of history. "This subject is so self-evident," John

25. *Post*, 28 October 1765, at 3, col. 1; [Bolingbroke,] *Freeholder's Catechism*, at 9; Lovell, *An Oration*, at 7–8.

26. [Molesworth,] *Denmark*, at 62–68.

27. 1 Bailyn, *Pamphlets*, at 43–44.

28. 38 *Gentleman's Magazine* (1768), at 434.

29. Corsica: *Gazette and Post-Boy*, 11 December 1769, at 2, cols. 1–3. Sweden: *Post*, 9 November 1772, at 2, col. 3.

30. *Bingley's London Journal*, 8 October 1774, reprinted in *Gazette and Post-Boy*, 12 December 1774, at 1, col. 1.

31. Speech of the duke of Argyle, Lords Debates of 6 March 1733, 8 *Parliamentary History*, at 1248. See also Robbins, *Commonwealthman*, at 104.

32. Anon., *Some Thoughts on the Land Forces*, at 25.

33. Anon., *Letter to Charles Townshend*, at 7–11; [Butler,] *Standing Army*, at 15; Speech of Sir Robert Walpole, Commons Debates of 3 February 1738, 7 *London Magazine* (1738), at 264.

Trenchard had asserted in 1697, "that I am almost asham'd to prove it: for if we look through the World, we shall find in no Country, Liberty and an Army stand together; so that to know whether a People are Free or Slaves, it is necessary only to ask, Whether there is an Army kept amongst them."[34]

The legacy of this history had been summed up by William Shippen as early as 1739. It was the constitutional maxim "that no government in this island can ever have occasion for keeping up a Standing Army in time of peace, unless it be to subdue the liberties of the people."[35]

That fear—a fear for "liberty"—was the legacy of demonstrable, historical "experience": seventeenth-century English experience under Stuart kings and "the known and universal experience of other countries in Europe."[36] To maintain a large standing army was to run the risk of "turning that civil government, under which we have for so many ages preserved our liberties, into a military sort of government, under which no country ever did, it is impossible that any country ever can, preserve either their liberties or their properties"[37]—that is, "bring on a total alteration of the frame of our government from a legal and limited monarchy to a despotick."[38] Sir John Conventry had expressed the fear in terms peculiarly English. "These red coats," he said in 1678, "may fight against *Magna Charta.*"[39]

Although the political debate had ended and standing armies had become part of the British constitution, the legacy of fear

34. [Trenchard,] *An Argument Shewing*, at 11–12.

35. Speech of William Shippen, Commons Debates of 14 February 1739, 10 *Parliamentary History*, at 1342.

36. Protest of 16 February 1722/23, 1 *Lords' Protests*, at 377.

37. Speech of the Marquis of Tweeddale, Lords Debates of 6 March 1733, 8 *Parliamentary History*, at 1238.

38. Protest of 16 February 1722/23, 1 *Lords' Protests*, at 377.

39. Speech of Sir John Coventry, Commons Debates of 30 April 1678, 5 *Grey's Debates*, at 287.

continued into the age of the American Revolution.[40] Today Sir William Blackstone is remembered as a tory, a conservative supporter of ministerial government. Yet, in the first volume of his *Commentaries*, published in 1765, he insisted that regular soldiers were like "slaves," threatening liberty by the fact they were both under arms and under orders. They should, he insisted "live intermixed with the people; no separate camp, no barracks, no inland fortress should be allowed."[41] It was not until 1792, more than a decade after Yorktown, that a program of building barracks in England was commenced.[42]

In the American colonies, where seventeenth-century English constitutionalism lingered on with a strength long since ebbed in the home islands, the legacy motivating Blackstone's prejudices was that much stronger.[43] Newspapers[44] and clergymen[45] were as apt to sound the alarm as were men that are remembered today as constitutional polemists: Samuel Adams, Josiah Quincy, and Alexander Hamilton.[46] Reluctant revolutionaries, they spoke not as colonials, not as whigs, not as Americans, but as Englishmen. Their fear was not paranoiac, *sui generis*, or fabricated to give constitutional gloss to economic discontent. The fear was both historically preordained and genuinely felt.

40. For statements expressing that legacy of constitutional fear by Englishmen associated with Massachusetts Bay, see, for example, [Bollan,] *Continued Corruption*, at 16; and Speech of Former Governor Thomas Pownall, Commons Debates of 8 May 1770, 16 *Parliamentary History*, at 987.

41. 1 Blackstone, *Commentaries*, at 401.

42. Omond, *The Army*, at 37.

43. For sources, see 1 Bailyn, *Pamphlets*, at 42n7, 71–76.

44. For example, *Boston Gazette*, 9 July 1770, at 2, col. 1.

45. For example, Howard, *Artillery-Election Sermon*, at 28.

46. Letter from the Massachusetts House of Representatives to Dennys de Berdt, 12 January 1768, 1 Adams, *Writings*, at 145–46; *Boston Gazette*, 26 December 1768, reprinted in 1 Adams, *Writings*, at 274; Quincy, *Observations with Thoughts*, at 400; Hamilton, *Farmer*, at 94.

The experience of all ages, and the observations both of the historian and the philosopher agree, that a standing army is the most ready engine in the hand of despotism, to debase the powers of the human mind, and eradicate the manly spirit of freedom. The people have certainly everything to fear from a government, when the springs of its authority are fortified only by a standing military force. Wherever an army is established, it introduces a revolution in manners, corrupts the morals, propagates every species of vice, and degrades the human character.[47]

Those words were written by an American, Mercy Otis Warren, long after quiet had returned to Yorktown. She published them in the nineteenth century, but they echoed a seventeenth-century fear. They were not eccentric, they were not extreme, and they stated a constitutional absolute subscribed to in every part of the English-speaking legal world. What Warren said in the nineteenth-century only repeated what a rebellious Irishman had said the very year Boston was occupied by British troops and what one of the most contented members of Britain's aristocracy had said thirty years before that date. "You must always remember," Charles Lucas wrote in 1768, "that STANDING PARLIAMENTS and STANDING ARMIES have ever proved the most dangerous enemies to civil liberty."[48] "Slavery and arbitrary power are the certain consequences of keeping up a Standing Army," the earl of Chesterfield had told his fellow lords. "It is the machine by which the chains of slavery are riveted upon a free people, and wants only a skilful and proper hand to set it a going."[49]

47. 1 Warren, *American Revolution*, at 62.
48. Lucas, *An Address to Dublin*, at 36.
49. Speech of the earl of Chesterfield, Lords Debates of 9 March 1738, 10 *Parliamentary History*, at 516.

❖ 13 ❖

IN COMMON WITH THE PEOPLE:

THE CONSTITUTIONAL IDEAL

Mercy Otis Warren called the standing army an "engine." The earl of Chesterfield used the word "machine." They were thinking of it as an instrument of executive force, more particularly as a tool of a ministry unaccountable to either Parliament or public opinion. First, a preliminary consideration must be underscored. There was an alternative, a constitutional ideal for avoiding the menace of standing armies. Most who favored that alternative during the prerevolutionary period took their theme from a Frenchman, the Baron de Montesquieu.

> To prevent the executive power from being able to oppress, it is requisite that the armies, with which it is intrusted, should consist of the people, and have the same spirit as the people, as was the case at Rome till the time of *Marius*. To obtain this end, there are only two ways, either that the persons employed in the army, should have sufficient property to answer for their conduct to their fellow subjects, and be enlisted only for a year, as was customary in Rome: or if there should be a standing army, composed chiefly of the most despicable part of the nation, the legislative power should have a right to disband them as soon as it pleased; the soldiers should live in common with the rest of the people; and no separate camp, barracks, or fortress, should be suffered.[1]

The second of Montesquieu's "two ways" was the constitutional compromise embodied by the Mutiny Act. The first was

1. 1 Montesquieu, *The Spirit of Laws*, book XI, chap. 6, at 229. For British application of this argument, see 1 Blackstone, *Commentaries*, at 401; *British Liberties*, at xxxviii.

the constitutional alternative generally supported by opponents of standing armies. In 1762 it was defined as "a constitutional militia, or such a number of men as the legislature thought requisite, to be chosen out of the whole body of the people by lot and rotation, not under military laws, nor to be marched out of their respective districts, except in cases of actual rebellion, or invasion."[2]

The constitutional theory was uncomplicated: the only safe way to defend freedom was with freemen,[3] to place "the Sword in the hands of the Subject,"[4] "by making the Militia to consist of the same Persons as have the Property."[5] Shaftesbury condensed the theory into a single sentence. "The *Militia* must, and can never be otherwise than for *English Liberty*, 'cause else it doth destroy it *self*, but a *standing Force* can be nothing but *Prerogative*, by whom it hath its *idle Living* and *Subsistence*."[6]

Like the constitutional fear, the constitutional ideal had its gainsayers. Scotland's duke of Argyle believed "a standing army of our own subjects can be no more dangerous than a well-ordered and a well disciplined militia;"[7] England's Sir Robert Walpole thought that "whilst our Army is commanded . . . by Gentlemen of the best Families and Fortunes" it was not a danger to the constitution but "one of its greatest Securities";[8] and Lord Chancellor Hardwicke, opposing a bill to train every Englishman for the militia, maintained "that a Nation of Merchants, Manufacturers, Artisans, and Husbandmen, defended by

2. 31 *London Magazine* (1762), at 202.

3. [Toland,] *Militia Reform'd*, at 18–25.

4. [Fletcher,] *Discourse of Government*, at 8; [Trenchard,] *An Argument Shewing*, at 13; [Bollan,] *Continued Corruption*, at 11.

5. [Trenchard,] *An Argument Shewing*, at 4.

6. [Shaftesbury,] *Parliamentman*, at 4.

7. Speech of the duke of Argyle, Lords Debates of 6 March 1733, 8 *Parliamentary History*, at 1245.

8. Speech of Sir Robert Walpole, Commons Debates of 3 February 1738, 7 *London Magazine* (1738), at 264.

an Army, is vastly preferable to a Nation of Soldiers."[9] These arguments were not persuasive with commonwealthmen and whigs of the old school, for whom the militia was not only an alternative to the professional army, but also a shield for civil liberty and a cherished part of their constitutional nostalgia.[10] The navy and the militia had defended England in better days and could do so again,[11] though some people had the odd idea it first might be necessary to restore feudal tenures.[12] After all, if one believed a standing army inevitably threatened tyranny, then it seemed reasonable to argue that "nothing can save us from following the Fate of all the other Kingdoms in *Europe*, but putting our Trust altogether in our Fleets and Militia's, and having no other Forces but these."[13]

The crux of the controversy, of course, was not whether militias could defend the nation from foreign invasion as competently as standing armies. Everyone granted professional soldiers had the advantage in warfare. It was whether or not a people policed by standing armies could be free. This question lay at the core of constitutional fears during the prerevolutionary era, and it was not new. If regular troops were employed to enforce law or punish sedition, it had been said in the 1690s, "the Lords, Gentlemen, and Freeholders of *England*, are not fit to be trusted with our own Laws, Lives, Libertys, and Estates."[14] According to John Trenchard, the reason was that a professional army

9. [Hardwicke,] *Two Speeches*, at 53.

10. "Philonomos," *Liberty of the Subject*, at 33; Schwoerer, *No Standing Armies*, at 194; Robbins, *Commonwealthman*, at 104–5.

11. Protest of 7 March 1732, 1 *Protests of the Lords*, at 421; Webb, *Military Treatise*, at 2; Gardiner, *Two Stuarts*, at 8; Omond, *The Army*, at 42.

12. Anon., *Independency of Military Officers*, at 59; Dalrymple, *Military Essay*, at 11–13. See also, [Hardwicke,] *Two Speeches*, at 53–54: Speech of Lord Noel Somerset, Commons Debates of 3 February 1738, 10 *Parliamentary History*, at 388.

13. [Fletcher,] *Militias and Standing Armies*, at 28.

14. Johnson, "Standing Army," at 149.

serving as enforcer of police regulations made government "violent" and "against Nature." The practice could not "possibly continue" in a free state where "the Constitution must either break the Army, or the Army will destroy the Constitution."[15]

In the third decade of the eighteenth-century, Lord Bathurst added an argument destined to become more weighty as the years increased. "The militia of the kingdom are the people of the kingdom," he theorized, "and it is impossible to make use of the people for oppressing the liberties of the people; but a standing army of regular forces soon begin to look upon themselves as a body separate and distinct from the people."[16] The militia not only could enforce the laws as effectively as a standing army, but to use the militia, the people, for police would insure better laws. The reason was that "where laws are to be executed by the militia, the government must take care to enact no laws, but such as are agreeable to the majority of the people."[17]

If Lord Bathurst's words from the 1730s seem familiar, it is because, despite his toryism, they have an American ring. The colonists were to rebel for the type of law he sought, one "agreeable" to the people. "THE Militia," one would write in 1776, "is the natural support of a government, *founded on the authority of the people only.*"[18] "From a well regulated militia we have nothing to fear," John Hancock believed,[19] a fact clearly not true for standing armies. From them "what has not a state to fear?"[20]

15. [Trenchard,] *An Argument Shewing*, at 4.

16. Speech of Lord Bathurst, Lords Debates of 6 March 1733, 8 *Parliamentary History*, at 1249.

17. Speech of Lord Bathurst, Lords Debates of 9 March 1739, 10 *Parliamentary History*, at 545–50.

18. "Demophilus," *Genuine Principles*, at 23.

19. John Hancock's Oration (1774), *Massacre Orations*, at 51.

20. Ibid., at 50. See also James Lovell's Oration (1771), *Massacre Orations*, at 9.

One reason Americans had opposed a military establishment was that it was not needed. Their "real Defence and Protection," it was said, was "received from the Valour of their own native Militia."[21] More important was the matter of constitutional liberty. It was guaranteed by the constitutional alternative of the American militia, which, Robert Viner told the House of Commons in 1754, was composed "of the gentlemen, freeholders, farmers, and master tradesmen of the country."[22] "[T]he troops which have been raised, or may hereafter be raised in America," William Beckford contended in the same debate,

do, and always must consist, so far as relates to the common soldier at least, of men of a very different character from those of our regular army here at home. In the latter we seldom, if ever, have any gentlemen, especially gentlemen of fortune serving as common soldiers; but on the contrary, they are generally men who had no character, or perhaps a bad one, before they listed in the army; whereas, in the former there will, I hope, be many gentlemen of some fortune, and almost all of them men of some substance and character before they listed in the army.[23]

On this difference alone, without even having to take into account their constitutional inheritance from the mother country, American whigs could have built their case for the constitutional alternative. If nothing else, the difference could have told them that British regulars were not the type of men colonists wanted enforcing their laws. "Who can be surprised," Josiah

21. Ray, *Importance of the Colonies*, at 15; [Bollan,] *Mutual Interest Considered*, at 11. See also, *Post*, 4 November 1765, at 1, col. 2.

22. Speech of Robert Viner, Commons Debates of 9 December 1754, 15 *Parliamentary History*, at 378.

23. Speech of William Beckford, Commons Debates of 9 December 1754, 15 *Parliamentary History*, at 388–89.

Quincy asked, "that princes and their subalterns discourage a martial spirit among the people, and endeavour to render useless and contemptible the militia, when this institution is the natural strength, and only stable safeguard, of a free country?"[24]

Quincy's words reveal much about transatlantic political vocabulary. From their English legacy, Americans had inherited a manner of speaking. The seventeenth-century English fear became, during the 1760s, their fear. In Massachusetts, the newly fearful sought refuge within the same constitutional alternative that had seemed promising to the fearful of the mother country. Resolutions and sermons urged "placing the sword in hands that will not be likely to betray their trust." Militia men, it was urged, unlike professional troops, "have the strongest motives to act their part well, in defence of their country, whenever they shall be called for."[25] If the words could have come from seventeenth-century England, so could their meaning. They spoke of defending the nation, but the concern was not about foreign enemies. "As Englishmen, as well as British subjects," the colonists regarded standing armies "as dangerous to their civil liberties."[26] Their constitutional fear was that "Soldiers may ruin the Liberties of America."[27]

From the British legacy, Americans had received a double inheritance. Along with the constitutional fear of seventeenth-century England, they inherited the same constitutional alternative still intriguing a political minority of eighteenth-century Great Britain. "[T]he Sword," the town of Boston would vote in 1773, "should never be entrusted but to those who combat *pro aris et focis*, and whose interest is to preserve the public Peace."[28]

24. Quincy, *Observations with Thoughts*, at 411.

25. Howard, *Artillery-Election Sermon*, at 28.

26. Letter from the Massachusetts House of Representatives to Dennis De Berdt, 11 January 1768, *Boston Gazette*, 4 April 1768, at 2, col. 1.

27. *Extract of Letter to De Berdt*, at 13.

28. Instructions of the Town of Boston, 5 May 1773, *Gazette and Post-Boy*, 10 May 1773, at 1, col. 2.

That was the seventeenth-century English fear, thrust into the governance of eighteenth-century Massachusetts. The constitutional issues were not only taxation and who decided how the colonies were to be defended. More immediate, now that troops patrolled Boston's streets, were questions as to what they could do and whether what they did would be legal. "The use of the military power to enforce the execution of the laws, is," the House of Representatives resolved, "inconsistent with the spirit of a free constitution, and the very nature of government. Nor can there be any necessity for it; for the body of the people, the *posse comitatus* will always aid the magistrates in the execution of such laws as ought to be executed."[29]

❖ 14 ❖

A CONSTITUTIONAL INNOVATION:
THE ARMY AND BRITISH LAW

It would be well to reiterate a central point. The words of the Massachusetts House are instructive. Two statements were made more reminiscent of seventeenth-century English than of eighteenth-century British legalism. One, of course, occurred when the House implied that some laws ought not to be enforced. The second had to do with employing military power to execute law. Such employment, it was said, would be "inconsistent with the spirit of a free constitution and the very nature of government." What must be understood is that the Massachusetts House was referring to the ancient, Gothic constitution. It was speaking much as John Hampden or John Pym might have spoken when

29. Message from the Massachusetts House to Governor Francis Bernard, 13 June 1769, *Boston Chronicle*, 15 June 1769, at 191, col. 2.

opposing the prerogative laws of Charles I. To use the military as police, the House was saying, would be "inconsistent with the spirit of a free constitution and the very nature of government," making the force of "law" mere power. Enforcement by the militia, by contrast, meant enforcement by the people themselves, which provided "law" with the moral support of popular consent. That basis for authority was much more preferable during the eighteenth century than was command.

The words of the Massachusetts House should be understood as their authors meant them to be understood, not as historians tend to interpret them. They contain more legal substance and less political propaganda than has been thought. By way of illustrating their constitutional nature, they should be compared to statements made in the mother country, one during the seventeenth century, the other in the eighteenth. In the first, in 1697, John Trenchard had used two words similarly to show how the House used them in 1769. To execute law with military force, he asserted, made government "violent," and therefore, "against nature." If the practice continued, "the Constitution must either break the Army, or the Army will destroy the Constitution."

The meaning of "constitution" as used by both Trenchard and the Massachusetts House should be contrasted to the meaning used by the duke of Newcastle in 1760. To placate a revival of constitutional fears, there had been a movement in Great Britain to revitalize the militia as a constitutional alternative for the professional army.[1] The effort failed, and one of those opposing it had been Newcastle. He had been alarmed on learning that tories were using militia musters to rally support among the property classes for opposition candidates to Parliament. These "little sparkes of opposition," arising from the militia, convinced the duke "that the establishment of the militia (and any con-

1. Omond, *The Army*, at 47.

tinuance establishes the principle) would be, in time, the ruin of our Constitution."[2]

It is obvious that Newcastle's constitution was not the customary constitution of John Trenchard and the Massachusetts House of Representatives. It was the constitution of parliamentary supremacy. To be more precise, it was a narrow version of that constitution, equating supremacy not only with Parliament, but also with Parliament as then constituted. For the electorate to follow new patterns of canvassing was, in Newcastle's vocabulary, to threaten not merely current government, it threatened the "constitution" itself. This definition of "constitution" obtained its most dilated form in 1769 when Parliament not only declared John Wilkes ineligible for election, but seated in his stead the government candidate to whom the electors had given scant support.[3]

It would not do to draw too rigid a line. The dichotomy between the legal minds of seventeenth-century England and eighteenth-century Great Britain was less hard and fast than has been implied. There were many in the mother country who defined "constitution" and "law" similarly to John Trenchard or American whigs, and opposed the definitions of the duke of Newcastle. "Military Power," a London-published pamphlet argued in 1768, "is not the proper aid, and can rarely, if ever, be called to the assistance of the civil magistrate, without infringing the constitution, or endangering our liberties, which flow from

2. Letter from the duke of Newcastle to Lord Hardwicke, 20 October 1760, quoted in Namier, *Age of Revolution*, at 134n3.

3. Interestingly, criticizing the Commons for seating a man not elected by the eligible voters, *Junius* used yet a third meaning of the word "constitution." "They have rejected the majority of votes, the only criterion, by which our laws judge the sense of the people; they have transferred the right of election from the collective to the representative body; and by these acts, taken separately or together, they have essentially altered the original constitutions of the house of commons." 2 "Junius," *Junius*, at 51–52.

the law, and can only be preserved by it."[4] Historians have termed the party sponsoring these theories "radicals," "real whigs," or "commonwealthmen." Their jurisprudence deserves closer attention than it has received from students of the American Revolution. They were, true enough, champions of an earlier constitutionalism,[5] but, unlike their counterparts in the colonies, they were not stubbornly insisting that the seventeenth-century constitution was still law. They knew of Newcastle's "constitution," and were either contending it was an usurpation or demanding the restoration of the seventeenth-century constitution.[6]

To no other constitutional innovation were commonwealthmen more opposed than employment of troops to quell domestic disturbances. "Instead of the ancient and legal civil police," a Middlesex petition of 1769 complained, "the military [are] introduced at every opportunity, unnecessarily and unlawfully patrolling the streets, to the alarm and terror of the inhabitants."[7] This theory—that only the "ancient civil police" were "legal"— was historical as well as jurisprudential. The customary constitution of the seventeenth century had not known a standing army, and could not, therefore, have used one to regulate civilian behavior. During early decades of the century, when law was changing, supporters of the standing army, arguing it should be

4. "Philonomos," *Liberty of the Subject*, at 5.

5. In 1749, for example, a London writer used words almost identical to those just quoted. Military force, he said, "is not the proper aid, and can very rarely, if ever, be called to the assistance of the civil magistrate, without infringing the constitution, or endangering our liberties." Linebaugh, "Tyburn Riot," at 100.

6. From that perspective, it is difficult to justify the term "radical." Although defenders of personal liberty against government power, commonwealthmen were, like the Americans, the constitutional conservatives of the 1760s. Like the Americans, also, they sought to restrain executive authority by reactivating the king's prerogative. In that sense, they were (like the Americans) constitutionally anachronistic and Britain's last royalists.

7. Middlesex Petition, reprinted in 39 *Gentleman's Magazine* (1769), at 290.

strong enough to crush rebellion,[8] reinforced their case by saying the troops could be employed to apprehend smugglers and quell mobs.[9] In fact, Robert Walpole thought smuggling proved regulars were needed as police. "In most of our maritime Counties," he pointed out, using words later echoed by Massachusetts' Governor Francis Bernard, "I do not know but that the Militia would protect the Smugglers, instead of bringing them to Justice, . . . and in every County, I am convinced, the Militia would protect the illegal Retailers of spirituous Liquors, instead of protecting those who serve the Publick by informing against them."[10] Professional troops, it was argued, had to be employed,[11] and one reason is that British smugglers were quite different than colonial smugglers. American historians have made much of colonial smuggling to prove lawlessness, but seldom have noted the material factor in which it differed from British smuggling. It was not deadly. In both England and Scotland, customs officers were killed.[12] That was surely a prime reason London believed the "misrepresentations" of Bernard and the customs commissioners about conditions in Boston. Officials performing the same tasks at home were in peril and the crowd on British streets was vicious.[13]

From the small beginning of supporting the customs service, the standing army's role as a law enforcement agency had steadily increased. By the 1760s it had reached the point where commonwealthmen at home were protesting the rise of a new

8. [Tindal,] *Present Disaffection*, at 21.

9. Speech of Lord Noel Somerset, Commons Debates of 3 February 1738, 7 *London Magazine* (1738), at 262. For a discussion of the changing law, see 2 Clode, *Military Forces*, at 131–34, 619–28.

10. Speech of Sir Robert Walpole, Commons Debates of 3 February 1738, 7 *London Magazine* (1738), at 270. For Bernard, see *In a Defiant Stance*, at 74–84.

11. Bridges, *Smuglers Defeated*, at 9.

12. For example, England: 27 *Gentleman's Magazine* (1757), at 528; Scotland: *Boston Gazette*, 15 January 1770, at 1, col. 2.

13. *In a Rebellious Spirit*, at 72.

constitutionalism and American whigs were able to identify new methods of constitutional governance they could not permit in the colonies without risking their most cherished rights: English liberty and local autonomy.

❖ 15 ❖

IN SUPPORT OF AUTHORITY:

THE NEW CONSTITUTION

It is necessary to summarize a vast amount of material. We are less concerned with how troops were employed to enforce British law in the 1760s than constitutional objections raised to the practice. Yet a point must be made. Military qua police became, during the decades of the American controversy, a major force in British life that gave rise not only to a new political theory, but also to a new constitutionalism and possibly a new definition of law.

An historian of the empire might claim that the new constitution of the 1760s was not so new. It was really the old Irish constitution imposed on the home kingdom of Great Britain. All during the prerevolutionary controversy, Boston newspapers and London periodicals were filled with accounts of mobs roaming throughout the British Isles and of troops sent out to suppress them.[1] The situation was so acute that colonial whigs saw irony in the decision to police Massachusetts Bay, which gave them a chance to poke sarcasm at the imperial

1. *Gazette and Post-Boy*, 29 November 1773, at 1, col. 1; *Post*, 24 September 1770, at 1, col. 3; *Boston Gazette*, 5 February 1770, at 4, col. 1; *Gazette and News-Letter* (Extraordinary), 22 August 1765, at 1, cols. 2–3; *Boston Post-Boy*, 17 December 1764, at 2, col. 1; *Annual Register, 1769*, at [72]; 39 *Gentleman's Magazine* (1769), at 555; 35 *London Magazine* (1766), at 378.

government. "The Americans," a card printed in a Rhode Island newspaper read, "present their Compliments of *Duty* to the M[inistr]y, and humbly beg leave to ask, whether they think it has been quite consistent with *Reason, Policy,* or *common Sense,* to keep a STANDING ARMY in the town of *Boston,* while the principal Cities and Towns of *England* were in continual Danger from the Outrages of Mobs, and which the Civil Magistrates have found it impossible to suppress?"[2] It is even possible additional troops would have been ordered to Massachusetts Bay in 1768 had they not been needed to curb civil disturbances in the home islands.[3]

The crowds against whom soldiers were used in England and Scotland generally consisted of the working class: laborers pulling down buildings where the poor were employed,[4] weavers and other clothiers smashing looms,[5] colliers burning pits,[6] coal heavers[7] and sailors[8] demanding higher wages, groups of laborers battling and killing one another,[9] and people rioting against the price of food.[10] Other crowds against whom the government employed troops give a hint about what some people in eighteenth-century Great Britain thought about the established political order. Some attacked the homes of magistrates who had used soldiers to suppress mobs,[11] some rioted

2. Card from a Providence newspaper, reprinted in *Post* 26 June 1769, at 2, col. 2.

3. Christie and Labaree, *Empire,* at 124.

4. 35 *Gentleman's Magazine* (1765), at 392.

5. *Gazette and Post-Boy,* 11 December 1769, at 4, col. 2; *Annual Register, 1769,* at [106], [124]; 34 *London Magazine* (1765), at 262; 32 *London Magazine* (1763), at 559.

6. 35 *Gentleman's Magazine* (1765), at 488.

7. *Annual Register, 1768,* at [124]; 38 *Gentleman's Magazine* (1768), at 197.

8. 38 *Gentleman's Magazine* (1768), at 242, 441; 32 *London Magazine* (1763), at 559.

9. *Annual Register, 1768,* at 57–58, 92, 105–14, 119, 120.

10. 38 *Gentleman's Magazine* (1768), at 245, 298; Letter from Horace Walpole to Horace Mann, 25 September 1766, 5 *Letters of Walpole,* at 12.

11. 38 *Gentleman's Magazine* (1768), at 243; *Annual Register, 1768,* at 101.

against executions of convicted felons and destroyed property belonging to prosecutors,[12] and some resisted with force and violence the execution of the militia laws.[13]

The rulers of Britain were not unaware of the class aspects of the new constitutionalism that employed the military to quell riots. Alexander Wedderburn is an example. He was a Scots advocate who, as solicitor general of England, would support the ministry's decision to solve the American controversy with force. "The mob," he wrote two months before Hillsborough ordered the first soldiers to occupy Boston,

> has been made sensible of its own importance, and the pleasure which the rich and powerful feel in governing those whom fate has made their inferiors, is not half so strong as that which the indigent and worthless feel in subverting property, defying law, and lording it over those whom they were used to respect. A Jack Straw, or a John Wilkes, are but the instruments of those whom they seem to lead; the leading principle of every mob is that impatience of legal rule which the relaxation of just authority, and the mutability of Government, that we have for some time experienced, never fail to produce in the minds of the inferior people. Has not the mob of London as good a right to be insolent as the unchecked mob of Boston?[14]

Perhaps no one expressed the class divisions more concisely than another Scot, Patrick Lindsay, member of Parliament for Edinburgh, the city in which John Porteous had been taken from Tolbooth Prison and lynched by a mob. Porteous had been captain of the town guard maintaining order on 14 April 1736

12. 34 *Gentleman's Magazine* (1764), at 300; 32 *London Magazine* (1763), at 445–46.

13. *Annual Register, 1770,* at [71].

14. Letter from Alexander Wedderburn to George Grenville, 3 April 1768, 4 *Grenville Papers,* at 264.

when a man convicted of smuggling was hanged in public. The crowd pelted his men with stones and mud until some soldiers began firing their weapons, even shooting at people during their withdrawal to barracks. Nine of the populace were killed. Porteous was tried for murder, convicted, and condemned to be hanged.[15] "The mob," according to Lindsay, knew he would never be executed, "that because no person of rank and condition had been killed, therefore would this barbarous murderer (as they called him) escape from justice by the favour of persons of condition."[16] That, of course, was what happened and why the crowd rescued Porteous from prison to hang him. What tells our story is Lindsay's explanation, not only why the "mob" acted as it did, but also why "persons of condition" petitioned the crown to pardon Porteous. It was, Lindsay told the House of Commons,

> not so much out of tenderness to this man, that they thought his case hard, as from another motive, a motive of a public nature; and that was, Sir, should this sentence have taken effect, the mob would become more insolent, when they found that the civil magistrate, or other persons acting under his authority, were in no better case than they who resisted the civil magistrate in the execution of the law; but if by this man's pardon, if by the interposition of mercy from the crown, they were convinced, that every person who acted by law, to put the laws in execution, acted safely, and that every person that acted otherwise did it with a rope about his neck, that would effectually suppress the insolence of the multitude, and force obedience of the law, even from those base minds who by force alone are to be driven into a sense of their duty, Who then, Sir, of that country

15. Baird, "Drummond," at 22–24.
16. Speech of Patrick Lindsay, Commons Debate of 16 May 1737, 10 *Parliamentary History*, at 254–55.

[Scotland] approves of that wicked murder and riot? The mob only, by whom it was committed; persons who have no property, and therefore are fond of disorders, because they lose nothing by disorders, and if they can escape corporal punishment, are often gainers by public calamity and disorder.[17]

Granted, class prejudice was a cause why Great Britain's rulers hardened their legal values, made power an ingredient of right, and adopted the policy of restraining civilian conduct with military force. Class prejudice must not, however, be mistaken for the entire story. Changing definitions of law played as great a role. People thinking Parliament sovereign enough to deny John Wilkes his seat in the Commons despite popular election, also thought government sovereign enough to suppress the crowd that had taken over the streets of London in the name of "Wilkes and Liberty."[18] The factors generally overlooked are that the decision to employ soldiers as police was less easily made and was, in constitutional law, far more controversial than it would be in either the nineteenth or twentieth centuries.

New constitutional premises were being introduced into British life. The sense of uniqueness is indicated by two items written in London during that year of 1768 when troops were sent to occupy Boston. In a pamphlet, *Philonomos* argued "that Military Power is not the proper aid, and can very rarely, if ever, be called to the assistance of the civil magistrate, without infringing the constitution, or endangering our liberties, which flow from the law, and can only be preserved by it."[19] Again,

17. Ibid. Lindsay was opposing a bill that would have punished the corporation of Edinburgh on a theory of collective guilt, much as Boston would be punished for the Tea Party.

18. *Post*, 30 May 1768, at 1, col. 1, and 13 June 1768, at 1, col. 1; 38 *Gentleman's Magazine* (1768), at 197; 38 *London Magazine* (1769), at 179; 1 Adolphus, *History*, at 368.

19. "Philonomos," *Liberty of the Subject*, at 5. The imprint on the edition in the

attention should be paid to how the writer used the words "constitution" and "law," and it should not be assumed that he meant what we think he meant. The second item was a letter sent by Lord Weymouth, a secretary of state, to the magistrates of Surrey urging that they not hesitate to suppress riots with military help.[20] Earlier, he had signified the king's pleasure that troops be in readiness to assist civil authorities police greater London.[21] In the letter, made public by John Wilkes, "it was recommended to the magistrates, not to delay a moment, if there was occasion, to call in the aid of the military, and to make use of them effectively, if the civil power was trifled with or insulted; as a military force could never be employed to a more constitutional purpose, than in the support of the authority and dignity of magistary."[22]

Both sides could and did appeal to the constitution. Those opposed to soldiers as policemen called the system unconstitutional; those like Lord Weymouth thought "a military force

---

Huntington Library does not indicate the date of publication. The catalog suggests it was around 1780, but the work was reviewed as a new book in 1768. 39 *Monthly Review* (1768), at 85–87. Recently, however, the date has been attributed to 1749. Linebaugh, "Tyburn Riot," at 100.

20. 1 Adolphus, *History*, at 372; 38 *London Magazine* (1769), at 291.
21. Barrington, *Viscount Barrington*, at 120.
22. *Annual Register*, 1769, at 64*–65*.

I need not add that if the public peace is not preserved . . . the blame will be imputed to the want of prudent and spirited conduct in the Civil Magistrate. As I have no reason to doubt your caution and discretion in not calling for Troops till they are wanted, so, on the other hand, I hope you will not delay a moment calling for their aid, and making use of them effectually where there is occasion,—that occasion always presents itself when the Civil Power is trifled with and insulted. Nor can a Military Force ever be employed to a more constitutional purpose than in support of the authority and dignity of Magistracy.

Excerpts of a letter from Secretary of State Lord Weymouth to the Chairman of the Quarter Sessions, 17 April 1768, 2 Clode, *Military Forces*, at 628.

could never be employed to a more constitutional purpose." It is this aspect of the controversy that interests us, not the related but independent arguments that mobs were often constitutional safety valves, that rioting generally arose from genuine social grievances, and that government response should be reform rather than suppression.[23]

No event reveals attitudes toward employment of the standing army against civilians in peacetime more sharply than the bloodshed resulting from Lord Weymouth's order. As he had urged, the magistrates called out the military, the Riot Act was proclaimed, the soldiers fired, and rioters were killed. It is not the circumstances of these deaths that need to be examined, but what certain men said about them and what they thought about the use of military force to police the streets.

Lord Weymouth, *Junius* wrote, "had animated the civil magistrate beyond the tone of civil Authority, and had directed the operations of the army to more than military execution."[24] Petitions were circulated citing as a grievance use of regular soldiers to quell riots,[25] and members of Parliament were urged to enquire "whether any encouragement has been given to premature or injudicious military *alacrity*."[26] Edmund Burke, moving for an investigation in the Commons, predicted that if the enquiry did not lead to Weymouth's impeachment, it would at least be "an examination how far the military should attend on the civil magistrate, and probably bring on an Act to regulate that matter."[27]

23. "In a Defensive Rage," at 1050–52.

24. Letter 1, 21 January 1769, 1 "Junius," *Junius*, at 9; "Junius," *The Genuine Letters of Junius* (London, 1771), at 10.

25. The humble Petition of the Livery of the City of London to the King, 39 *Gentleman's Magazine* (1769), at 329–30.

26. "Instructions from the Citizens of London to their Representatives in Parliament," 10 February 1769, 39 *Gentleman's Magazine* (1769), at 74 [hereafter cited as Citizens' Instructions].

27. Speech of Edmund Burke, Commons Debate of 8 March 1769, 16 *Parliamentary History*, at 603.

Burke wanted the military's police role confined and regulated by statute. Constitutional purists, troubled by constitutional innovation, wanted the practice stopped by restoring the old constitution before the military became the force of government.[28] "Instead of the ancient and legal civil police," petitioners of Middlesex County complained, "the military [are] introduced at every opportunity, unnecessarily and unlawfully patrolling the streets, to the alarm and terror of the inhabitants."[29] The petitioners not only were saying that "the duty of the magistrate" was "transferred to the soldiery,"[30] but that it was performed with excessive force, even in trifling affairs.[31] Parliament was asked to end constitutional innovations by removing "every pretence for calling in a military force," and to redeem the former constitutionalism by putting "the civil magistracy on a more respectable footing, [and] by restoring the office of constable, or conservator of the peace, to its ancient power and authority."[32]

In America the whigs were defending the same "ancient authority" against the same new constitutionalism. When General Thomas Gage reported that troops were needed to police Massachusetts Bay, he was told by the House of Representatives that knowledge of the nature and history of British government "should have led him to enquire whether, the disorders complained of, have not arisen from an arbitrary disposition in

28. "That you use your utmost endeavours that the civil magistracy of this kingdom be put on a respectable footing, and thereby remove the *pretence* of calling in a military force, and preserve this nation from a calamity which has already been fatal to the liberties of every kingdom round us, and which we at this day are beginning to feel." Citizens' Instructions.

29. 39 *Gentleman's Magazine* (1769), at 290.

30. Letter of 21 January 1769, 1 *Junius* (London, 1794), at 12; 39 *Gentleman's Magazine* (1769), at 68.

31. Anon., *Conduct of the Minister*, at 30–31; [Bollan,] *Free Britons Memorial*, at 17; [Dowdeswell,] *Address to Electors*, at 8–9.

32. Instructions of the Borough of Southwark, 1 March 1769, 38 *London Magazine* (1769), at 133.

the Governor, rather than too great a spirit of democracy in the constitution."[33]

Past events might have taught Gage to be more cautious in his public statements. At one time, he had experienced the old constitutionalism in conflict with the new, and surely had learned, not only that in America the old still enjoyed majority support, but that it remained strong enough to undo the new. The one occasion when he had employed troops to police white civilians in the colonies occurred when New York officials asked him for aid in suppressing disturbances among tenant farmers. The military chased the rioters to the Massachusetts line, where the officer commanding the soldiers was visited by the sheriff of Berkshire County. The sheriff informed him the troops had crossed into Massachusetts and told them to leave the colony. That encounter presents a picture of the old constitution putting down the new, but that picture must not be viewed incorrectly. It is not represented by the scene of a civilian sheriff ordering the military to cease and desist. It was, rather, represented by three hundred fifty men accompanying the sheriff "to support his authority."[34] "The Regulars withdrew early in the Morning, and the People returned Home."[35]

33. Resolves of the Massachusetts House, 29 June 1769, *Speeches*, at 179.

34. Letter from Captain John Clarke to General Thomas Gage, 19 August 1766, Gage Papers.

35. *Gazette and News-Letter*, 4 September 1766, at 3, col. 2.

A TAX OF LIBERTY:

THE OLD CONSTITUTION

No historian would be so bold as to say when the new constitutionalism of coercive police power replaced the old constitutionalism of law by consensus or popular custom. In a sense, the tension between the two extended through the entire eighteenth century, and lasted even for a few years into the nineteenth. What can be identified are periods and events when the two constitutions were in direct conflict and supporters debated the merits of their premises.

No other topic so consistently brought the two constitutions into confrontation as the standing-army controversy. It occurred at least once each year when the government moved that the Mutiny Act be renewed. The sessions of 1738 and 1739, when the opposition questioned both the projected size of the standing army and the need to maintain it, are good examples of how the debate turned on the dual constitutionalism.

Speaking for maintaining a large standing army, William Yonge, the secretary-at-war, stated the need in terms of the new definition of law and constitution. "I cannot," he asserted, "remember a year when the reasons for keeping them up were so strong as they are at present. The insolence of the people in all parts of the kingdom is risen to a height that makes it unsafe for the civil magistrate to do his duty without the assistance of the military power."[1] Lord Hinton agreed. "[B]y the audaciousness of the disaffected and the seditious, and by the lenity of our laws, as well as of those in power, there is such a spirit of licentiousness spread among the lowermost sort of our people, that I believe, nothing could command their obedience to the laws of

1. Speech of William Yonge, Commons Debates of 3 February 1738, 10 *Parliamentary History*, at 431.

their country, but the regular troops we keep in pay."[2] Colonel Mordaunt also thought the situation grave, so grave in fact, he was "convinced" that without a standing army in Great Britain, "his Majesty could not live in safety in St. James's palace; nay, I doubt if our present royal family could remain three days in the kingdom."[3] Yonge summed up the case when he argued that

> if it were not for the number of land forces we keep up, we could not expect that they [the disaffected and seditious amongst us] would keep themselves within the bounds of law. They would openly, and in defiance of the civil magistrate, transgress, in the most flagrant manner, the known laws of the kingdom; because it would be impossible for any civil magistrate to put the laws in execution against them: the consequence of which would certainly be anarchy and confusion; and this would as certainly end in a dissolution of our constitution, and an establishment of arbitrary power.[4]

Ironically, Yonge was worried about the same thing that concerned those trying to resurrect the old constitution. They, too, thought the danger was arbitrary government, but saw the threat from an opposite source. When members of Parliament insisted a large standing army was needed to enforce the Gin Law, which was physically resisted by the working people it had been enacted to protect, Lord Bathurst protested that the wrong legal values were receiving priority. "It is a strange doctrine in a free country," he told the House of Lords,

2. Speech of Lord Hinton, Lords Debates of 9 March 1738, 10 *Parliamentary History*, at 530.

3. Speech of Colonel Mordaunt, Commons Debates of 3 February 1738, 10 *Parliamentary History*, at 452.

4. Speech of William Yonge, Commons Debates of 14 February 1739, 10 *Parliamentary History*, at 1335.

that because some laws have been enacted, or some things have been done, that are disagreeable to the people, therefore a numerous Standing Army ought to be kept up, in order to compel the people to submit. This is a doctrine, my Lords, I shall never approve of: even as to the drinking of gin, if it should be no way prevented, but by a Standing Army, I should be for leaving the people in possession of that darling liquor, rather than attempt to bereave them of it by such means; for in that case, an army that could take gin from them, could likewise, and probably would, take their liberties from them also.[5]

There were, of course, people unconvinced that extremes of arbitrary power had to follow if either the old or new constitutional theory dominated police law. A few, for example, willing to "keep up a Force sufficient to prevent our happy Constitution from being subverted by domestic Conspiracies or foreign Invasion," wanted statutes ensuring "that the Liberty of the Subject shall be as little endangered as may be from this military Establishment."[6] If that view had the future before it, it still had a past to overcome on both sides of the Atlantic. The perspective still depended on how one defined "law," and there were many lawyers as well as nonlawyers who resisted the notion that law was nothing more than the sovereign's command.

Back during the debates of 1738, a member told the House of Commons:

As to what the gentlemen who are for continuing the present number of our forces have so much insisted on, I

5. Speech of Lord Bathurst, Lords Debates of 9 March 1739, 10 *Parliamentary History*, at 549.

6. Anon., *Letter Relating to Mutiny*, at 3. See also Speech of Governor Thomas Pownall, Commons Debates of 14 December 1770, 16 *Parliamentary History*, at 1332.

mean the spirit of opposition to the civil magistracy on some occasion, it has, I am afraid, been too much owing to the conduct of the magistrates; and their opposition to some late laws is to be imputed, I believe, to the nature of the laws themselves. . . . Are gentlemen to suppose that a people will submit to laws which they look upon [as] oppressive and inconsistent?[7]

If this concept of "law" seems quaint today, it would not do to assume it was quaint to the prerevolutionary generation, even in Great Britain. *Junius*, for example, termed Lord Weymouth's policy that the magistrates use the military as policemen, "this illegal, inhuman doctrine."[8] Then, invoking the same definition of "law" to which American whigs adhered, *Junius* asserted that had George III reflected on the implications of Weymouth's policy, the king could not have boasted "that he had made the laws the rule of his conduct."[9] The jurisprudence of the opposition in Great Britain during the prerevolutionary era was a throwback to seventeenth-century whiggery. People opposed to rule by the ministry were not so much afraid the military would become the government, as that the military would make government more powerful than what they called "law."[10]

The blending of law into the governmental authority may have been established by 1768, yet it was still resisted by many factions and the concept triggering their fear was "power." In the vocabulary of British whigs before the nineteenth century, "power" was the opposite of "right," and "right" was the most essential ingredient instilling command with lawfulness.[11] Discussing Parliament's claim to tax Americans, Richard Bland

7. Speech of Sir William Pulteney, Commons Debates of 3 February 1738, 10 *Parliamentary History*, at 436–37.

8. Letter XXXVII, 19 March 1770, 2 "Junius," *Junius*, at 77.

9. Ibid.

10. For the seventeenth century, see Schwoerer, *No Standing Armies*, at 47.

11. "Power" was also the opposite of "consent." John Trenchard, Letter 95,

pointed out that "*Power* abstracted from *Right* cannot give a just Title to Dominion."[12] His distinction was a jurisprudential truism characteristic of the school of eighteenth-century legalism that sought restraint on government authority while acknowledging the legitimacy of coercive force. If power proved too strong to resist, it had to be obeyed, but that reality would not make either power or its exercise "right." Discussing the question, "how far the Parliament, of right, might impose taxes upon them," Thomas Hutchinson shed light on what Bland and other American whigs had in mind. "[F]ew or none," he said, "were willing to admit the right, but the power and, from thence the obligation to submit none would deny."[13] Of course, events proved Hutchinson wrong, and the reason why he was wrong illustrates the distinction. Americans not only denied the right, they resisted the power, and did so because it could be resisted successfully. Parliament did not have the will to test its power to enforce the Stamp Act. Conversely, it was just as possible to assert the right, though lacking the power. For example, a theorist could argue that Parliament, to retain its sovereignty whole, had to insist it possessed the right to tax the colonies even if, either because of political inexpediency or lack of power, it could not enforce the right. This species of powerless right was described "as a *speculative* right merely, never to be *exerted*, nor ever to be *renounced*."[14]

---

22 September 1722, "Cato's Letters," at 229. "Consent," of course, was a test of "right" just as "right" was a test of "law."

12. Bland, *An Inquiry*, at 25.

13. Letter from Chief Justice Thomas Hutchinson to Former Governor Thomas Pownall, 8 March 1766, Morgan, *Prologue*, at 123.

14. Letter LXIV, 2 November 1771, 2 "Junius," *Junius*, at 296. Thomas Paine was wrong when he asserted that "Government on the old system is an assumption of power, for the aggrandizement of itself; on the new, a delegation of power, for the common benefit of society." *The Rights of Man*, quoted in Greene, "Paine and Modernization," at 80–81. What Paine called old was new.

There were differences in perceptions. Mere power could be seen as law without right, or as command that was not law. "Such Laws as require an armed Force to put them in Execution are unnatural," it was said in 1749,[15] and earlier Thomas Gordon had written much the same about laws "of tyrants." They were "not Laws, but wild Acts of Will, counselled by Rage or Folly, and executed by Dragoons."[16] If today's lawyers are puzzled by the meaning, it is because they cannot forgo twentieth-century constitutional eidolons. An explanation would require defining what the Massachusetts House of Representatives meant when it warned against "arbitrary Power,"[17] a concept that, in a negative sense, had much to do with eighteenth-century notions concerning liberty and political freedom. Laws requiring military enforcement had "more the Air of arbitrary Edicts than the voluntary Acts of a free People."[18] They were "inconsistent, with the spirit of a free constitution, and the very nature of government,"[19] not because the edicts lacked force and would be disobeyed, but because, even though obeyed exactly, they would be commands of mere power. William Bollan thought the difference so obvious every one acknowledged it. "[T]hey who pretend to learning and knowledge, and yet cannot discern any

---

The old idea was that the "only Rule" of power "is the Good of the People." Power was confined by law. Thomas Gordon, Letter 25, 15 April 1721, "Cato's Letters," at 71. Government was "not a Power, like that which we have over Beasts." [Burnet,] *Coronation Sermon*, at 5. For a lawyer making the distinction in 1642, see [Parker,] *Observations upon Some Answers*, at 3.

15. Anon., *Apology for Smugglers*, at 9.

16. Thomas Gordon, Letter 63, 27 January 1721, "Cato's Letters," at 141.

17. Message from the Massachusetts House of Representatives to Acting Governor Thomas Hutchinson, 24 April 1770, *Gazette and Post-Boy*, 30 April 1770, at 1, col. 2.

18. Anon., *Apology for Smugglers*, at 9.

19. Message from the Massachusetts House of Representatives to Governor Francis Bernard, 13 June 1769, *Speeches*, at 170.

difference between the use of civil and military force in a free state, are, I conceive, unworthy members of it."[20]

Some writers went even further than Bollan. He objected to military force; they objected to excessive force of any kind. There is no need to detail their arguments, for they were not concerned with the standing-army controversy, but their theories should be noted because they formed part of every opposition to the use of soldiers as policemen. For them, even though mobs were undesirable, they were "sometimes useful," and certainly less dangerous than the power of a magistrate to crush unruly crowds with force.[21]

As previously noted, Secretary-at-War Yonge was a spokesman for the constitutionalism of command. Indeed, he was, for 1738, something of an extremist. The fact there were mobs in England "so favoured by the country in general" no magistrate could "raise a posse strong enough . . . to have suppressed them," demonstrated, he believed, the need to maintain a standing army in peacetime.[22] Other people looked at the same facts and came to opposite conclusions: that they proved the need for reform, not force. Mobs were the evidence, not the cause, of social unrest. They were, in fact, "not the most dangerous symptoms of the disease; such breakings out have been often regarded, by able statesmen, as a favourable crisis, by which nature throws off the peccant humours in the body politic."[23] The task for governors was not to crush the crowd, but to learn its grievance and effect the cure. At the very time troops were assembling in Ireland for embarkation to Boston, it was contended that "when the real spirit of our constitution is adhered

20. [Bollan,] *Continued Corruption*, at 19.

21. *Boston Gazette*, 12 September 1768, at 2, col. 2 (quoting a member of Parliament).

22. Speech of William Yonge, Commons Debates of 3 February 1738, 10 *Parliamentary History*, at 431. See also 35 *London Magazine* (1766), at 35.

23. Anon., *Conduct of the Minister*, at 31.

to, and *suitably* executed, its decisions are always valid, always respected; for no people are more jealous of their constitution, than the English. But when our laws are remissly carried into execution, or when they are perverted to wrong intentions, the body politic sensible of the disorder, becomes agitated, and confusions ensue. In such a situation to plead the necessity of restoring quiet by turning the military force upon the people, can only proceed from weak heads or base hearts."[24] An American clergyman made almost the exact same argument when denying that troops sometimes might be needed to support civil government.

> But whoever considers, that the design of government is the good of the people, and the great improbability there is, that a people, in general, should be against measures calculated for their good, and that *such* measures only ought to be enforced, will look upon this as the idlest pretense. For rulers to use a military power, to enforce measures of a contrary tendency, is one of the wickedest and most unjustifiable kinds of offensive war; a violation not only of the common laws of justice and humanity, but of their own sacred engagements to promote the public good.[25]

The legal theory why force should not be applied in these situations was that power, by making magistrates contemptuous of the people, encouraged oppression. "If," a member told the House of Commons, "a Tumult happens from a just Cause of Complaint, the People ought to be satisfied, their Grievance ought to be redressed, they ought not surely to be immediately knocked on the Head, because they happen to complain in an irregular Manner."[26]

One final point must be stressed. The tension between the two constitutional traditions was not geographical, it was not

24. 39 *Monthly Review* (1768), at 85.
25. Howard, *Artillery-Election Sermon*, at 28.
26. *Boston Gazette*, 12 September 1768, at 2, col. 2.

between two parts of the British Empire divided by the Atlantic Ocean. There were in the colonies supporters of the constitutionalism of sovereign command, just as in Great Britain there were supporters of the constitutionalism of customary restraints to power. Disorders had to be put down, Governor William Franklin warned the New Jersey General Assembly, or the crowd would put down government. "Laws, the best Cement of Societies, will be broken with Impunity. . . . Anarchy and Confusion will then ensue, and the most despotic and worst of all Tyrannies—the Tyranny of the Mob—must at length involve all in one common Ruin."[27] Franklin's words foretold the future. Order and force would determine the course of nineteenth-century politics and law.[28] But in 1768 the future was not clear. The seventeenth-century fear of arbitrary power lingered on, and colored legal theory well into the eighteenth century. "There is," a London pamphlet argued in 1766, "no Country which has long enjoyed Freedom, in which the publick Tranquility has not, at Times, been interrupted by the Licentiousness of some disorderly Members of the Community: . . . this Inconvenience seems to be a disagreeable Condition annexed to Liberty, and a Tax paid for its Enjoyment."[29]

❖ 17 ❖

IN TIME OF PEACE:
THE ENGLISH SUSPICION

The dichotomy was not what it appears. Twentieth-century concepts of "law and order" were not being debated. What were

27. Speech of Governor William Franklin to New Jersey Council and General Assembly, 16 March 1770, *Gazette and Post-Boy*, 16 April 1770, at 4, col. 3.
28. See Appendix.
29. Anon., *To Committee of the London Merchants*, at 27.

in contention were eighteenth-century concepts of "law and liberty." Speaking of "the Pretense of calling a Military Force" to police civilians in peacetime, a petition submitted by London voters urged Parliament to put the civil magistracy "on a respectable footing" in order to "preserve this Nation from a Calamity which has already been Fatal to the Liberties of every Kingdom round us, and which we at this Day are beginning to feel."[1]

The peril was to liberty, not to order; the danger was from power, not from anarchy. Adding a dimension to the argument just discussed, *Junius* thought the problem was not only power to suppress riots, but power employed in a manner that provoked riots. "Ill-usage may rouse their indignation, and hurry them into excesses," he wrote of British mobs, "but the original fault is in government. Perhaps there never was an instance of a change, in the circumstances and temper of a whole nation, so sudden and extraordinary as that which the misconduct of ministers has, within these few years, produced in Great Britain."[2] A perfect example of such a minister, *Junius Americanus* agreed, was Lord Hillsborough. "Instigated" by misrepresentations from Governor Francis Bernard and the commissioners of the American customs, "but above all, by that truly constitutional spirit of administration, which taught them effectually to support the civil Magistracy by military force," he wrote Hillsborough, "your L[ordshi]p commenced hostilities in form, both by sea and land, against the town of *Boston*."[3]

Both *Junius*, the unknown Briton, and *Junius Americanus*, a Virginian, wrote of the same constitutional malfeasor, the ministry. They did so because they wrote from the perspective of the

1. Instructions to the Representatives in Parliament for London, 11 February 1769, *Boston Post-Boy*, 17 April 1769, at 2, col. 3.

2. Letter I, 21 January 1769, 1 "Junius," *Junius*, at 3–4.

3. Letter to Lord Hillsborough, 12 October 1769, [Lee,] *Junius Americanus*, at 16.

same constitutional inheritance, distrust of power. It was a fear John Wilkes often utilized when addressing his supporters. "[A]ll my grievances," he told the freeholders of Middlesex, "have arisen from various acts of arbitrary power exerted by the minister."[4] And again, "In the whole progress of ministerial vengeance against me for several years, I have shewn, to the conviction of all mankind, that my enemies have trampled on the laws, and been actuated by a spirit of tyranny and arbitrary power."[5]

The constitutional complaint was not just a matter of constitutional innovation: that the king's ministers had, on their own initiative, without parliamentary authorization, introduced "new and dangerous powers into the state" when employing soldiers as policemen.[6] It was also a matter of constitutional misgivings. One of the changes wrought by the new constitutionalism had been the emergence of executive government and the rapid decline of parliamentary policymaking.[7] Moreover, the ministers in charge of departments served remarkably short tenures in office.[8] Hillsborough had just assumed the position of secretary of state for the colonies when he ordered troops to Boston. In what appeared an offhanded manner, he carried out a program of military coercion that his predecessor would never have adopted. To hostile observers, it seemed that fateful decisions were made on personal whim or arose from the advice of faceless, often unknown, subministers. Even more troublesome was the question to whom these men answered. "A new sys-

4. Address of John Wilkes to the gentlemen etc. of the County of Middlesex, 3 November 1768, *Annual Register, 1768,* at [183].

5. In an address to the freeholders, published in June 1768, *Annual Register, 1768,* at [127].

6. [Bollan,] *Free Britons Memorial,* at 17.

7. Robson, *American Revolution,* at 149.

8. Wickwire, *Subministers,* at 6.

tem," *Junius* lamented, "has not only been adopted in fact, but professed upon principle. Ministers are no longer the public servants of the state, but the private domestics of the Sovereign."[9]

Missing from the current constitution was the principle of accountability. The Commons, no longer subject to frequent elections and rejecting John Wilkes as a member even though he had won at the polls, was responsible to no one. The crown had lost its authority to check Parliament, and the two Houses were so faction ridden they lacked leadership to direct the executive. "Corruption" and "usurpation," critics could charge, had "invaded the prerogatives of the crown, and the rights of the kingdom," and had "intercepted all due communication between the King and his people, and transferred the respect and attention of the subject, from the Sovereign to his minister."[10] The charge had validity when the existing government is evaluated by the premises of the seventeenth-century constitution.[11]

We must not wander far afield. Our theme restricts us to the question of how government-by-ministry affected the standing-army controversy. When we encounter an influential writer such as *Junius* referring to the "offenses"[12] and "crimes"[13] of the ministry, the connection is readily seen. Power unchecked by accountability could become absolute when able to employ the military as a civil police force. "By a numerous army and a severe riot act," Josiah Quincy quoted a member of the Commons, "you may indeed prevent mobs and riots among the people; but if this method be pursued for a long time, you will make your ministers tyrants and your people slaves."[14]

9. Letter XXXIX, 28 May 1770, 2 "Junius," *Junius*, at 105.

10. [Ruffhead,] *Considerations*, at 5.

11. As, for example, did Catharine Macaulay. See 42 *Monthly Review* (1770), at 390.

12. Letter XXX, 17 October 1769, 1 *Junius* (London, 1794), at 182.

13. Letter XXX, 1 Wade, *Junius*, at 239.

14. Quincy, *Observations with Thoughts*, at 427n (quoting Sir John Bernard).

The concern was not new. Lord Noel Somerset had voiced it back in 1738 when Robert Walpole was providing Great Britain with its first experience of government by ministry.

> [W]hatever Regard and Esteem I may have for those who are at present the Officers of our Army, yet when I consider how easy it is for a wicked Minister to garble and make the Army fit for his Purpose, I must think the Honour of a mercenary Army but a precarious Dependence; a Dependence which the People of this Nation ought never to rely on, because, by our present Establishment, that Army must be under the absolute Direction and Command of that Sort of Men, who have always been, and always will be, the greatest Enemies to our Liberties and Constitution.[15]

William Bollan argued for exactly the same principles shortly after Boston had been occupied by British troops, explicitly basing them on the old constitutionalism.[16]

> [I]f our ministers have it in their power to lay aside the civil judicature, with its proper officers, and take our lives into their hands, and the hands of the soldiery, with the bare intervention of a justice of the peace, whom they can with so much ease make, inspirit and prepare for their purpose, it is a vain thing for us any more to mention, unless with lamentation, our constitution, laws, liberty and security.[17]

The British suspicion was twofold: the ministry was capable of corruption and the military was corruptible. On the ministry side of the connection, having "lost the art of making themselves

---

15. Commons Debates of 3 February 1738, in 7 *London Magazine* (1738), at 247.

16. "That, according to the English constitution, the authority of the civil government is to be supported by the civil power, including the *posse comitatus*, when the occasion requires." [Bollan,] *Free Britons Memorial*, at 16.

17. Ibid., at 16–17.

beloved, they seem resolved to make themselves feared by the people."[18] On the military side was the indisputable fact "that [the] Army must in some measure be slaves to the crown, or rather to the ministers of the crown," and will not "have a regard for the liberties of the people."[19]

> When there is any difference between rulers and subjects, they [the standing army] will generally be on the side of the former, and ready to assist them in oppressing and enslaving the latter. For though they are really servants of the people, and paid by them; yet this is not commonly done in their name; but in the name of the supreme magistrate. The KING'S BREAD, and the KING'S SERVICE, are familiar expressions among soldiers, and tend to make them consider him as their only master, and prefer his personal interest to that of the people.[20]

"Self-love in officers and soldiers, will hardly prefer their precarious state under parliaments, who, jealous of their liberties, may incline to diminish or disband them, and think it mighty grievous to allow them half-pay, to the security of the continuance, and probably the increase of their pay, by bestowing an absolute power, for the defence of which they must necessarily be kept up."[21]

These arguments may seem extreme today, but, before concluding they are groundless, it would be well to ask if our judgment is colored by contemporary predilections. The same fears, when expressed by American whigs, have been interpreted by historians as symptoms of a conspiracy syndrome

18. Speech of George Barclay, Commons Debates of 3 February 1738, 10 *Parliamentary History*, at 376.

19. Speech of Lord Bathurst, Lords Debates of 9 March 1739, 10 *Parliamentary History*, at 543.

20. Howard, *Artillery-Election Sermon*, at 27.

21. [Erskine,] *Shall I Go to War?*, at 28–29.

which, arising from apprehensions unfounded in fact, transformed American grievances from "constitutional arguments to expressions of a world regenerative creed."[22] The error is to equate the eighteenth-century British constitution with the constitution of the twentieth-century United States. The British opponents of military coercion were not paranoiac extremists, and American whigs were not victims of conspiratorial delusions. They both were making legal arguments within a constitutional framework that restrained power by appealing to precedents or by resisting innovations, not by providing forums empowered to grant specific relief, or by balancing branches of government. Many techniques were utilized, including citations to history and appeals of reason. One of the most effective was to argue against constitutional novelties by postulating the worst event that a novelty might produce. *Junius* was a master of the art. "I do not doubt," he told Lord North, "that there is a deliberate plan formed.—Your lordship knows best by whom;—the corruption of the legislative body on this side—a military force on the other—and then, *Farewell to England!*"[23]

Similar arguments were made on both sides of the Atlantic, and all arose from the same constitutional problem: restraining ministerial abuse of military power. In fact, they were often related because danger to one was danger to the other. A clergyman was not unique when warning the duke of Portland in 1775 that there was "a regular plan of despotism," of which ministerial measures against the American colonies were but "one link in the chain."[24] Nine years earlier, a pamphlet published in London spun a far more elaborate plot.

Should an aspiring Minister, at any Time in full Career of extending his Power, beyond all legal Limits, and establish-

---

22. 1 Bailyn, *Pamphlets*, at 82.

23. Letter XL, 22 August 1770, 2 "Junius," *Junius*, at 111.

24. Robson, *American Revolution*, at 16 (quoting the Reverend Robert Bramley).

ing lawless Domination, by subverting the Liberties of his Country, perceive, that the reigning virtue of the Nation afforded him no Hopes of Success, by Means of Bribery or Corruption, and attempt to avail himself of Force and Violence, it is not likely he would begin at Home. . . . He might discover the Reasonableness and Utility of the Advice lately given by *Pacificus*, of sending Troops to *America*, and putting the People under Military Government, and probably the Plan of Operations against *British* Liberty might there be first executed: Slavery being once securely fixed in the Colonies, the Minister might readily discover the Conveniency of raising an Army of the conquer'd *Americans*, for opening and carrying on a Campaign in *Ireland*: Liberty effectually subdued there, the Transition to *Scotland* would be easy; thence to *England*, though more difficult, perhaps not impractible.[25]

If a writer in London could concoct such a scheme for ministerial absolutism in the British Isles, it is no wonder that Samuel Adams could excogitate the far more probable scenario of military power subduing American liberties.

[T]he time may come, in some future reign, when a favourite minister may gain such an ascendency over his master, as to have it in his power to trifle with the royal prerogative; at least to dispose of the army in America as he pleases: With an air of sovereignty, he may dismantle garrisons, remove the troops from those stations where alone the service of the public may call them, and order them to be marched into the very heart of well settled provinces, and quartered even in cities in a time of profound peace; there to erect standing armies, or at least to maintain such a military force, as he

25. Anon., *To Committee of the London Merchants*, at 8–9.

may think sufficient to awe the civil authority, and subdue the people of America to his schemes of arbitrary and despotic power.[26]

Adams was writing three months after British troops landed in Boston and two years after the pamphlet quoted just above had been published in London. The similarity is striking, and it might be guessed that Adams borrowed his conjectures from that earlier pamphlet. It would be a mistake to think so. The arguments are similar because the purpose was similar. Both writers were seeking to solve the same constitutional dilemma: how to restrain military power under a constitution in which it was permissible for ministers, accountable to no authority except perhaps the king, to employ troops to police civilians in time of peace.[27]

❖ 18 ❖

A CASE IN POINT:

THE CONSTITUTIONAL APPREHENSION

When constitutional observers of the eighteenth century postulated their most extreme arguments about standing armies, their apprehensions were less centered on mobs and police enforcement than on political influence and the Houses of Parliament. The time could come, John Trenchard predicted in 1720, "when ministers will endeavour to bribe the Electors in the Choice of

26. *Boston Gazette*, 26 December 1768, reprinted in 1 Adams, *Writings*, at 275–76.

27. Many others, considering the dilemma, made arguments that today seem as farfetched as those just quoted. Alexander Hamilton is an example. Hamilton, *Farmer*, at 94.

their Representatives, and so to get a Council of their own Creatures; and where they cannot succeed with the Electors, they will endeavour to corrupt the Deputies after they are chosen, with the Money given for the publick Defence."[1] Among those "exposed to temptations," thirty-three protesting members of the House of Lords pointed out in 1734, were army officers serving in the Commons, "especially should we have the misfortune to see an imperious, all-grasping, and power-engrossing minister, who may make their political submission to his oppressive and destructive schemes, the only test to their merit, and the only tenure of their commissions."[2] The constitutional danger, other protesting lords insisted, was ministerial influence.

> [A]ll influence over either House of Parliament, except that which arises from a sense of those duties which we owe to our King and country, are improper; . . . and naturally must in course of time, become extremely pernicious both to the Crown and to the people. For, first, although this influence appears to be that of the Crown, it may become virtually that of the minister, and be applied to deceive the Prince as well as to oppress the people. If ever a corrupt minister should have the disposition of places and the distribution of pensions, gratuities, and rewards, he may create such an influence as shall effectually deprive the Prince of the great advantage of knowing the true sense of his people; and a House of Parliament being prevailed upon to approve such measures as the whole nation dislikes, so may be confirmed in the pursuit of them, and for the sake of an unworthy servant, lose the affections of his people, whilst he imagines that he both deserves and possesses them.[3]

1. John Trenchard, Letter 17, 18 February 1720, "Cato's Letters," at 55. See also at 53.

2. Protest of 13 February 1734, 1 *Protests of the Lords*, at 443.

3. Protest of 21 March 1730, 1 *Protests of the Lords*, at 409–10.

The constitutional apprehension had respectable stirps. It had been strong enough during the parliaments of William III for Place Acts—including a clause in the Act of Settlement—to be passed. These barred from membership in the House of Commons persons holding offices of profit from the crown.[4] During the reign of Anne, however, the prohibition had been removed for army and naval officers.[5] This left what opponents of ministry influence perceived as a serious constitutional defect. "Considering what vast sums of money, and what extensive powers have been put into the hands of the Crown," Lord Noel Somerset lamented in 1738, ministers might easily "apply them towards managing and purchasing votes at elections, or even in Parliament," which would give the executive control of both Houses. The army, of course, provided a major portion "of these lucrative posts and employments, . . . a consideration that of itself is sufficient to put gentlemen upon their guard against too numerous a standing army."[6] Indeed, in 1741, when the Commons voted eleven new regiments with 362 new commissions, the earl of Chesterfield was quoted as charging they were intended as "bribery at the ensuing election."[7] For colonial whigs, Josiah Quincy summed up the same constitutional apprehension on the eve of the American Revolution, when he wrote:

> New forces have oftener than once been raised in England more for civil than military service; and as elections for a new Parliament have approached, this door has been opened to introduce a large body of commissioned pensioners. What hath been the consequence? A constant majority of placemen meeting under the name of a Parliament, to

4. 12 and 13 William III, cap. 2; Harris, *Eighteenth-Century England*, at 43.

5. 6 Anne, cap. 7, sec. XXVIII; Harris, *Eighteenth-Century England*, at 68n1.

6. Speech of Lord Noel Somerset, 3 February 1738, 10 *Parliamentary History*, at 387.

7. 2 *Protests of the Lords*, at 1.

establish grievances instead of redressing them,—to approve implicitly the measures of a court without information,—to support and screen ministers they ought to control or punish,—to grant money without right and expend it without discretion?[8]

The constitutional apprehension had changed, but not the unconstitutional instrument that was feared. It was still the standing army. Once the fear had been that the crown could employ it to impose arbitrary government. Now it was feared ministers would use the king's discretionary power of revoking military commissions to control the votes of army officers in the House of Commons. This aspect of the constitutional apprehension was especially vivid, at least in London, during the prerevolutionary era, a time when old whigs and commonwealthmen were captivated by the idea that British liberty could be lost only by a corrupt Parliament.[9]

The apprehension probably received its fullest discussion during 1734, when several members of the House of Lords lost their regiments for voting against the administration. "[T]he greatest danger to this nation, from a standing military force," dissentient lords contended, "must arise from the abuse of power which now subsists of cashiering officers, without any crime proved or alleged, and of garbling the army at pleasure."[10] It was, they added, "absolutely necessary for the preservation of the Constitution, that every member should be free and independent,"[11] and a bill to shield commissions from ministerial or royal vengeance, was entitled "An Act for the better securing the Constitution."[12] The bill was not passed and, although the

8. Quincy, *Observations with Thoughts*, at 433–34.
9. Sainsbury, "Pro-Americans," at 428.
10. First Protest of 13 February 1734, 1 *Protests of the Lords*, at 440–41.
11. Ibid., at 441–42.
12. Protest of 13 February 1734, 1 *Lords' Protests*, at 100.

apprehension continued to be voiced,[13] it was not a serious constitutional issue again until the first half of the 1760s. At that time, during the controversy about John Wilkes and the legality of general search warrants, several officers were stripped of military commissions or relieved of their regiments for voting against the administration. Among them were two men of special interest to Americans because they would play prominent roles in the prerevolutionary debate between Parliament and colonial whigs. One was Isaac Barré, champion of colonial claims in the Commons and the man who coined the appellation "sons of liberty."[14] The other was Henry Seymour Conway, who also denied Parliament's constitutional right to tax Americans and would be secretary of state during the Stamp-Act crisis.[15]

For purposes of understanding the constitutional grievance, only the Conway case needs to be considered. It reveals the issues and the arguments. Conway termed his dismissal "extraordinary news,"[16] his cousin Horace Walpole thought it "a violent step,"[17] and a pamphleteer described it as "a blow to public liberty."[18] Why such strong language and why did the

13. Speech of the earl of Westmoreland, Lords Debates of 9 March 1739, 10 *Parliamentary History*, at 538–41; Protest of 9 December 1740, 1 *Protests of the Lords*, at 496; Protest of 3 February 1741, 2 *Protests of the Lords*, at 4–5; 33 *London Magazine* (1764), at 66; Knollenberg, *Origin*, at 93.

14. Barré did not have a regiment, but was on half pay. He had recently been appointed adjutant general and governor of Stirling Castle. When relieved of that sinecure, he resigned his half pay, losing a total income of more than £4000 a year. Britton, *Authorship of Junius*, at 18, 40; 3 *Walpole Letters*, at 258n(a); *Gazette and News-Letter*, 30 May 1765, at 1, col. 3.

15. Conway was deprived of a regiment and of civil sinecures that were in the crown's gift.

16. Letter from Henry Seymour Conway to the earl of Hertford, 23 April 1764, 3 *Walpole Letters*, at 317.

17. Letter from Horace Walpole to the earl of Hertford, 2 December 1763, 3 *Walpole Letters*, at 254.

18. [Guthrie,] *Dismission of a General Officer*, at 40.

case arouse public interest?[19] One answer was that property had been taken from Conway without trial, the ministry acting arbitrarily on its own initiative. A military officer of senior rank, James Adair pointed out, had earned his posts and sinecures as a result of years of service, and to be dismissed for doing what he was elected to do—exercising his judgment as a representative of the people—meant that constitutionally he owed his loyalty to a minister, not to the crown.[20]

Although few writers were bold enough to assert that members of Parliament should obey ministers or suffer the consequences, there were wide ranging differences of opinion. The earl of Hertford, who was both Conway's brother and the crown's ambassador to Paris, tried to take a middle ground. He did not approve his brother's conduct, Hertford told George Grenville,

> but I own to you that I did not foresee or imagine that the offence would be followed with such consequences, or that the merits of his military character could ever be obliterated by his Parliamentary conduct; civil offices are supposed to be conferred from favour or purchased by civil services, and it is natural to imagine that they may be forfeited by opposite causes; but employments in the army have commonly been thought to be out of the reach of Ministerial influence.[21]

19. For example, 34 *Gentleman's Magazine* (1764), at 362–69.

20. [Adair,] *Dismission of Officers*, at 17. To be historically accurate, it should be noted that the facts in the Conway case did not support the constitutional apprehension as it pertained to fear of ministerial rule alone. George III, not a minister, had insisted on Conway's dismissal. See letters, diary entries, and notes quoted in 2 *Grenville Papers*, at 162, 166, 224, 229, 231, 297n1.

21. Letter from the earl of Hertford to George Grenville, 26 April 1764, 2 *Grenville Papers*, at 308.

William Guthrie thought Hertford's distinction "absurd."[22] Army officers, he wrote,

> who engage in civil business, or who have civil connections, cannot but think that he [Conway] should have given his assistance to government if he expected their support; and as for those who are neither engaged themselves, nor have any interest with those who do, they will soon bring themselves to be of opinion, that as he went out of his way, and of his profession, to perplex and harass the servants whom the king thought proper to employ, it is no wonder that in [sic] some sort of retaliation should take place.[23]

Guthrie's argument was one extreme: that ministers had to have authority to dismiss, otherwise officers "would soon begin to think they have a legal right to their commissions and their pay" and would become independent.[24] After all, the entire standing-army controversy had revolved around the constitutional necessity of securing their dependence.[25] At the other extreme was the view of Horace Walpole. "Such doctrines," he complained,

> are new and never were *avowed* before. They clash with all parliamentary freedom; they render the condition of officers in Parliament most abject, slavish, and dishonourable; they alarm all thinking men, and, I will do them the justice to say, do not seem universally the sentiments of the

22. [Guthrie,] *Dismission of a General Officer*, at 21.

23. Ibid., at 20.

24. Ibid., at 16. Conway said that the only explanation he heard why he was dismissed from all his posts was "that if I was turned out of the bedchamber, and not my regiment, it would be a *sanction* given for military men to oppose." Letter from Henry Seymour Conway to the earl of Hertford, 1 May 1764, 3 *Walpole Letters*, at 321.

25. [Guthrie,] *Dismission of a General Officer*, at 16.

Ministers themselves, as so many generals and officers in Parliament, who are avowedly in opposition, retain their commissions.[26]

Thomas Pitt said much the same as Walpole. "Alarming would it be, indeed, to every friend of liberty," he wrote, "if we could conceive an English Minister uniting the two propositions, 'that an officer voting in Parliament according to his conscience was *therefore* unfit to serve,' and 'that the King did not dare to trust his army in any hands but of such as were ready at any time to vote in Parliament against their consciences.' "[27] To say a minister held and acted on such principles was to allege unconstitutional behavior. The reaction of George Grenville indicates how sensitive some ministers were to the charge. He might be expected not to care. He was one of those new leaders enforcing civil law with troops,[28] and he kept tabs on how military men voted in Parliament.[29] Yet Grenville did care, and cared very much. This is evident from the trouble he took to clarify his statements about when it was constitutional for government to revoke the commission of a military man for votes in Parliament. As leader of the administration, Grenville took much of the criticism for Conway's dismissal. His efforts at redeeming his reputation were directed mainly toward ensuring that his theory of proper constitutional behavior not be misinterpreted.

Grenville's defense reveals how ministers, willing to assert military power and exact political obedience from military officers, perceived the constitutional apprehension of those who

26. Letter from Horace Walpole to Thomas Pitt, 5 June 1764, 2 *Grenville Papers*, at 342. For similar arguments, see Anon., *Some Late Dismissions*, at 27, 30.

27. Letter from Thomas Pitt to Horace Walpole, 10 June 1764, 2 *Grenville Papers*, at 349.

28. Letter from George Grenville to Charles Jenkinson, 22 August 1764, 2 *Grenville Papers*, at 432.

29. Letter from George Grenville to the earl of Northumberland, 26 November 1763, 2 *Grenville Papers*, at 169.

feared both standing armies and government by influence. First, he insisted no officer could be dismissed for opposing the administration on one or two issues, denying General Conway's claim he never "gave a single vote against the ministry, but in the questions on the great constitutional point of the warrants."[30] "No officer," Grenville hoped, "would be dismissed from the King's service for giving his opinion upon this or that particular measure agreeable to his conscience." But, when a "gentleman of high rank," such as Conway, "engage[s] in an open, regular, and systematic opposition," he had to be dismissed. And the reason, Grenville explained, was that "a military command, in factious hands, would be more dangerous to the public safety than most civil offices could possibly be." Tipping his constitutional predilections, Grenville contended that an officer voting as Conway had could not be trusted to police "tumults and insurrections against the Government."[31]

Shades of interpretation made all the difference. Grenville put up his constitutional defense on hearing that he was quoted as saying "that if General Conway voted in Parliament according to his conscience, he was unfit to have any command in the King's army."[32] The man doing the quoting, Horace Walpole, claimed Grenville also had said that "the King cannot trust his army in the hands of those that are against his measures."[33] Grenville confronted Walpole and denied making the statement. "I asked him repeatedly," Grenville later wrote,

30. Letter from Henry Seymour Conway to the earl of Hertford, 23 April 1764, 3 *Walpole Letters*, at 318. Publicly, it was said he had been dismissed for "having voted on a constitutional Point against the Administration." [Walpole,] *Dismission of a General Officer*, at 14.

31. Letter from George Grenville to Thomas Pitt, 15 May 1764, 2 *Grenville Papers*, at 321.

32. Ibid., at 324.

33. Letter from Horace Walpole to Thomas Pitt, 5 June 1764, 2 *Grenville Papers*, at 335.

whether he thought that an officer who approved in any degree of the doctrines contained in that paper [Wilkes's North Briton #45], and who dissaproved of the censure of it, or of the punishment of the author, would be a proper person to be trusted at the head of a regiment of guards to quell a tumult and insurrection occasioned by the burning of it. This was pressed by me more than once, and at last produced the following answer, with some heat and peevishness: "Good God! what do you intend to do with the army?" to which I replied, to defend the King and the Commonwealth, and to carry the laws into execution.[34]

Grenville's sensitivity indicates something of the awareness of the constitutional grievance among ministers. More to the point were Walpole's question and Grenville's answer. Walpole wanted to know what would be done with the army, and Grenville did not hesitate to reply the army would execute "the laws." Had they known of it, old whigs and commonwealthmen might have been more troubled by the answer than by the original dismissals. To say the military was "to carry the laws into execution" was to state a constitutional imperative why officers had to be free of ministerial influence. Apprehensions could be compounded, one constitutional danger leading to another. Surely, *Junius* insisted, "it is not less crime, nor less fatal in its consequences to encourage a flagrant breach of the law by a military force, than to make use of the forms of parliament to destroy the constitution."[35]

In that state of abandoned servility and prostitution, to which the undue influence of the crown has reduced the other branches of the legislature, our ministers and magistrates have in reality little punishment to fear, and few

34. Letter from George Grenville to Thomas Pitt, 19 June 1764, 2 *Grenville Papers*, at 355–56.
35. Letter XXX, 1 Wade, *Junius*, at 240.

difficulties to contend with, beyond the censure of the press, and the spirit of resistance, which it excites among the people.[36]

The British constitution was being amended. The Conway case brought the constitutional apprehension to the surface, and the public debate focused attention on the dual problem. A constitutional trade-off took place. Grenville set the tone for the future. On one hand, the ministry would employ military force as he said it could be used; on the other, the government now realized that army commissions were too sensitive to be made pawns in parliamentary politics. Henry Seymour Conway was the last military officer dismissed for voting against the court's policy as a member of Parliament.[37] As with all constitutional conventions, the rule could emerge only over time when people recognized that a power had been abandoned by nonusage. It was still too early for William Beckford to know of the change by 1770 when he rose in the Commons to support a motion placing the military in the colonies under the constitutional control of civilian government. Unwittingly, he summed up an old constitutional rule, and stated an old apprehension, when reserving the right to speak again. If necessary, he said, he wanted "to answer anything which may be urged against it, by placemen or pensioners; for such, notwithstanding the apparent wisdom of the measure, may prefer their paltry wages to the voice of conscience, or the circumstances of reputation."[38]

36. 1 "Junius," *Junius*, at xiv–xv.

37. Sir William R. Anson, *Law and Custom of the Constitution* (Oxford, Eng., 1907), vol. 2, part 1, at 125; Omond, *The Army*, at 49–50.

38. Speech of William Beckford, Commons Debates of 8 May 1770, 16 *Parliamentary History*, at 995.

❖ 19 ❖

IN A MANNER OF SPEAKING:
THE AMERICAN INHERITANCE

There were observers in Great Britain who hoped the constitutional apprehension could be palliated by stationing troops in North America. "Our colonies," an open letter told Charles Townshend, "are at too great a Distance for Soldiers or Officers to feel any undue Influence either of ministerial or sovereign Authority. Wisely, therefore, either to prevent a real Danger, or obviate the Suspicion of Danger, to our Liberties, has the Mass of our military Strength been transferred to *Ireland and America.*"[1] For American whigs, the suggestion was another example of how some in the mother country would safeguard their own civil liberties by jeopardizing those of their fellow subjects in the colonies. Americans belonged to the same constitutional world as did the writer to Townshend, and, because of that constitution, knew that the step he proposed to preserve liberty in Great Britain could destroy it in the colonies. "What regular government can America enjoy," Josiah Quincy asked, "with a legislative a thousand leagues distant, unacquainted with her exigencies, militant in interest, and unfeeling of her calamities? What protection of property—when ministers under this authority shall overrun the land with mercenary legions?"[2]

American whigs realized that, if the rising influence of ministers was changing the British constitution, it was changing America's as well.[3] The implications of the Conway case were not missed, for there was a connection between the influence the

1. Anon., *Letter to Charles Townshend*, at 10.
2. Quincy, *Observations with Thoughts*, at 400.
3. "[W]ithin these few Years the Ministry seems to have considered the Governors of this Province, not as Crown Officers with Commissions under the Great Seal, but as Officers within their Department and under their Direction."

ministry exercised over Parliament and soldiers quartered in some of the colonial seaports. "When we complain of the violent proceedings in the late administrations," William Hicks insisted a few months before Boston's occupation,

> let us consider the alterations which a century has produced in our constitution. We have now a standing army of one hundred and twenty regiments. Scarce a family of rank but what has some military connections; and even in the house of commons there are too many gentlemen of the sword. No wonder then that we are alarmed with such *spirited resolves*—that execution is to proceed judgment; and that the inhabitants of a colony are regarded as *dependent vassals*, . . . points of honour now take place of points in law, and *Magna Charta* itself must give away to that *furor militaris* which so universally prevails.[4]

As heirs of seventeenth-century England, eighteenth-century colonial whigs inherited not only the English fear of standing armies but the English mistrust of military power. "As Englishmen, as well as British subjects," the Massachusetts House asserted, "they have an aversion to an unnecessary standing army, which they look upon as dangerous to their civil liberties; and considering the examples of ancient times, it seems a little surprising, that a mother state should trust large bodies of mercenary troops in her colonies, at so great a distance from her, lest, in process of time, when the spirits of the people shall be depressed by the military power, another Caesar should arise and usurp the authority of his master."[5] "I always look[e]d upon

---

Message from the Massachusetts Council to Governor Thomas Hutchinson, 1 February 1774, *Gazette and Post-Boy*, 7 February 1774, at 1, col. 3.

4. William Hicks, in *Pennsylvania Journal*, reprinted in *South Carolina Gazette*, 4 April 1768, at 1, col. 4.

5. Letter from the Massachusetts House to Dennys de Berdt, 12 January 1768,

a standing Army," Samuel Adams told Christopher Gadsden, "especially in a time of peace not only a Disturbance but in every respect dangerous to civil Community."[6]

Even colonial prejudice against the standing army because it was staffed by foreigners owed much to inherited attitudes. The troops sent by Great Britain to America, Josiah Quincy wrote, "are in every view foreigners, disconnected with her in interest, kindred, and other social alliances."[7] His complaint was understood by British officers,[8] for he was saying what Englishmen had said before and would say again.[9] "[M]aintaining Foreign Troops in our Pay," some lords protested in 1730, "must be owing to the Advice of Ministers less cautious and less concerned for the true Interest of this Kingdom than their Duty obliged them to be."[10] Robert Walpole, defending the standing army of 1738, took pains to argue that the troops he had in mind would not support "arbitrary and oppressive Government." Put in nonconstitutional terms, it would not be an army "of foreign mercenary Troops, or an Army composed of the Scum of the People."[11] Later, in an effort to free British regulars for service in the American Revolution, George III lent Great Britain Ger-

---

1 Adams, *Writings*, at 145–46. This letter was published as a pamphlet in London the year of the Boston Massacre. *Extract of a Letter to De Berdt*, at 12.

6. Letter from Samuel Adams to Christopher Gadsden, 11 December 1766, 1 Adams, *Writings*, at 111.

7. Quincy, *Observations with Thoughts*, at 405.

8. Gage wrote of the disorders in Boston in 1770, "The officers and soldiers are Britons, and the people found no advocates amongst them." Robson, *American Revolution*, at 88.

9. In the Lords, the earl of Chatham said: "If I were an American, as I am an Englishman, while a foreign troop was landed in my country, I never would lay down my arms—never—never—never." Don Higginbotham, "The American Revolution: Yesterday and Today," 31 *Historical New Hampshire* 1, 7 (1976).

10. Protest of 17 April 1730, 2 *Lords' Protests*, at 71–72.

11. Speech of Robert Walpole, Commons Debates of 3 February 1738, 7 *London Magazine* (1738), at 264. The type that suppressed Danish liberty: "A

man troops for stationing in Gibraltar and Minorca. The loan, members of both Houses protested, was unconstitutional,[12] nineteen lords particularly stressing the point that the soldiers were foreigners.

> That Hanoverian troops should, at the mere pleasure of the ministers, be considered as a part of the British military establishment, and take a rotation of garrison duties through these dominions, is, in practice and precedent, of the highest danger to the safety and liberties of this Kingdom, and tends wholly to invalidate the wise and salutary declaration of the grand fundamental law of our glorious deliverer, King William, which has bound together the rights of the subject and the succession of the Crown.[13]

Xenomilitary fears, so much a part of the British constitutional psyche, inevitably were inherited by colonial whigs. Statements that have seemed extreme to American historians become less extreme when evaluated in the perspective of their intellectual heritage. Josiah Quincy intended making a serious point when he wrote, "By the aid of mercenary troops, the sinews of war, the property of the subject, the life of the commonwealth have been committed to the hands of hirelings, whose interest and very existence depend on an abuse of their power."[14] In an American context, what Quincy says has little meaning. To make sense, it belongs in a British context, for it describes an English fear.

New England's memories of Governor Edmund Andros's administration provide another instance of Americans thinking

---

standing Army composed for the most part of Foreigners, who have no value for the Natives, nor any concern for their welfare." [Molesworth,] *Denmark*, at 244.

12. Omond, *The Army*, at 50.

13. Protest of 26 October 1775, 2 *Protests of the Lords*, at 162.

14. Quincy, *Observations with Thoughts*, at 401.

what would be nonsensical thoughts had they not been inherited from a different English past. The people were said to have been "genuinely afraid" of Andros. It was also said that the first British regulars many of them ever saw were those he brought with him in 1686.[15] The connection between the constitutional fear and the soldiers is not hard to make if it is realized that what people feared was an inherited English rather than an indigenous American fear—fear of executive power and of governance by military force.[16] Increase Mather, who knew everyone involved, made the point when explaining why, when Boston rose up against Andros, the rebels arrested and imprisoned his soldiers.[17]

Then comes the disbanding of the *Standing Forces*: A word not so very grateful to the pallate of English Parliaments. *Standing Forces*! Whom do they mean? what *Coats* did these Forces wear? do they mean those that were brought a thousand Leagues to keep the Country in awe? A crew that began to teach *New-England* to Drab, Drink, Blaspheme, Curse and Damn.[18]

To gain some measure of the extent of inherited fears and inherited doctrine, the evidence of language must be considered.

15. Breen, *Good Ruler*, at 145n31.

16. Stephen Saunders Webb, "Army and Empire: English Government in Britain and America, 1569 to 1763," 34 *William and Mary Quarterly* 1, 24 (1977).

17. "And tho' tis judged that our Indian Enemies are not above 100 in Number, yet an Army of One thousand English hath been raised for the Conquering of them; which Army of our poor Friends and Brethren now under Popish Commanders (for in the Army as well as in the Council, Papists are in Commission) has been under such a Conduct, that not one Indian hath been kill'd, but more English are supposed to have died through sickness and hardship, than we have Adversaries there alive; and the whole War hath been so managed, that we cannot but suspect in it a Branch of the Plot to bring us low." "Declaration of the Gentlemen," at 181.

18. Mather, *Vindication*, at 49–50. At least one of Andros's "red-coats" was "a Dutchman." "Letter of Samuel Prince, 22 April 1689," in *Narratives of the Insurrections, 1675–1690*, at 188.

If the fears of American whigs were these of their English forefathers, it is not surprising that their words were as well. The two groups shared a manner of speaking that misleads historians who mistake constitutional alarm for paranoiac exaggeration. During the summer of 1766, British regulars assisted New York authorities to suppress a tenant riot. "On Saturday the 26th of July Instant," an eyewitness wrote, "Hermanus Schyler, Sheriff of the County of Albany, and Robert Van Ranslear, of Cleverack, attended with about 250 of General Gage's Light Infantry, arm'd with Guns, Swords, Pistols, one Field Peice [sic], and three Swivels, came in a hostile Manner to Nobletown, to the House of Andrew Stalker, which they broke down."[19] Language and the choice of words are revealing. The military officer in charge attempted to use restraint and avoid conflict, yet the writer says the troops "came in a hostile Manner." He is referring to the fact that they came at all—armed soldiers to police civilians—not to what they specifically did or threatened to do.

This inherited rhetoric colored the constitutional discussions of the prerevolutionary era by providing statements with a tone that today rings extreme, but suited the predilections of the audience for which they were written. "It hath been unanswerably proved," a Rhode Island clergyman said of the British people before knowing that the army had been ordered to Boston, "that they have no more power over us than we have over them, yet relying on the powerful logic of guns and cutlery ware, they cease not to make laws injurious to us; and whenever we expostulate with them for so doing, all the return is a discharge of threats and menaces."[20]

The clergyman was speaking constitutionally, not factually. The threats and menaces of which he wrote arose from the po-

19. "Extract of a letter from Egremont," 30 July 1766, *Gazette and News-Letter*, 14 August 1766, at 2, col. 2.
20. [Downer,] *Discourse in Providence*, at 8.

tential of power, not from recorded experience. Just to contemplate military coercion could be upsetting. "To have a standing army!" a Boston Congregational minister wrote a friend in London. "Good God! what can be worse to a people who have tasted the sweets of liberty!"[21] The friend needed no elaboration. The message had as much constitutional currency in London as in Boston. "Because," thirty-three dissentient lords had explained in 1734, "no free People should, on any Occasion whatever, vest in any Person an unlimited Power for an indefinite Time, and whenever they do, they at the same Time resign their Liberty."[22]

Two constitutional opposites were in conflict, and military force could tip the constitutional balance. One was liberty, the other power. "I say," Andrew Fletcher wrote in 1697, "if a Mercenary Standing Army be kept up, . . . I desire to know, where the Security of the Liberties of *England* lies, unless in the good Will and Pleasure of the King."[23] A "standing Army in Time of Peace," protesting lords asserted almost two generations later, "must be always burthensome to the People and dangerous to their Liberties," constitutional truisms "so obvious, in our Opinion, that they must occur upon the least Reflection to every *Englishman* who loves his Country and his Freedom."[24]

What appeared on one level to be a matter of localism and parochialism was, on another, a matter of how "freedom" and "free government" were defined. "A Standing Army is Inconsistent with A Free Government," John Trenchard had written in 1697.[25] "Free Government," Benjamin Franklin agreed seventy-

21. Letter from Andrew Eliot to Thomas Hollis, 27 September 1768, Eliot, "Letters," at 428.

22. Protest of 29 March 1734, 2 *Lords' Protests*, at 116.

23. [Fletcher,] *Militias and Standing Armies*, at 14.

24. Protest of 23 March 1729/30, 2 *Lords' Protests*, at 71. See also, 1 Blackstone, *Commentaries*, at 395.

25. Quoted in Schwoerer, *No Standing Armies*, at 1. And in 1782 an English

three years later, "depends on Opinion, not on the brutal Force of a Standing Army."[26] "For to live under a Force," Samuel Johnson explained in 1698, "and yet to enjoy Liberty or be a Freeman at the same time, is an utter impossibility and a contradiction in Terms."[27] "What a deformed monster is a standing army in a free nation!" Josiah Quincy echoed on the eve of the American Revolution. "Free, did I say! what people are truly free, whose monarch has a numerous body of armed mercenaries at his heels? who is already absolute in his power,—or by the breath of his nostrils may in an instant make himself so?"[28]

The language was both familiar and antique. Defending their version of seventeenth-century constitutionalism against the threats and menaces of Parliament's standing army, American whigs spoke of the same "constitution" as had Andrew Fletcher when objecting to William III's standing army. " 'Tis pretended, we are in hazard of being invaded by a powerful Enemy," he wrote. "Shall we therefore destroy our Constitution? What is it then we would defend?"[29] Fletcher would have had no difficulty understanding what the Massachusetts House of Representatives meant by "constitution" when it used the word in a message sent Francis Bernard in 1769. "The experience of ages," the House told the governor, "is sufficient to convince that the military power is ever dangerous, and subversive of free consti-

---

lawyer added that "no people can be really and substantially free, whose freedom is so *precarious*, in the true sense of the word, as to depend on the protection of the soldiery." Jones, *Suppressing Riots*, at 10.

26. In the *Public Advertiser*, 1 February 1770, reprinted in *Franklin's Letters to the Press*, at 193.

27. [Johnson,] *A Confutation of a Late Pamphlet*, at 6. "[W]e apprehend, that the keeping up, in time of peace, a greater number of forces than can be well governed by the established laws, is inconsistent with the notion of the government of a free people." Protest of 24 February 1732, 1 *Protests of the Lords*, at 419.

28. Quincy, *Observations with Thoughts*, at 412.

29. [Fletcher,] *Militias and Standing Armies*, at 21.

tutions."[30] When Parliament in 1718 voted to maintain a peacetime army of 16,347 men, four spiritual and twenty-six temporal lords protested that "so numerous force is near double to what hath ever been allowed within this Kingdom," and "may, we fear, endanger our constitution, which hath never yet been entirely subverted but by a standing army."[31] That maxim and that constitution were on the minds of Bostonians the first fourth of July after the British army had occupied their town. "[R]emove the Military Power now amongst us," they petitioned George III. It was "a Power unnecessary—a Power unfavourable to Commerce, destructive to Morals, dangerous to Law, and tending to overthrow the Civil Constitution."[32]

❖ 20 ❖

FOR THE GOOD OF THE STATE:

THE COLONIAL CONSTITUTION

The colonial inheritance of the English constitutional tradition opposing armies in peacetime had been part of the American constitution long before British troops entered Boston. At a time when the American military establishment was still a rumor, the Massachusetts House of Representatives had termed

30. Message from the Massachusetts House of Representatives to Governor Francis Bernard, 31 May 1769, *Speeches*, at 167. "A Standing Army," John Trenchard had said in 1697, is "absolutely destructive to the Constitution of the English Monarchy." Quoted in Schwoerer, *No Standing Armies*, at 1.

31. Protest of 24 February 1718, 1 *Protests of the Lords*, at 241.

32. For the Boston resolves, 4 July 1769, see *Post-Boy*, 10 July 1769, at 1, col. 1. For the petition, see *Post-Boy*, 24 July 1769, at 2, col. 2. For a collection of citations documenting American whig fear of standing armies, see 1 Bailyn, *Pamphlets*, at 42n7.

it "an unconstitutional measure."[1] To raise and keep "a standing army within this Province, in time of peace," the House later added, "is *equally* against law."[2] From the lowest to the highest public forum, the principle was understood. "Voted," the small New England town of Boxford resolved shortly after the Boston Massacre, "That the quartering [of] troops in this province in a time of profound peace, under pretence of aiding the civil magistrate, when justice, until they were quartered here, was so impartially administered, and the civil magistrate no ways impeded in the administration thereof, is a great grievance."[3] "*Resolved*," the First Continental Congress voted, "that the keeping a standing army in several of these colonies, in time of peace, without the consent of the legislature of that colony in which such army is kept, is against law."[4]

The words varied—"a great grievance" and "against law"— but their meaning was not vague. They meant what the Massachusetts House had meant back in 1764 when it termed the rumored American establishment "an unconstitutional measure."[5] But if the legal principle was unambiguous, its validity,

1. Letter from the Massachusetts House of Representatives to Agent Maudiut, 13 June 1764, quoted in Tudor, *Otis*, at 166.

2. Message from the Massachusetts House of Representatives to Lieutenant Governor Thomas Hutchinson, 7 April 1770, *Chronicle*, 30 April 1770, at 140, col. 2.

3. Boxford Resolves, 24 May 1770, *Post*, 9 July 1770, at 4, col. 1.

4. Resolves of 14 October 1774, *Extracts from the Votes and Proceedings of the American Continental Congress, Held at Philadelphia, Sept. 5, 1774*, (New York, 1774), at 5; 1 *Journals of the Continental Congress 1774–1789* (Washington, 1904), at 73.

5. The standard British constitutional treatise of the era employed the expression "contrary to law" when discussing the oath administered to William and Mary, and when observing that that oath determined that it "was unconstitutional" for the crown "to keep up a standing army in time of peace." De Lolme, *Constitution*, at 36. And, of course, the annual Mutiny Act stated that "the raising or keeping a Standing Army within this Kingdom, in Time of Peace, unless it be with the Consent of Parliament, is against Law." 4 George III, cap. 3.

❖ 157 ❖

as a rule of law, was not. The Continental Congress might resolve that a standing army, kept in a colony without consent of the local legislature, "is against law," Ambrose Serle complained, but the congressmen were speaking of "*their* law," not his, "for no law of the constitution, common or statute, says any such thing."[6] New Jersey's Thomas B. Chandler, an Anglican clergyman and outspoken loyalist, elaborated.

[W]hat are we to understand by the expression *against law*, is not easy to determine. If they mean by it, contrary to any laws that have been enacted in the Colonies, I conceive, that an attempt to point out such laws, would puzzle the Congress. . . .

If they mean, contrary to the *common law* of England, the position is more than they can defend. . . . But allowing that the Colonies are entitled to the *common law* of England; yet there is an act of Parliament, now in force, that declares, that the *government* of the military forces (which includes the *assignment* of their *posts* and *stations*) *within* ALL *his Majesty's realms and dominions, ever was and is the undoubted right of his Majesty, and his royal predecessors, the Kings and Queens of England; and that both or either House of Parliament cannot nor ought to pretend to the same.*" If this always or *ever was* the case, as the act of Parliament asserts; then it is certain that the *common law* of England can afford no pretence for this claim of the Congress.[7]

The words of Serle and Chandler delineate the legal issue that is the central theme of this book. True, Chandler's use of the Restoration statute[8] as authority for his argument may be questioned. Surely, it had lost much force during the Glorious Revolution. Also doubtful is whether the statute supported

6. [Serle,] *Liberty*, at 31–32.
7. [Chandler,] *What Think Ye of Congress?* at 33.
8. 13 & 14 Charles II, cap. 3.

Chandler's point. It authorized the deployment of troops, not their maintenance. Maintenance, not deployment, had been the concern of the Continental Congress's resolve. The Mutiny Act would have provided Chandler better authority. What is pertinent here, however, is not their mistakes, but that Serle and Chandler stumbled upon the theme of this book by defining the word "law" differently than did the whig bodies they criticized, and the reason is that they cited one constitution; the whigs depended upon another.

Chandler's constitutional theory is to the point. Although himself anachronistic, relying on a 113-year-old statute for a rule of law beyond its scope, he does not note that the American theory was (to him) more properly related to the seventeenth- than the eighteenth-century constitution. Chandler's theory of legal authority must be reemphasized lest it be overlooked. In a straight-forward argument of eighteenth-century constitutionalism, he cited a parliamentary enactment and expected its provisions to resolve all doubts.

Undoubtedly just about every English and Scots lawyer of that day assumed the same constitutional premises as Chandler. But their misreading of the American brief does not prove American whigs wrong. The colonial contention that the constitution was not as simple as Chandler thought should not be dismissed out of hand, as some historians would.[9] That the seventeenth-century constitution of customary rights would never be reestablished as the constitution of Great Britain does not prove that the eighteenth-century British constitution of parliamentary supremacy had been established in the North American colonies.[10] Whether it had or not was the basic

9. See, for example, Leder, *Liberty*, at 145–46.

10. The arguments made in some histories bear little relation to the law they supposedly explain. One historian, for example, rejects the American argument against parliamentary supremacy by relying on evidence of Parliament's lawmaking authority in the nineteenth century. See Robert Livingston Schuyler,

jurisprudential question dividing Serle and Chandler from the voters of Boxford and the majority of the Continental Congress.

The constitutional case of the American whigs was made by several alternative arguments. Some were based on the seventeenth-century English customary constitution, some on the eighteenth-century customary colonial constitution, and some on the eighteenth-century British constitution of the Glorious Revolution. Together these arguments offered evidence of meaning of the imperial and colonial constitutions, the prime sources of American rights. By universal whig interpretation of that constitution, one of those rights was the right not to have standing armies quartered in their midst without the consent of the local assembly.

The source of authority underlying both the seventeenth-century English constitution, and the contemporary American constitution that colonial whigs were defending against the eighteenth-century British constitution, was custom. In jurisprudence, custom obtains the force of law by a combination of time and precedent. Whatever had been done from time immemorial in a community was legal; whatever had been abstained from was illegal.[11] To say an action was unprecedented was to say it was illegal. "[T]he hearts of your people," the Commons told Charles I in 1628, "are full of fear of innovation and change of government and accordingly possessed with extreme grief and sorrow."[12] One matter of concern that year was the troops being raised by the duke of Buckingham and quartered in private homes by executive fiat. "Innovations in all states are dangerous," Sir John Suckling warned, "especially where there is a diminution of the laws, or a fear to execute

Parliament and the British Empire: Some Constitutional Controversies concerning Imperial Legislative Jurisdiction (New York, 1929).

11. Pocock, Ancient Constitution.

12. Remonstrance of Charles I, 14 June 1628, 4 Commons Debates, 1628, at 314.

justice, through too much liberty given to soldiers."[13] A hundred and forty years later Americans were facing the same constitutional innovation. "Resolved," the Massachusetts lower House voted, "That a standing army is not known as a part of the British constitution in any of the King's dominions;[14] and every attempt to establish it has been esteemed a dangerous innovation, manifestly tending to enslave the people."[15]

In the jurisprudential context of "custom," "precedent," and "innovation," the occupation of Boston in 1768 was, to American whigs, both unprecedented and an attempt to create a precedent that, if not remonstrated, would legalize itself. Consider the argument. "[U]nder a Pretence of aiding and assisting the Civil Authority," the troops had been sent to Massachusetts as part of "an Endeavour to establish a Standing Army here without our Consent." Because the "Endeavour" was both "highly dangerous to the People," and "unprecedented," it was "unconstitutional."[16] If accepted by the people or, at least if not resisted, it could become both a precedent and constitutional.

Discussion in this chapter has, until now, been confined to the negative test of constitutional custom. By that test, a harmful innovation was unconstitutional, and the reason it was unconstitutional was that it was an innovation. There also was a positive argument identifying constitutional custom that colonial whigs employed to prove that standing armies, such as the one sent to

13. Sir John Suckling, "A Letter written to the Lower House of Parliament (1628)," 4 *Somer's Tracts*, at 111.

14. This statement was applicable to Great Britain as well as the colonies because of the Mutiny Act compromise, which made the peacetime army legal though "against law."

15. Massachusetts Resolves, 29 June 1769, *Speeches*, at 178; *Post Boy*, 3 July 1769, at 1, cols. 1–2. See also Resolves of the Representatives of Massachusetts-Bay, 8 July 1769, *Chronicle*, 10 July 1769, at 210, col. 1; *Gazette and Post-Boy*, 10 July 1769, at 2, col. 1.

16. Resolves of the Massachusetts House of Representatives, *Post-Boy*, 3 July 1769, at 1, col. 2.

Boston, were unconstitutional and could not be made legal except by approval of the local legislature. The customary American constitution, by this argument, had existed for over a century and a half and had long performed functions Parliament and the British ministry were attempting to assume.[17] "[O]ur several colonies," a London pamphlet pointed out, "have a compleat legislature, subordinate to that of Great-Britain, which has a power of forming militias, raising troops, &c. and as they ought to be the best judges of their own wants, it would seem natural to leave the affair of regular troops to their own option, to be raised and paid as they shall find most convenient, or not to be raised at all, unless it be requisite."[18] The Massachusetts House stated the same principle in more constitutional language when it resolved

> that the British constitution admits of no military force within the realm, but for the purposes of offensive and defensive war; and, therefore, that the sending and continuing a military force within the colony, for the express purpose of aiding and assisting the civil government, is an infraction of the natural and constitutional rights of the people, a breach of the privilege of the General Assembly, inconsistent with that freedom with which this House, as one branch of the same, hath a right, and ought to debate,

17. Often, the constitutional test combined positive and negative standards. "Our wise forefathers," it was said, "drew a line between the supreme legislative power of the Mother-Country and the constitutional rights of her colonies, as free-born *English* Subjects." It was a constitutional innovation when, "[i]n the year 1764, the Parliament of *England* first declared its determination to pass that line, and grant to his Majesty a revenue out of the property of his *American* Subjects." *Extract of Letter to De Berdt*, at 16–17. The reference is to the Sugar Act, and a positive test of constitutionality would be to restore colonial rights to what they had been "before the act of the 6th of George the 2d, commonly called the sugar-act." Boston Merchants, *Observations*, at 20.

18. Anon., *Necessity of Repealing the Stamp Act*, at 13.

consult, and determine, and manifestly tends to the subversion of that happy form of government, which we have hitherto enjoyed.[19]

The Massachusetts House was saying that, for the British government, on its sole authority to maintain a standing army in the English-settled colonies,[20] violated the American customary constitution. Reference to the British constitution did not make the argument inconsistent. British constitutional principles, together with English constitutional rights, provided much of the substance of the American customary constitution. Moreover, the British constitution was an alternative authority in the colonial case against ministerial standing armies. As much as the people of London, Edinburgh, and Cardiff, American whigs were heirs of the Glorious Revolution. Privileges guaranteed English subjects by the Bill of Rights and the Act of Settlement[21] belonged as much to them as to those remaining behind in the mother country.

The argument was not absolute. Americans could, of course, claim that standing armies acting in peacetime as civilian police, were "most contrary to the spirit of the British constitution," and rest their case on the historical authority of the revolutions against Charles I and James II.[22] They could also state what seemed to them undeniable constitutional truisms, that, for example, "[s]uch is the delicacy of the *British* constitution, that it instantly dies under the hands of such *executive red coats*, and every privilege wings it's flight."[23] The difficulty was that doctrines ordained by the Glorious Revolution, of which the

19. Resolution of the Massachusetts House of Representatives, 21 June 1769, *Speeches*, at 174.

20. As distinct from those conquered from France and Spain.

21. 1 William and Mary, session 2, cap. 2, and 12 & 13 William III, cap. 2.

22. *Post*, 28 October 1765, at 3, col. 1.

23. *Post-Boy*, 15 July 1765, at 2, col. 2.

unconstitutionality of standing armies was one, were not as firmly established in the American colonies under the British constitution as they were at home.

American whigs could not lay claim to all the constitutional benefits of the Glorious Revolution. They wished to do so, of course, but were on weak grounds regarding some, such as *habeas corpus*[24] and judicial tenure *quam diu se bene gesserint* with salaries "ascertained and established."[25] It was generally accepted by English lawyers that neither of these two provisions of the current British constitution were applicable in the colonies. These legal conclusions were theorized on the authority of sovereign power or of custom or of both. The validity of the first authority depended on a constitutional argument American whigs rejected: that Parliament was supreme for all the empire. For English lawyers, if that body had not granted *habeas corpus* to the colonies, it followed that Americans could not claim the writ under the imperial constitution. The case was even stronger for tenure *bene gesserint* because Parliament had done more than fail to extend it to the colonies. Parliament and the ministry had always insisted that the colonies did not enjoy the right even under the American constitution, and, whenever an assembly voted judicial tenure for good behavior, the crown disallowed the bill. The second authority English lawyers utilized to prove that Americans did not possess these rights was custom: that they had never enjoyed or exercised them as Americans. It is this second authority that is of interest here because of the way it could be turned around. If English lawyers could cite custom to prove tenure *bene gesserint* was not a right guaranteed Americans by the British imperial constitution, American whigs could do

24. 31 Charles II, cap. 2. *Habeas corpus* was, during the Glorious Revolution, confirmed as a constitutional right by the very statute that temporarily suspended it. 1 William and Mary, cap. 2.
25. 12 & 13 William III, cap. 2, sec. III.

the same to prove that, under the British imperial constitution, they possessed the right of not receiving standing armies in peacetime. They could do so, that is, if they were correct in their facts. The factual argument was that ever since Governor Edmund Andros had been arrested and his two companies of soldiers disarmed, during New England's version of the Glorious Revolution, imperial troops had not been employed as police in the colonies unless requested by the local government.

Distinctions about to be made, it is vital to note, are distinctions of law, not of fact. The same facts were used to prove two different propositions of law. The factual argument seeking to establish that, under the customary British imperial constitution, standing armies were illegal unless voted by the local assembly was the same factual argument used to prove them illegal under the customary American constitution. What was different was the constitutional conclusion. By citing seventy-nine years of experience between the arrest of Andros in Boston in 1689 and the decision in 1768 by Lord Hillsborough to send troops back to the same town, one could argue the existence of a customary privilege under the colonial constitution. The same facts could be argued as evidence demonstrating that the prohibition against standing armies in peacetime (made part of the English constitution by the Bill of Rights) had been extended to the North American colonies by the doctrine of nonuse. The imperial government had never stationed standing armies in the colonies during peacetime. With time, that policy of restraint became a custom establishing a right under the British imperial constitution.

The American whig contention that the provision in the Bill of Rights making unconstitutional the maintenance of peacetime standing armies had been extended to the English-settled colonies contained two elements. The first was that the British constitution ran in British North America, a proposition easily applicable to the standing-army controversy. "Resolved," the Massachusetts House voted,

> That the establishment of a standing army, in this colony, in a time of peace, without the consent of the General Assembly of the same, is an invasion of the natural rights of the people, as well as of those which they claim as free born Englishmen, confirmed by magna charta, the bill of rights, as settled at the revolution, and by the charter of this province.[26]

It was, Mercy Otis Warren later explained, the opinion of the House "that the British constitution admits no armed force within the realm, but for the purpose of offensive or defensive *war*. That placing troops in the colony in the midst of profound peace was a breach of privilege, an infraction on the natural rights of the people, and manifestly subversive of that happy form of government they had hitherto enjoyed."[27] Saying the same in slightly more legal terms, it was "manifestly subversive of that happy" customary colonial constitution.

There was a second component to the American constitutional argument, an element difficult to prove by custom and one that Britain's lawyers could never have been persuaded was law. It was that, when the Bill of Rights declared standing armies "against law" unless "with consent of Parliament," what was meant was consent by the colonial assemblies in America, not just consent by the imperial Parliament sitting in London. "The Bill of Rights," the Massachusetts House of Representatives asserted,

26. Resolutions of the Massachusetts House of Representatives, 29 June 1769, *Speeches*, at 178. For a similar resolution, worded slightly differently, see Resolves of 8 July 1769, *Post-Boy*, 3 July 1769, at 1, col. 1; and *Gazette and Post-Boy*, 10 July 1769, at 2, col. 1. Cf. *Chronicle*, 6 July 1769, at 216, col. 2, to *Chronicle*, 10 July 1769, at 219, col. 1.

27. 1 Warren, *American Revolution*, at 73.

expressly declares that the raising and keeping a Standing Army, within the Kingdom in a Time of Peace, without the Consent of Parliament, is against Law. And we take this Occasion to say with Freedom, that the raising and keeping a standing Army within this Province, in a Time of Peace, without the Consent of the General Assembly is equally against Law.[28]

This was the unacceptable claim: that American legislatures were the constitutional equals in local affairs of the British Parliament. Revolution would come partly because of the inability of London to compromise the doctrine of parliamentary supremacy. That tale, however, must await the telling of the constitutional history of the American Revolution. In the narrower story of the standing-army controversy, there is only one more point to be added. It is that American whigs, wishing to stake their case against the legality of standing armies on the British constitution, did not have to depend on the Bill of Rights and argue that by custom the provision against standing armies in the Bill of Rights had become part of the imperial constitution. They could rely upon the British constitution alone, without cluttering up their case with evidence of custom or nonusage. There were two broad doctrines of English constitutionalism supporting the colonial argument that it was unconstitutional to use troops as police in the English settlements of North America. They were the doctrine of consent and the doctrine of equality.

When American whigs asserted that standing armies in peacetime were unconstitutional unless voted by colonial assemblies, they generally were not arguing that the word "Parliament" in the Bill of Rights meant colonial assembly. They were think-

28. Message from the Massachusetts House of Representatives to Lieutenant Governor Thomas Hutchinson, 24 April 1770, *Gazette and Post-Boy*, 30 April 1770, at 1, col. 2.

ing, rather, of the ancient principle of English constitutionalism requiring consent by representation for binding legislation.
"[K]eeping up a Standing Army in this Province, in Time of
profound Peace, without the Consent of the General Assembly,"
the inhabitants of Taunton, Massachusetts, voted, was "subversive of the first Principles of the British Constitution."[29] "And
whereas," the town of Boston said of the Bill of Rights,

> it is declared, That the raising or keeping a standing Army,
> within the Kingdom in Time of Peace, unless it is with the
> Consent of Parliament, is against Law: It is the Opinion of
> this Town, that the said Declaration is founded in the
> indefeasible Right of the Subjects to be *consulted*, and to *give
> their* free *Consent*, in Person, or by Representatives of their
> own free Election, to the raising and keeping a standing
> Army among them; And the Inhabitants of this Town,
> being free Subjects have the same Right, derived from
> Nature and confirmed by the British Constitution, as well
> as the said Royal Charter; and therefore the raising or
> keeping a standing Army, without their Consent, in Person
> or by Representatives of their own free Election, would be
> an Infringement of their Natural, Constitutional and Char-
> ter Rights; and the employing such Army for the enforcing
> of Laws made without the Consent of the People, in Person
> or by their Representatives, would be a Grievance.[30]

If the argument does not impress twentieth-century lawyers,
it is because it states a constitutional theory denying parliamentary supremacy. The taught historical assumption has been not

29. Taunton Town Meeting, 21 May 1770, *Boston Gazette*, 4 June 1770, at 4,
col. 2.

30. Resolutions of Boston, 13 September 1768, *Post-Boy*, 19 September 1768,
at 1, cols. 2–3. See also articles in *Boston Gazette*, 19, 26 December 1768,
reprinted in 1 Adams, *Writings*, at 269, 273–74; and in *New Hampshire Gazette*,
23 March 1770, described in 1 *Revolution Documents*, at 76.

to take seriously American constitutional pretensions because the constitution was what Parliament declared it to be. That was the constitution British lawyers knew, but they thought of "law" only from London's experience. Except in the areas of trade, imperial defense, and some minor matters, the authority of Parliament to bind the North American colonies had not been established by custom or precedent. To say that Americans, because they were virtually represented, consented to Parliament's statutes, was to equate "consent" with the eighteenth-century constitution of parliamentary command, not with the consent of custom and community consensus inherent in seventeenth-century constitutionalism. The fact that one constitutional theory was British, and the other American, did not make the first "right" and the second "wrong." They remained theories until established as law. From the American whig perspective, the special nature of the danger may have made consent even more necessary for standing armies than for other legislation. In addition to the constitutional requirement of representation, there were the problem of control, the question for whose benefit decisions were made, and the matter of assumption of risks. "If," James Lovell pointed out, "the *British* parliament consents from year to year to be exposed, it doubtless has good reasons. But when did *our* assembly pass an act to hazard all the property, the liberty and lives of their constituents? what check have *we* upon a *British* army? can *we* disband it? can *we* stop its pay?"[31]

That Parliament, rather than the crown, made the decision was not a constitutional consideration mitigating the fears of American whigs. Without representation, one authority was as constitutionally objectionable as the other. The royalist Edward Hyde could well have been talking for prerevolutionary colonial whiggery when he warned in 1648 that Parliament went too far

---

31. James Lovell's Oration (1771), in *Massacre Orations*, at 10.

when it demanded control of the militia. Should the king consent, Hyde predicted, he would abandon the people of England

> to an Arbitrary and unlimited Power of the Two Houses, for ever, concerning the Leving of Land or Sea Forces, without stinting of Numbers, or distinction of Persons. . . . Is this the *Militia*, that the KING contends for: or, did ever any King of *England* pretend to, or seek for, such a Power? surely no: But, this is a new *Militia*, and take heed, lest this should prove like the Roman *Praetorian Cohorts*, that what they did in choosing and changing Emperours, these do not to this Government, by moulding and altering it according to their Fancies.[32]

This fear was a symptom of the seventeenth-century constitution of customary restraints. The menace to freedom about which he warned had constitutionally been corrected in eighteenth-century Great Britain by the principle of control through representation. Ironically, the very doctrine of representation, which had solved the crisis of the English customary constitution by taking arbitrary power from the crown and granting it to Parliament, was the most persuasive argument why American whigs could not accept the constitution of parliamentary supremacy and had to rely on the seemingly anachronistic seventeenth-century constitution. They were not represented. Hyde's fear was as real for them as it had been for him. In that sense, their constitutional theory was not as anachronistic as British lawyers may have thought. In the eighteenth century, Americans were still encountering seventeenth-century constitutional dangers.

Representation in Parliament might also have muted the second British constitutional doctrine that American whigs thought had been violated when Lord Hillsborough sent troops to police

32. [Clarendon,] *An Answer to a Pamphlet*, at 5.

Boston in time of peace: the doctrine of equality. A committee of Bostonians summed up the constitutional principle:

> But as we are free British Subjects, we claim all that Security against arbitrary Power, to which we are entitled by the Law of God and Nature, as well as the British constitution. And if a Standing Army may not be posted upon the Subjects in one Part of the Empire, in Time of Peace, without their Consent, there can be no Reason why it should in any other; for all British Subjects are, or *ought to be*, alike free.[33]

The principle was simple enough. Even the constitutionally inept Benjamin Franklin understood that it was "equality." "As to the Standing Army kept up among us in time of Peace, without the Consent of our Assemblies," he wrote Samuel Cooper,

> I am clearly of Opinion that it is not agreeable to the Constitution. Should the King, by the aid of his Parliaments in Ireland and the Colonies, raise an Army, and bring it into England, quartering it here in time of Peace without the Consent of the Parliament of Great Britain, I am persuaded he would soon be told, that he had no Right so to do, and the Nation would ring with Clamours against it. I own, that I see no Difference in the Cases: And while we continue so many distinct and separate States, our having the same Head, or Sovereign, the King, will not justify such an Invasion of the Separate Right of each State to be consulted on the Establishment of whatever Force is proposed to be kept up within its Limits, and to give or refuse its Consent, as shall appear most for the Public Good of that State.[34]

33. *Appeal to the World*, at 25; "Report of October 1769," at 320.
34. Letter from Benjamin Franklin to Samuel Cooper, 8 June 1770, 5 Franklin, *Writings*, at 259.

❖ 21 ❖

A RESTRAINT OF LAW:

THE CONSTITUTIONAL INHERITANCE

The time has come to turn from the general to the particular. We must ask what the constitutional legacy meant in terms of one event, the military occupation of Boston in 1768. But first, to set the stage for that question, it is necessary to examine further the meaning of the tension between the two constitutions in rules of positive law. The newer constitutional tradition, in which law was equated with sovereignty and power, saw no reason why troops should not police English as well as Irish streets. The older, customary constitution, based on fear of arbitrary government, was too suspicious of the standing army to admit the legality of regular soldiers exercising force against civilians. We must linger a few pages more with that tension between constitutional theories to see what it meant for the British governance of colonial America and how it contributed to the coming of the American Revolution.

The constitutional tension requiring a constitutional compromise may be summarized by recalling an incident that occurred during the Stamp Act crisis. The only mainland colony in which any stamps had been distributed was Georgia, a feat that Governor James Wright accomplished with the aid of regular troops. Again, it is not the incident, but how individuals reacted to it that reveals the constitutional tension. General Gage was full of praise for the governor's success. "You have very great trouble & uneasiness in putting the Stamp Act in Execution," he wrote Wright, "but you have this Consolation, that you are the only Gover[nor] from the Province of Massachusetts Bay to Georgia, who has Enforced the Law in One Instance."[1] In the remainder

1. Letter from General Thomas Gage to Governor James Wright, 26 April 1766, Gage Papers.

of this book, a fact that is going to be stressed emphatically is
that Thomas Gage was a man of law who adhered scrupulously
to constitutional mandates. His comment that Wright had "Enforced the Law" deserves special weight. It takes on a different
color, however, when contrasted to what Wright was told by his
superior in London, the earl of Shelburne. Although necessary
to protect the prerogatives of the crown, the secretary of state
admonished the governor, "it is the Duty of His Majestys
Governors so to conduct themselves as not to create groundless
Jealousies or suggest Suspicion that they are capable of. . .
wishing to restrain the just and decent Exercise of that Liberty
which belongs to the People."[2]

The contrast between what these men said may not be startling, but surely it was unexpected. Although both were servants
of the king and were enforcing the same law, their ideas about
how to do the job were not the same. Gage thought "law" was
being enforced even if troops did the enforcing. Shelburne
questioned if "groundless Jealousies" and "Suspicion" made
enforcement worthwhile. He was concerned about constitutionally sensitive people like the voters of London's Southwark
Borough who, alarmed by the use of regular troops to police
crowds, three years later instructed their member of Parliament
to "endeavour to quiet the apprehensions of the public, arising
from the idea of an intended exertion of the *obsolete claims* of
the crown."[3]

Jurisprudential premises motivating the concern of Lord Shelburne and the voters of Southwark deserve reemphasis. They
combined the doctrine of constitutional restraint with a political
theory stressing appearances—the appearance of mild government and the appearance of ruling without excessive force. "An

2. Letter from the earl of Shelburne to Governor James Wright, 22 September
1766, quoted in Maier, *Resistance*, at 144 [hereafter cited as Shelburne Letter].
3. Instructions of the Borough of Southwark, 1 March 1769, 38 *London
Magazine*, at 133.

Administration founded on large Principles of Public Good,"
Shelburne advised Wright, "will give Dignity to Power[,] insure
the Reverence and Affections of the Governed . . . and make it
unnecessary to have recourse to lesser and more narrow Means
of Government."[4]

Shelburne was thinking eighteenth-century thoughts, and the
one to stress is the notion that restraint gave "Dignity to
Power." The word "dignity" seems somewhat odd in the context, but expressed the idea precisely. It would, dissentient lords
had contended, be "an indignity" to the king to say he could not
rule without increasing the size of his "standing force."[5] Samuel
Adams did not use the term but had the concept in mind when
asking the earl of Hillsborough why he had sent the soldiers to
occupy Boston. "Has his lordship then been told," he wrote,
"that the civil magistrates of the province have been deserted by
the people, their only constitutional aid, in the legal exercise of
power, and that a military force is become necessary to support
the King's authority in it?"[6]

There were two separate aspects to Shelburne's admonition of
restraint on "Liberty" belonging "to the People." If his words
mean anything, he was saying that the fears of antimilitary
commonwealthmen were unfounded. The constitutionalism of
police command need not mean all old values would be swept
away. Tories and imperialists, as well as whigs and commonwealthmen, were on guard that the price of maintaining a
standing army would not be the loss of English liberty. An
anonymous writer calling for restraint deserves to be quoted. He
clarifies the concern best, not only because he writes of troops
enforcing British law in North America but also because his
concepts of British supremacy were as extreme as any published
during the prerevolutionary era. The Americans had no right of

4. Shelburne Letter.
5. Protest of 7 March 1732, 1 *Protests of the Lords*, at 421.
6. *Boston Gazette*, 26 December 1768, reprinted in 1 Adams, *Writings*, at 276.

representation in Parliament, the pamphleteer tells us. From that fact, two conclusions followed: the colonists were not constitutionally equal, and need not be treated equally with the king's subjects in the home islands. Even so, although the right was absolute, there were limits to the power. That Parliament had authority to command with arbitrary legislation did not mean Americans could be compelled by arbitrary force.

> We cannot send our fleets and armies there to put them under military execution; that is not the method of treating the free-born subjects of Britain: no: we must make a law, that law will be put into the hands of the civil magistrate, and if the execution of it is impeded by the tumultuous, and rebellious insurrections of the people, the military power will then, in a due course of law, be called on, and will act under and assist the civil magistrate in the execution of it. These are the only methods of raising money on a free people—these are the privileges of British subjects.[7]

American whigs would not have appreciated the privilege. Government without consent was as unconstitutional as government by the sword. But whigs would have understood reluctance to use military force unless ordered by a civil magistrate. The difference was that they questioned the constitutionality of troops. The writer doubted only the constitutionality of using troops without constitutional restraint.

The words of two military men may illustrate the difference. "Employing the troops on so disagreeable a service always gives me pain," Secretary-at-War Barrington wrote after soldiers fired on and killed rioters in London; "but the circumstance of the times makes it necessary."[8] Lord Jeffrey Amherst, commander in chief in North America before Gage, warned one of his staff

7. Anon., *Constitutional Considerations*, at 10.

8. Letter from Lord Barrington to the Field Officer, et al., 11 May 1768, *Annual Register, 1768*, at 111.

not to use troops to put down antimilitary riots in Philadelphia. "As to their preventing any tumults," he wrote, "I apprehend it is entirely foreign to their command and belongs of right to none but the civil power."[9]

Barrington and Amherst may not have disagreed about the constitution, but wrote as if they did. The war minister thought troops quelling civilian disturbances constitutional, yet found the reality distasteful. The field officer, who ironically was destined to end the old constitutionalism in Great Britain,[10] spoke much as if the military had no constitutional role to play. It was more than a matter of distaste. To prevent tumults, he said, "is entirely foreign to their command and belongs of right to none but the civil power."[11]

Constitutional values were in competition, and law could not ignore either tradition. From this historical background and legal reality came the constitutional rule determining how British regulars in North America would be utilized during the prerevolutionary crisis. Soldiers were prohibited from policing civilian misbehavior unless requested and directed by a civil magistrate.[12]

9. Quoted in J. C. Long, *Lord Jeffery Amherst: A Soldier of the King* (New York, 1933), at 124.

10. He would be the commander of troops who, during the Lord Gordon Riots, were ordered to introduce Irish constitutionalism in London and "to act without waiting for directions from the Civil Magistrates and to use Force for dispersing the illegal and tumultous assemblies of the People." Ibid., at 289; 2 Clode, *Military Forces*, at 166; Finlason, *Riot or Rebellion*, at 7–13.

11. If his words mean what they seem to say, Amherst can be compared to General Ralph Abercromby, who would be removed from command of the British forces in Ireland when he insisted that his men should conduct themselves under constitutional supervision familiar to English, Scottish, and American law, but unknown in Ireland. *In a Defiant Stance*, at 114–15, 148–54.

12. The whigs, of course, interpreted the law more narrowly than did imperialists. The Massachusetts council, for example, said the soldiers could act "only as part of the posse comitatus under the direction of the civil magistrate." Letter from Massachusetts Council to the earl of Hillsborough, 15 April 1769, *Chronicle*,

The constitutional rule was summarized in nonlegal terms by the London agent of the Massachusetts House of Representatives. He had met with Lord Hillsborough, he reported, a month before the first soldiers arrived in Boston, and

> expressed my fears that some arbitrary transactions of the military might be the means of inflaming the people. His Lordship assured me they had strict orders to preserve the peace, and act in concert with the civil magistrate; and I might depend, no measures would be taken, but what were entirely constitutional, and executed with as much lenity as the law would admit.[13]

Just a few days earlier, another man had spoken with Hillsborough. The secretary had said, the man wrote, that the troops were to act only under civil magistrates, "and that no unconstitutional Method shall be taken."[14]

❖ 22 ❖

TO OBEY THE MAGISTRATE:

THE CONSTITUTIONAL RULE

The earl of Hillsborough said no "unconstitutional Method" would be employed in Boston. The answer to what he meant is not hard to find. For him, the constitutional method was the constitutional compromise spawned by the tension between the

---

3 August 1769, at 246, col. 2. See also BENEVOLOUS, in *Boston Gazette*, 14 November 1768, at 1, cols. 2–3.

13. Letter from D. De Berdt to the Speaker of the House, 29 August 1768, *Speeches*, at 162.

14. Letter from London, 16 August 1768, *Boston Gazette*, 12 December 1768, at 3, col. 2.

two constitutional traditions. Simply stated, military force could not be employed to police civilian behavior unless called out and acting under the authority of a civil magistrate.

For constitutionalists of the school of Lord Hillsborough, the constitutional method relieved the constitutional tensions. To opponents of coercive government, the method still had a tinge of unconstitutionality. "It is time for that magistrate to resign," a Boston clergyman told his congregation after the Boston Massacre, "who cannot depend on the assistance of his *neighbours* and *fellow-citizens* in the administration of justice."[1] What he said was no different than what the electors of Bristol had instructed their members of Parliament the year before:

> We request you to use all your influence, to recommend such justices of the peace, as are men of fortune and approved integrity, thereby to put the *civil* magistracy on a respectable footing; as we apprehend this will be the most effectual means of preserving a due obedience to the laws, and thereby prevent the military from becoming dangerous to our *civil* liberty.[2]

It is reasonably certain that the earl of Hillsborough was aware of the constitutional tension. He tried to avoid antagonizing old-school whigs and tories, who were suspicious of ministerial soldiers enforcing ministerial law. There is, however, little else about that minister and the law that can be substantiated. The fact may not be credited, but all the modern evidence indicates that the leaders of the British government gave little thought to the law, either imperial or local, to what troops were to do, or even to what they could do, once garrisoned in Boston.

Today no one can even be certain Hillsborough thought about law and constitutional restraints when making his decision to

1. Lathrop, *Innocent Blood*, at 7.
2. Instructions to the Members of Parliament from Bristol, 15 March 1769, 38 *London Magazine* (1769), at 193.

occupy Boston. The House of Lords said the troops were "to support and protect the civil magistrate, and the officers of his Majesty's revenue."[3] The Commons thought they were "to enforce a due obedience to the Laws, to restore order and good government where they have been disturbed, and to establish the constitutional dependence of the Colonies, on Great Britain."[4] One account of Lord Barrington's explanation to the Commons has the secretary-at-war speaking across the constitutional traditions—from the old to the new. "[T]he peculiar necessity . . . for employing a military force in America," he explained, was that

> the laws of this *country* were despised, were trampled upon in most of the provinces.—A desperate band of hypocrites had poisoned the minds of the people—universal anarchy was prevailing, and there appeared a general resolution of shaking off the British government.—Was not this, therefore, a period that called for the interposition of the military power? was not this a time to take coercive measures?—The gentlemen in opposition say no.—In the solemn assembly of parliament, they pronounce it criminal to execute parliamentary acts, and are complaining to us that the ministry have supported our honour, contended for our justice, and enforced our resolutions.[5]

Although not giving the constitutional "method" as much thought as it deserved, Hillsborough had a fairly clear idea of

3. Lords' Address to the King, *Chronicle*, 20 March 1769, at 90, col. 3. In Boston, Jonathan Sewall, lawyer and future loyalist, cited the same purpose. "His Majesty's Troops are come," he wrote, "to support his authority, and protect his Commissioners, and other Officers who are commissioned to exact and collect certain duties granted him by Act of Parliament." *Post*, 26 December 1768, at 2, col. 3.

4. Address of the House of Commons to the King, 8 November 1768, 16 *Parliamentary History*, at 474.

5. Caius Sulpicius, in "Debates of a Political Club," 39 *London Magazine* (1770), at 545.

what he wanted to happen. On making the decision to occupy Boston, he ordered General Gage to use *"such Force as you shall think necessary . . .* to be QUARTERED in that Town, and to give every legal Assistance to the Civil Magistrates in the Preservation of the public Peace; and to Officers of the Revenue, in the Execution of the Laws of Trade and Revenue."[6] The troops, Gage was told, "will strengthen the hands of government in the province of Massachusetts Bay, enforce a due obedience to the laws, and protect and support the civil magistrates and the officers of the Crown in the execution of their duty."[7] Hillsborough surely thought these objectives could be accomplished. A month later, informing Bernard soldiers were on the way, he expressed frustration at hearing of official helplessness when faced by the Boston mob. From now on, Hillsborough wanted no more talk about government being in the hands of the whig crowd. "Full responsibility thus rests with you," the secretary warned the governor, "and terror and danger in execution of your office will not be an excuse for remission of duty."[8]

A dimension missing from accounts of the American Revolution is how much officials mistook the law. Lord Hillsborough is a case in point. His words are clear enough. Once soldiers had arrived in Boston, he expected Bernard to enforce the acts of Parliament. So too, it must be suspected, did every other member of the imperial ministry. Few people in the mother country seem to have realized that constitutional law had to be taken into account. One man who seems to have done so was familiar with North America. Asked if he thought six-and-a-half regiments

6. Letter from the earl of Hillsborough to General Thomas Gage, 8 June 1768, *Boston Gazette*, 11 December 1769, at 2, col. 1.

7. Letter from the earl of Hillsborough to General Thomas Gage, 8 June 1768, 9 Jensen, *Documents*, at 717. For a summary of Hillsborough's orders, see Zobel, *Massacre*, at 85.

8. Letter from the earl of Hillsborough to Governor Francis Bernard, 11 July 1768, Cary, *Warren*, at 79.

"would be sufficient to quell the Bostonians," he replied that "the money they would spend there . . . was the only good they would perform."[9] Ironically, another person expressing constitutional doubts was Lord George Sackville, the man who, as Lord George Germain, would later direct the British army's efforts to defeat the rebelling American states. "They talk of vigour, and two regiments are embarked for Boston," he wrote about eight days before the first soldiers arrived in the colony, "but . . . applying this military force . . . is a point of such delicacy in our constitution that I doubt much of its being properly executed."[10] Events would prove that Sackville was nearer the constitutional mark than Lord Hillsborough.

Not all responsibility was placed on the unwilling shoulders of Francis Bernard. The man who had to contend with what Sackville termed the "delicacy" of the British constitution was General Gage. As commander in chief of the king's forces on the continent, Gage occupied an office of such nature "that the incumbent might be called the principal representative of the British Empire in North America."[11] Like Lord Hillsborough, he believed that what was needed to bring Massachusetts whigs into line was an application of military force. Reporting to Hillsborough that he had obeyed his orders and had sent the regiments to the Bay Colony, Gage referred to

> the Mutinous Behaviour of the People of Boston, and of the Treasonable and desperate Resolves they have lately taken. They have now delivered their Sentiments in a Manner not to be Misunderstood, and in the Stile of a ruling and Sovereign Nation, who acknowledges no Dependence.

9. A London newspaper, 15 October 1768, quoted in *Post-Boy*, 2 January 1769, at 1, col. 3.

10. Letter from Lord George Sackville to Irwin, 22 September 1768, quoted in Shy, *Toward Lexington*, at 298.

11. Randolph G. Adams, "New Light on the Boston Massacre," 47 *Proceedings of the American Antiquarian Society* 259 (1936).

Whatever opinion I may form of the Firmness of these Desperadoes, when the Day of Tryal comes, that the two Regiments ordered from Halifax, shall arrive at Boston; I am taking Measures to defeat any Treasonable Designs, and to support the Constitutional Rights of the King and Kingdom of Great Britain, as far as I am able. Whilst Laws are in force, I shall pay the obedience that is due them, and in my Military Capacity confine Myself Solely to the granting Such Aids to the Civil Power, as shall be required of me; but if open and declared Rebellion makes it's Appearance, I mean to use all the Powers lodged in my Hands, to make Head against it.[12]

Thus Thomas Gage summed up the constitutional dilemma: he would enforce the law while obeying the law. To what "Power" he was referring, Gage did not indicate. There can be little doubt, however, that he believed the ministry's decision to resort to military force in its quarrel with Boston would prove to be successful. "I know of nothing," the general wrote in the conclusion of that letter to Hillsborough,

that can so effectualy quell the Spirit of Sedition, which has so long and so greatly prevailed here, and bring the People back to a Sense of their Duty, as Speedy, vigorous, and unanimous Measures taken in England to suppress it. Whereby the Americans shall plainly perceive, that it is the general and determined Sense of the British Nation, resolutely to support and Maintain their Rights, and to reduce them to their Constitutional Dependence, on the Mother Country.[13]

12. Letter from General Thomas Gage to the earl of Hillsborough, 26 September 1768, 1 Gage, *Correspondence*, at 196.
13. Ibid., at 197. See also Letter from General Thomas Gage to Lord Barrington, 4 February 1769, 2 Gage, *Correspondence*, at 499.

By the middle of 1770, after his troops had been in Boston almost two years, General Gage was no longer certain that the "Speedy, vigorous, and unanimous Measures taken in England" would bring the whigs to heel. Still, he was confident that the military could do the job if only given the chance. "You have found," he wrote Lord Barrington,

> that lenient Measures, and the cautious and legal Exertion of the coercive Powers of Government [in Massachusetts Bay], have served only to render them more daring and licentious. No Laws can be put in Force; for those who shou'd execute the Laws, excite the People to break them, and defend them in it. Nothing will avail in so total an Anarchy, but a very considerable Force, and that Force empower'd to act.[14]

Vocabulary is a problem—for Gage as well as for us. His definition of "law" left him with a distorted conception of his enemy. In his letter to Barrington, he treated legality as if it were white and illegality black, but he did not ask if others accepted his definitions. Gage complained that the "coercive Powers of Government" had failed to crush the whigs because "those who shou'd execute the Laws, excite the People to break them, and defend them in it." He was not referring to rabble-rousers or anonymous street orators, but was placing fault with the justices of the peace. The army was in Boston to support their efforts to uphold the law, but the law it came to enforce was not their law and the time would never arrive when a justice of the peace would call for military assistance.

---

14. Letter from General Thomas Gage to Lord Barrington, 6 July 1770, 2 Gage, *Correspondence*, at 547. Even as late as September, 1774, when the situation was desperate—government was at a standstill, the councillors in hiding, the courts closed, and the people at arms—Gage believed force could restore imperial law and order. Letter from General Thomas Gage to the earl of Dartmouth, 2 September 1774, 1 Gage, *Correspondence*, at 371.

It was "those who shou'd execute the Laws" who created what Gage and his fellow imperial officials called "Anarchy." The dilemma was not caused by having too few men or by lack of material support; it was legal. Of course Gage, as he told Lord Barrington, desired "a very considerable force." Like most army officers, he felt he needed more soldiers than were on hand. But what he wanted even more than additional men was that the forces he commanded, whether large or small, be "empower'd to act."

It is important to understand the man, for he may not have been as narrow as we assume. If he had prejudices against lawyers, they were no greater than ours against the military. While serving as governor of Quebec, Gage had been a member of the provincial supreme court. It was a duty he had not relished, mainly because of the lawyers who, he complained, stressed points of law and insisted on making long arguments. Gage wished to decide cases according to plain fairness, and lawyers deprived him of the unhindered use of his own modest abilities.[15] Although this plaint sounds like a typical military man's impatience with civilian law, he probably was referring only to the technicalities of trial procedure and to the long, drawn-out process of private litigation. When confronted by constitutional law, his extant interpretations seem to have been as narrow and precise as any that could have been formulated by an eighteenth-century special pleader. No whig lawyer in Boston could fairly charge that he flouted a constitutional convention or ignored individual rights. Thomas Gage was typical of the officials sent out by London to govern the North American colonies: he was a ruler who ruled by the rule of law.

Bostonians who worried that the troops might curb their civil liberties would have been put at ease had General Gage's orders been published in their newspapers. Instead, it was Samuel

---

15. Alden, *Gage in America*, at 57.

Adams whose words were printed by the *Gazette*, and he greeted the army with some rather biting remarks. The townspeople had lost their liberty, Adams implied, for

> where *military power* is introduced, *military maxims* are propagated and adopted, which are inconsistent with and must soon eradicate every idea of *civil government*. Do we not already find some persons weak enough to believe, that an officer is *oblig'd* to obey the orders of his superior, tho' it be ever AGAINST the law! And let anyone consider whether this doctrine does not directly lead even to the setting up that superior officer, whoever he may be, as a tyrant.[16]

Because truth in political propaganda meant little to Adams, it probably would not have troubled him to learn that seldom had he been so wrong. Few members of any occupying army have had less chance to be tyrants than the British officers stationed in prerevolutionary North America.

In a sense, it is surprising that Gage ever acted to suppress civilian disturbances. The orders that he received from London were of a quality that might have justified him throwing up his hands in exasperation, keeping his men in the barracks, and ignoring the political situation. Consider, for example, the instructions sent by Secretary of State Henry Seymour Conway during the Stamp Act crisis, when, for the first time, American mobs challenged British imperial authority. His words take on added meaning when it is recalled that he, too, was a general military officer used to issuing commands. The tensions between the two constitutional traditions are reflected in the vagueness of his directives.

> It is with the greatest concern, that his Majesty learns [of] the disturbances which have arisen in some of The North American colonies: these events will probably create appli-

16. *Boston Gazette*, 17 October 1768, reprinted in 1 Adams, *Writings*, at 252.

cation to you, in which the utmost exertion of your prudence will be necessary; so as justly to temper your conduct between that caution and coolness, which the delicacy of such a situation may demand on one hand, and the vigour necessary to suppress outrage and violence on the other. It is impossible at this distance, to assist you by any particular or positive instruction, because you will find yourself necessarily obliged to take your resolution as particular circumstances and emergencies may require. . . .

If, by lenient and persuasive methods, you can contribute to restore that peace and tranquility to the provinces, on which their welfare and happiness depend, you will do a most acceptable and essential service to your country: but having taken every step which the utmost prudence and lenity can dictate, in compassion to the folly and ignorance of some misguided people, you will not, on the other hand, where your assistance may be wanted to strengthen the hands of government, fail to concur in every proper measure for its support, by such a timely exertion of force, as may be necessary to repel acts of outrage and violence, and to provide for the maintenance of peace and good order in the provinces.[17]

Although today one might wonder what Conway meant by these orders, it is known how Gage interpreted them. "[W]hen obliged by the sollicitation of the Civil Magistrate to grant the assistance of a Military Force for the suppression of Riots," neither he nor any subordinate military officer was "to act by his own authority, but to be in every thing obedient to the Orders of the Civil Magistrate, with respect to the marching or quarter-

17. Letter from Henry Seymour Conway to General Thomas Gage, 24 October 1765, in Anonymous, *An Impartial History of the War in America Between Great Britain and Her Colonies From Its Commencement to the end of the Year 1779* (London, 1780), Appendix, at 8–9. See also 2 Gage, *Correspondence*, at 28–29.

ing his Troops, the opposing the Rioters, or repelling force with force."[18] The constitutional rule, therefore, was that the military lawfully could police civilians only under the direction of civil authorities; the army was not to act as an independent or separate force.

In orders to his commanding officer in South Carolina during the Stamp Act crisis, when mobs roamed the streets of Charles Town, Gage explained that all decisions were to be made by civilians:[19]

> First, the Officer Commanding is directed to take no Step whatever with Respect to the Marching or Quartering the Troops under His Command, but at the Express Requisition of the Civil Magistrates; Secondly, That when so Marched and Quartered, the Forces are to take no Step whatever towards opposing the Rioters but at the same Requisition. And Thirdly They are not to Repel Force with Force unless in case of absolute necessity, and being thereunto required by the Civil Magistrates. You are to observe the above relates to quelling Riots and Disturbances only. If People are in actual Rebellion, every Military Officer is to attack and quell Rebels by every means in His Power.[20]

18. Letter from General Thomas Gage to Lord Barrington, 16 January 1766, 2 Gage, *Correspondence*, at 334.

19. There was one exception. Troops "should not upon any requisition whatever be drawn out, without His Majesty's express command, in aid of the civil magistracy in the colonies unless in cases of absolute and unavoidable necessity, nor until it has been clearly shown that every power existing in the colony where the danger arises has been exerted without effect." If the military commander judged that these conditions were not satisfied, he was authorized to refuse compliance with the requisition. Letter from the earl of Dartmouth to General Frederick Haldimand, 14 October 1773, 6 *Revolution Documents*, at 234–35.

20. Letter from General Thomas Gage to Captain-Lieutenant Ralph Phillips, 19 January 1766, Gage Papers.

The rule was uniform everywhere in North America, in the backcountry as well as in the populous seaports.[21] Instructing his junior officers, Gage laid down rigid standards of legal conduct—standards to which they were expected strictly to adhere. "And if matters should come to an Extremity," Gage wrote a commanding officer ordered to suppress a frontier disturbance in Pennsylvania during 1764, "you will take care that it shall appear, that any Mischief which shall happen has been thro' the Management and Orders of *Civil Authority*, and that the Military are in no way concerned, but in obeying the *Civil Magistrates*, and in supporting them in the due Execution of the Laws."[22]

21. Gage followed the doctrine of civil control over civilians even in the backcountry, beyond the Proclamation Line of 1763, at a time when the British army supposedly had jurisdiction. In 1764, before passage of the Mutiny Act of 1765, Colonel Henry Bouquet apprehended a man named Hicks beyond the frontier line of Pennsylvania. Bouquet's instructions were to try Hicks by court-martial as a spy, and hang him if found guilty. On reviewing the case, Gage altered these instructions.

> I wish the Evidence against Hicks was a little more plain, there is nothing to prove him a Spy but his own Confession extorted from him by Threats of Death. I can't therefore, confirm the Sentence. Both He and his Brother have been in Arms. And you will endeavour to get what Proofs you can of this that they may be tried as Traitors to their Country. But these trials must be in the Country below by the Civil Magistrates, to whom they should be given up. The Military may hang a Spy in Time of War, but Rebels in Arms are tried by the Civil Courts.

Letter from General Thomas Gage to Colonel Bouquet, 15 October 1764, quoted in Carter, "Commander in Chief," at 186.

22. Letter from General Thomas Gage to Captain John Schlosser, 6 February 1764, quoted in Carter, "Commander in Chief," at 204.

❖ 23 ❖

IN EXECUTION OF OUR DUTY:
THE CONSTITUTIONAL DILEMMA

To comprehend the limitations of the coercive power of British imperial government in the coming of the American Revolution, it is necessary to appreciate the narrow scope of military authority and the restricted role the army could play in enforcing imperial law. A justice of the peace, the local official closest to the people, alone had authority to call out troops to suppress civil violence. Even orders from the colonial governor, the royal official closest to the king, were not sufficient justification for soldiers to use their weapons: troops were not to fire upon civilians unless a civil magistrate on the spot gave the command.[1] Indeed, the rule of law was more strict in eighteenth-century America than it is today. Army officers were instructed, when confronted by civilians, to repel "force with force" only in obedience "to the Orders of the Civil Magistrate."[2]

For most practical purposes, these regulations meant that the soldiers, when confronted by civilian rioters, could not fire at all. Most justices of the peace were whigs and did not see matters in the same light as imperial officials. Generally the justices supported those whom Gage or Bernard called "rioters" and thought they were within their rights to be on the streets.[3] Even when the crowd's actions went beyond what the magistrates deemed acceptable, they would not call for troops or read the Riot Act.[4] "No magistrates to act, or do any thing to keep the

1. Letter from General Thomas Gage to Captain John Schlosser, 6 February 1764, quoted in Carter, "Commander in Chief," at 204.

2. Letter from General Thomas Gage to Lord Barrington, 16 January 1766, 2 Gage, *Correspondence*, at 334.

3. *In a Defiant Stance*, at 79–81; "In a Defensive Rage," at 1088–90.

4. 1 Hutchinson, *Diary*, at 179; Miller, *Origins*, at 286–87; Zobel, *Massacre*, at 230.

Peace," was how Gage summed up the situation.[5] It was a constitutional dilemma that sorely tried the patience of military men. "It is a very disagreeable Business," an officer wrote from the Pennsylvania frontier, "to be employed against the King's Subjects as bad as they may be, particularly as the Law of that Country to which we have the honour to Serve, keeps allways our hands tied, in the execution of our Duty in Such Cases."[6]

An event on that same Pennsylvania frontier illustrates the legal caution of military men, even when faced with threats of deadly violence. The people of the backcountry were a particularly unruly lot, scornful of the Quaker-dominated assembly, and bitter toward the British army, both of which, they said, protected the Indians from them rather than protecting them from Indians.[7] A party known in history as the Paxton Boys fell on a village of peaceful settlement Indians and killed many of them.[8] When survivors fled to Philadelphia and were given protection,[9] a large force of frontiersmen began a march toward the city. With terror spreading, trenches being dug, and Quakers arming themselves, the governor of Pennsylvania asked the commander of the king's troops if he and his men would protect the Indians in Philadelphia.[10] "He answered, NO: But if the assembly would pass a riot act,[11] he would defend them to the

5. Letter from General Thomas Gage to General Burton, 5 November 1765, Gage Papers.

6. Letter from Captain John Schlosser to Colonel Henry Bouquet, 16 March 1765, quoted in Shy, *Toward Lexington*, at 208 [hereafter cited as Letter].

7. 34 *Gentleman's Magazine* (1764), at 197; *Post-Boy*, 16 April 1764, at 3, col. 1.

8. "Extract of a letter from Philadelphia, Dec. 30 [1763]," *South Carolina Gazette*, 14 January 1764, at 2, col. 2; *Post*, 12 March 1764, at 1, cols. 1–3; "Extract of a Letter from a Gentleman at Philadelphia to his Friend in London," 14 March 1764, *Gazette and News-Letter*, 2 August 1764, at 2, col. 3.

9. *South Carolina Gazette*, 28 January 1764, at 4, col. 3.

10. [Barton,] *Conduct of the Paxton-Men*, at 12; *Post-Boy*, 27 February 1764, at 2, col. 3.

11. For the significance of the Riot Act during the prerevolutionary controversy, see Zobel, *Massacre*, at 52–53.

last."[12] The officer knew his duty and surely did not expect to be reprimanded for cooperating with the colonial government against the frontiersmen. Yet, needing orders "with Sufficient Civil Power,"[13] he refused to be involved until all technical aspects of law were covered and he was formally—and legally— authorized to use soldiers against civilian rioters. Meeting his demands, the Pennsylvania assembly enacted a riot act,[14] the endangered Indians were housed with the troops, and General Gage ordered the army to protect them as long as necessary.[15]

Gage has not fared well with many historians. They have not credited his role as a man of law. A recent writer, viewing him from the bias of preconceived prejudice rather than from evidence, says that "[f]rom the outset," Gage sought an opportunity to put Boston "under military domination."[16] Nothing could be further from the truth. He wanted Boston dominated by imperial, not whig, law, true enough, but he had no ambition to rule by military law. Subordinate officers often complained about legal restraints, but their remonstrances were wasted on Gage. "I am," the commander of his troops in Boston wrote after occupying the town for one year, "in hourly uneasiness about the temper prevalent here and I am sorry to hear from different channels that the officers of the Revenue are the objects of the public resentment. I cannot help believing that in case a riot should ensue, the Magistrates here would be very backward in appearing effectually for their preservation or protection."[17]

12. *Post*, 5 March 1764, at 2, col. 2.

13. Letter, *supra*, note 6, at 208. The officer was less worried about his superior than the law. With a riot act, he would better be able to defend himself in a private action of trespass or battery.

14. *Post*, 5 March 1764, at 2, col. 3; Shy, *Toward Lexington*, at 206.

15. *Gazette and News-Letter*, 10 May 1764, at 4, col. 1; *Post*, 7 May 1764, at 3, col. 1.

16. Foner, *Labor and Revolution*, at 96.

17. Letter from Lieutenant Colonel William Dalrymple to General Thomas Gage, 17 September 1769, Gage Papers. Earlier, Dalrymple's predecessor as

Gage was sympathetic toward those harassed by the constitutional dilemma, but not to any suggestion that he relax the constitutional rule. "Your Situation amidst all this Confusion," he replied to his subordinate, "every body will allow to be a critical one, but I cannot take it upon me to send you directions to grant a regular military aid toward the Suppressing any riots without the Intervention of the Civil Power."[18] The officer at Boston wrote back, indicating that he had understood Gage's answer to his complaint. "It is," he said, "not for us to arrogate powers to ourselves, but I thought it my duty to state the difficulty and have your sentiments upon it."[19]

Thomas Gage's sentiments were sentiments of law, as he understood the law. It was a theory of law adhered to by all the imperial rulers of British North America in the two decades preceding the American Revolution. The maxim underlying their constitutional rule and creating their constitutional dilemma—one that Gage repeatedly stressed to his subordinates—was the principle that civilian authority is superior to military authority in almost all things during peacetime and regarding almost every question involving the nonmilitary population. From this doctrine, neither the commander in chief nor the British army ever wavered.

---

commander in Boston had suggested the justices would call for military aid only if the mob "were pulling down their own houses." Letter from Major General Alexander Mackay to General Thomas Gage, 12 June 1769, Gage Papers.

18. Letter from General Thomas Gage to Lieutenant Colonel William Dalrymple, 25 September 1769, Gage Papers.

19. Letter from Lieutenant Colonel William Dalrymple to General Thomas Gage, 1 October 1769, Gage Papers.

❖ 24 ❖

IN A CONSTITUTIONAL VOID:

THE IRRELEVANCE OF THE ARMY

The impotency of the army as a colonial police force in pre-revolutionary North America may be measured by considering the one significant occasion when local authorities requisitioned it to suppress white, civilian rioters in peacetime. It occurred in New York, during an uprising of tenant farmers.[1] Sir Henry Moore, the colony's governor, requested "a little Military Assistance" from General Gage,[2] who ordered Major Arthur Browne of the Twenty-eighth Regiment to assist the civil authorities to suppress the riot.[3] "[Y]our Excellency," Browne replied, "may depend upon my executing your orders with the greatest Punctuality, and that I shall be particularly cautious in this case to be entirely directed by the Civil officers."[4]

Because of the location of the riots, Gage gave Browne a special injunction, a "caution" he called it. It was "a caution not to be led out of this Government into that of Massachusetts without having the proper Officers of the province you shall act in, along with you. This I think may be the more necessary to mention to you, as you are just upon the borders of the two Governments, who I find seem to think differently upon the present Subject of Dispute."[5] As did the rioters, Browne crossed

1. *Gazette and News-Letter*, 15 May 1766, at 3, col. 2.

2. Letter from Governor Henry Moore to the Lords of Trade, 12 August 1766, 7 *Documents of Colonial New York*, at 849.

3. Kim, *Landlord and Tenant*, at 394.

4. Letter from Major Art. Browne to General Thomas Gage, 23 July 1766, Gage Papers. How completely Browne thought himself under the supervision of civilians is revealed by his statement that he would "march to such Parts of this Province, as the Sheriff or other Civil Magistrate, who shall be order'd on this service, shall require." Ibid.

5. Ibid. Should the rioters flee into Massachusetts Bay, Gage explained, "the

the line and was ordered by Massachusetts officials to retreat—
even though he as well as New York's civilian authorities
wanted to pursue them. "The Sheriff of New York who conducted the Troops," Gage reported to London,

> tendered to some of those [Massachusetts] Magistrates the
> Proclamation issued in this Province against the Rioters,
> and a Warrant from two Justices of the Peace in Conse-
> quence of the Proclamation but they refused to accept it so
> that the Rioters have found a safe Retreat in the Province of
> the Massachusett's Bay.[6]

Gage expressed annoyance at the turn of events, but did not
criticize his officers. They had obeyed the constitution. When
the civil authorities of Massachusetts refused to cooperate, the
army had had no legal option except to withdraw.

Even when a royal governor sought military assistance, Gage
required that the request be made through constitutional channels so that the government would accept full responsibility for
conducting any operations undertaken against civilians. At the
height of the Stamp Act crisis, when New York City was experiencing what tories considered mob rule, Lieutenant Governor
Cadwallader Colden gave Gage an oral hint that soldiers were
necessary to restore imperial authority. "It's needless for me to
tell you," Gage replied in writing,

> that the Military can do nothing by themselves; but must
> act whol[l]y and solely in obedience to the Civil Power.

Troops had Orders not to pursue them, unless attended by the Civil Magistrates
of that Province." Letter from General Thomas Gage to the duke of Richmond,
26 August 1766, 1 Gage, *Correspondence*, at 103.

6. Ibid. The New York sheriff presented a Massachusetts magistrate with "the
proclamation and a warrant from the two Justices in Consequent of the Proclamation to be renew'd—but he absolutely refused it." Letter from Captain John
Clarke to General Thomas Gage, 19 August 1766, Gage Papers.

I can do nothing but by Requisition of that Power, and when Troops are granted to such Requisition they are no longer under my command, [n]or can the officers do anything with their Men, but what the Civil Magistrate shall command.[7]

Under the British constitution, Gage explained, the maintenance of law and order was the responsibility of civilian authority, which had to direct the military because the army could not initiate actions on its own. The one exception, as the general told Hillsborough just before his troops arrived in Boston, occurred "when People go into open Rebellion." Then, he assured Colden, "other Measures are taken."[8]

In reply to Gage's letter, Colden reminded the general that New York municipal officials were not likely to request military

7. Letter from General Thomas Gage to Cadwallader Colden, 31 August 1765, quoted in Carter, "Commander in Chief," at 205 [hereafter cited as Gage-Colden Letter]. Two years later, Colden would mistakenly recall that the idea had been Gage's, that Gage wrote him complaining of treasonous newspaper articles and "concluding with an Offer of any military Assistance which should be thought necessary." [Colden,] *Conduct*, at 458.

8. Gage-Colden Letter. Because of the realities of the political situation, military officers knew they would have to decide themselves when rebellion broke out; they would probably not be able to anticipate a gubernatorial proclamation or guidance from local magistrates.

> I shall . . . pay due regard to the precautions, your Excellency appraises me of, observed by the Secretary at War, when the civil power demands Military aid to sup[p]ress riots and disturbances, tho in the present state of Matters here [Charles Town, South Carolina], it will be hard to distinguish the time when riots cease and Rebellion begins, when it become the duty of every officer to attack and quel[l] Rebels, by every Means in his power; if this Province should bring itself into this unhappy situation, which is possible, and no requisition made to me by the Lieut. Governour which is probable, I beg to have your Excellency's orders for my conduct.

Letter from Captain-Lieutenant Ralph Phillips to General Thomas Gage, 8 March 1766, Gage Papers.

interference to suppress Stamp Act riots. "In case the civil Magistrates cannot or are not willing to do their duty, you must Judge what is incumbent on you as well as on me in such case, when all civil Authority is at an end."[9] Gage needed no reminder. If 5,000 troops had been on hand and ready for duty during the Stamp Act riots, he later observed, the magistrates of New York would not have called for their assistance.[10] Yet until they made a request there was nothing he or the army could or should constitutionally do.

It has been suggested that each man, Colden and Gage, "was trying to shift the responsibility for using force to the other."[11] A better explanation is that both wanted to employ troops to put down what they regarded as insurrection,[12] but neither knew how to do so legally under the current constitution. Colden could not make a formal request without the advice and consent of the council,[13] which he could not obtain from its whig membership.[14] When Colden asked, the council replied "that it will be more safe for the Government to shew a Confidence in the People; than to discover its Distrust of them by calling in any Assistance to the Civil Power."[15] "You know Sir," the lieutenant governor wrote Sir Jeffrey Amherst, "that the Military

9. Letter from Lieutenant Governor Cadwallader Colden to General Thomas Gage, 2 September 1765, 2 *Colden Papers*, at 30–31. Also quoted in Shy, *Toward Lexington*, at 210–11.

10. Letter from General Thomas Gage to Secretary of State Henry Seymour Conway, 16 January 1766, 1 Gage, *Correspondence*, at 81–82.

11. Shy, *Toward Lexington*, at 211.

12. Letter from Lieutenant Governor Cadwallader Colden to the Board of Trade, 2 *Colden Papers*, at 79.

13. A general constitutional rule in the colonies. For discussion, see *In a Rebellious Spirit*, at 74–85.

14. All the council had to do was delay consideration and the governor's hands were tied. See sources cited in "In a Constitutional Void," at 14n53.

15. Advice from the New York Council to Lieutenant Governor Cadwallader Colden, 4 September 1765, Gage Papers.

Power cannot act but in assisting the civil. When I proposed the calling in the Military Assistance, the Council & Magistrates insisted that there was no danger from Mobs & there was no need of assistance."[16]

Colden apparently hoped that the constitutional stalemate between himself and the council created a constitutional emergency of sufficient danger to free Gage from all constitutional restraints. The general disagreed. No matter what the political or constitutional situation, even as commander in chief with power independent of the civilian governors and responsible only to the crown, he alone had no authority to order the military to police civilians except in case of rebellion. Government might be helpless, but mass violence—even on the scale of the Stamp Act riots—was not legally a revolution. "Gage," his biographer concludes, "believed in a 'country of liberty' the military was rightly subject to the civil power, with the exception noted, of course."[17]

These constitutional premises, tested in New York during the Stamp Act crisis and found wanting, still prevailed at the time the British army was ordered to occupy Boston during 1768. Before the troops had even embarked for Massachusetts, Gage did his best to ascertain that everyone concerned understood the law. Confusion between civilian governors and military officers over their respective power to command troops, he knew, had been the cause of recent political disputes in North America.[18] To avoid animosities arising in Massachusetts, he sent precise

16. Letter from Lieutenant Governor Cadwallader Colden to Sir Jeffrey Amherst, 13 January 1766, 2 Colden Papers, at 92.

17. Alden, Gage in America, at 114.

18. Letter from General Thomas Gage to the earl of Halifax, 27 April 1765, 1 Gage, Correspondence, at 56. Letter from General Thomas Gage to Lord Barrington, 28 March 1766, 2 Gage, Correspondence, at 342–43. See also Letter from General Thomas Gage to Lord Barrington, 28 March 1768, ibid., at 457–58; Letter from General Thomas Gage to Lord Barrington, 10 September 1768, ibid., at 487.

instructions to the colonel in command[19] and then repeated the details to Governor Bernard:

> The officer Commanding the Troops ordered into your government, is informed, that he is sent thither to strengthen the hands of Government in the Province of Massachusett's Bay, enforce a due Obedience to the Laws, and protect and support the Civil Magistrates in the preservation of the public Peace, and to [assist] the Officers of the Revenue in the Execution of their duty, and is directed to give every legal Assistance to the Civil Magistrates in the preservation of the public Peace, and to the Officers of the Revenue in the Execution of the Laws of Trade and Revenue. The Use that shall be made of the Troops to effect these Purposes I am to leave to the Direction, and Management of the Civil Power.[20]

❖ 25 ❖

A LEGAL UNCERTAINTY:

THE CONSTITUTIONAL VACUUM

The time has come to focus attention on the most famous standing army in prerevolutionary North America, the troops

---

19. "[T]o strengthen the hands of Government, to enforce a due obedience to the Laws and to protect and support the Civil Magistrates and the Officers of the Crown in the Execution of their Duty. You are therefore to give every legal Assistance to the Civil Magistrates in the preservation of the publick peace, and to the Officers of the Revenue, in the Execution of the Laws of Trade and Revenue." Instructions from General Thomas Gage to Colonel Alexander Mackay, 24 November 1768, Gage Papers.

20. Letter from General Thomas Gage to Governor Francis Bernard, 12 September 1768, quoted in Carter, "Commander in Chief," at 208.

Lord Hillsborough sent to Boston in 1768. They had not been long in Massachusetts Bay before the officers in charge discovered that General Gage's interpretation of their constitutional role deprived them of any chance to be an effective force. After about a year, their commanding officer requested permission to employ the soldiers as necessity required. Gage replied that he agreed with the arguments that the officer made: he too expected fresh riots at any moment; he knew that most Bostonians were fond of "anarchy & licentiousness"; and that the "tyranny of the people appears to be confirmed in opposition to order justice and every mark of a regular government." He could not, however, order his men to suppress rioting unless requested to do so by some civil authority. "Had I proper authority to act in these cases," he assured his junior colleague,

> I should have interfered in matters that have occurred here [New York City] lately, wherein I think everything has happened but a declaration of war against Great Britain. . . .[1] You will feel the same indignation & resentment which such proceedings must occasion in the breast of every Briton here, who has the least love or regard for his country, but if they do not rouse a proper spirit at home, what can we do here?[2]

The question of "what could the army do" was asked by tories as well as whigs. What was the legal function and utility of the troops once stationed on official duty in Massachusetts Bay? Ironically, both sides gave the same answer: the military could do little or nothing to support imperial law or coerce the political opposition.

1. Gage, writing from New York, was referring to the forcible seizure there, by members of a nonimportation association, of goods imported into New York by nonsigners of the association, and of crowd attacks on two customs officials.

2. Letter from General Thomas Gage to Lieutenant Colonel William Dalrymple, 25 September 1769, quoted in Alden, *Gage in America*, at 170.

IN DEFIANCE OF THE LAW

The American whig answer, of course, was to collocate all the arguments from the seventeenth-century English constitution that are examined in this book, and contend that troops could do nothing because they had no constitutional function, either in a political dispute or as civilian police in peacetime. The imperialist answer was first provided by the commissioners of the customs, and was not encouraging for the future of British rule in North America. The fact must be stressed that the commissioners were largely responsible for the troops being sent to Boston. Even more than Governor Bernard, they had mounted the propaganda campaign that convinced London of Boston's lawlessness and the need for an imperial police force in the colony. It is no exaggeration to suggest that had the commissioners not resided in Boston the soldiers would never have been ordered to the town, for it was their protection as much as any other consideration that persuaded Lord Hillsborough to issue the command. Before the troops arrived, the commissioners had fled the town and taken refuge at Fort William and Mary, on Castle Island in Boston harbor. Until they were protected, they wrote London, they would not be safe in Boston and would not return.[3] The idea that seems to have been in the minds of the imperial ministry was that the troops, if they accomplished nothing else, would at least protect these revenue men and make it possible for them to perform their official duties. They might be no more popular than they had been before the soldiers arrived, but no Yankee mob would dare chase them out of town again. Surprisingly Governor Bernard endorsed this theory—at first. "We have got two Reg[iments] from Halifax landed at Boston," he optimistically wrote to Lord Barrington, "[s]o that

3. The argument has been made that they fled Boston and refused to return in order to create probative facts that would convince Hillsborough Boston was unsafe and troops were necessary for their protection. *In a Rebellious Spirit*, at 100–126.

❖ 200 ❖

the Persons of the Crown Officers arc safe as I believe: tho' that is still doubted."[4]

The first indication of doubt came from the comissioners themselves. Secure behind the guns of Castle Island, they had had time to weigh local, or whig, law against imperial, or tory, order, and had come to the conclusion that as long as the people of Boston did not want them in town they would be wiser to stay away. Even Thomas Gage could not coax them back.

> The Commissioners of the Customs are still in Castle-William, and upon being asked about their Return to Boston, one of them said, there were Troops now to Support them, but desired to know, if there was any or what Civil Officer, who would undertake to ask the Assistance of the Troops, if there should be occasion for it? The Governor and Lieutenant Governor were present, but neither could be answerable that any Civil Officer would undertake it.[5]

The lieutenant governor was Thomas Hutchinson and his answer takes on more weight when it is recalled that he was also chief justice of the province, a man quite knowledgeable in the law and an official dedicated to upholding British supremacy through the rule of law.[6] What Gage reports that he and Governor Bernard said to the customs commissioners surprised no one who was present. They had said it before and would say it again. They could guarantee the safety of no British official inasmuch as the reins of government were not in their hands.

It may be suspected that the commissioners did not believe they were in danger, that they refused to come ashore because

4. Letter from Governor Francis Bernard to Lord Barrington, 20 October 1768, Bernard and Barrington, *Correspondence*, at 179.

5. Letter from General Thomas Gage to the earl of Hillsborough, 31 October 1768, 1 Gage, *Correspondence*, at 205.

6. See discussion in "Book Review," 48 *New York University Law Review* 593 (1974).

they were creating a factual case to support certain demands they wished to press upon London.[7] The puzzle is what they hoped to obtain. Surely they knew better than ask that Irish military law be imposed on Massachusetts Bay. Martial law was one solution they would not have rejected, but as realistic men they could not have been hoping for the impossible. Undoubtedly they sought to impress London,[8] perhaps seeking some assurance, now that troops were on hand, that the military would be called upon to act should it be necessary. If so, they were requesting a pledge that Bernard, Hutchinson, and Gage could not give. The difficulty lay with the justices of the peace. Magistrates who would not try to disperse mobs by reading the Riot Act were not likely to take the more drastic legal step and call for force to suppress riots. The troops might be in Boston, but they would remain of marginal utility unless the justices of the peace would employ them.

The dilemma that the magistrates posed was not caused merely by the fact that Gage would not permit his soldiers to fire upon the civilians unless ordered to do so by a justice "on the spot." Just as crucial was the fact that no other official thought himself empowered to call out the army. Because the justices of the peace were the responsible local officers who most often were available to represent civilian authority, the riot law de-

7. *In a Rebellious Spirit*, at 100–126. During the Stamp Act crisis, one of the commissioners, while serving as customs collector of Rhode Island, had gone aboard a naval vessel and refused to come ashore until he had exacted from the authorities the terms he wanted. Stout, *Royal Navy*, at 94–96.

8. They came ashore on 8 November, a time when nothing had changed and when they were no more "safe" than before. It was, however, time enough to be certain letters had been dispatched, by both civil and military authorities, informing London of their fear and impressing Hillsborough with "evidence" that, despite the troops, Boston was in the hands of the mob. Entries for 9 and 13 November 1768, Rowe "Diary," at 70–71; *Journal of the Times*, 8 November 1768, at 20, col. 1.

pended on their judgment and hence on their cooperation. When they refused to take a hand, the system for bringing military force to bear on the whig population could not function.

If justices of the peace could not be counted on to call out troops, only two alternatives remained. One was the sheriff, whom General Gage believed had at least the constitutional authority to request military assistance in situations of potential disorders.[9] It is not clear, however, that he thought sheriffs were authorized to command soldiers to fire on civilians. In truth, the authority was constitutionally vague. Some colonial riot statutes authorized sheriffs to proclaim riots, others implied that they could, yet it seems to have been a rule of custom that they did not do so. During the New York tenantry riots, magistrates had accompanied the troops even though a sheriff was present. Although other explanations are possible, it is most likely that the sheriff was there to take custody of civilian prisoners, the magistrates to lend legality to whatever force was exerted. Besides, in many Massachusetts counties—if not most of those in America—the sheriff often leaned more toward the whig than the tory persuasion.

The second alternative to the justices was the governor. It was undisputed that he could order out troops if the council consented. What was not certain was whether he had power to act on his own authority without consulting the council. Such authority might be implied either from his commission as captain-general of the province, from his instructions, or from the fact that he, like the justices of the peace, was a magistrate.

Both Bernard and Hutchinson, who succeeded Bernard first as acting governor and then as governor, had no doubts about the question, and each steadfastly based his official conduct on

9. Letter from General Thomas Gage to Lieutenant Colonel William Dalrymple, 19 August 1770, Gage Papers.

the premise that he had no constitutional power to call the military out against civilians unless the council concurred. Former Massachusetts Governor Thomas Pownall disagreed. During 1774 he made a speech in Parliament declaring that he had

> as Governor, without communion of power with the Council, done every civil act of Government, which the King, actuating the powers of the Crown, does here within the Realm. And as to the military, if it had been my misfortune to have been Governor in these times [i.e., the week of the Boston Tea Party], and if the interposition of the military had been necessary, I would not have applied to them for their aid—I would have sent them an order.[10]

Hutchinson, who was in London at the time of the speech and had published a history of Pownall's administration, was astonished. Confronting the former governor, Hutchinson challenged him to name one occasion when he applied force without the advice and consent of his council. Pownall replied he had done so in every instance. Recollect one, Hutchinson demanded. Again, Pownall said "All" and the discussion ended.[11]

Another former governor believing he had the authority to use troops without consulting his council was George Johnstone of West Florida. Where Pownall had found the power in both the colonial charter and his commission as governor, Johnstone drew his from the instructions issued by the ministry to each new appointee. Criticizing Hutchinson for not acting to prevent the Boston Tea Party, Johnstone asserted that "there is a volume of instructions to every Governor on this subject, whereby he is commanded under the severest penalties, 'To give all kind of protection to trade and commerce, as well as to the officers of his

10. Speech of Former Governor Thomas Pownall in the House of Commons, 22 April 1774, 1 *American Archives*, at 75; 17 *Parliamentary History*, at 1285.
11. Entry for 19 July 1774, 1 Hutchinson, *Diary*, at 194–95.

Majesty's Customs, by his own authority, without the necessity of acting through his Council.' "[12]

After learning what had been said by both Pownall and Johnstone, Thomas Hutchinson met the solicitor general of England and discussed yet another constitutional theory: that a colonial governor was invested with the power of a justice of the peace to "call upon the troops to fire, in case of any riotous, violent resistance of the people." Expressing his own doubts, Hutchinson requested a legal opinion. The solicitor general answered that "the King's Law Servants seemed generally to be of that opinion, and, mentioned [the] Lord Chancellor in particular, but says he, I own *I am in doubt* or *not without a doubt*."[13]

There is no need to stop to untangle these legal contradictions. If they are puzzling today, it is not as before when the mistake was made of thinking of constitutionalism in twentieth-century terms. The doubts of England's solicitor general were not caused by conflict between the eighteenth-century jurisprudence of Governor Pownall and any lingering seventeenth-century constitutionalism in the jurisprudence of Governor Hutchinson. The doubts of the solicitor general were caused by no more subtle a reason than that there was no definite answer. The imperial constitution of eighteenth-century British North America was not as precise as today's historians insist it must have been. It was not precise because no institution was empowered to resolve conflicts except Parliament, and that body was content to leave matters as they were.

12. Speech of Former Governor George Johnstone in the House of Commons, 25 March 1774, 1 *American Archives*, at 55.
13. Entry for 5 July 1774, 1 Hutchinson, *Diary*, at 183.

✦ 26 ✦

ATTENDED WITH CONSEQUENCES:

THE RESTRAINT OF LAW

There is a dimension yet to be added. Constitutional law rendered the king's soldiers relatively impotent in prerevolutionary North America, true enough, but that is only part of the story.[1] The civil and criminal juries also played a role.[2] Army officers were being more than constitutionally scrupulous when demanding that a justice of the peace be on hand before they faced a civilian crowd. More to the point, they were afraid of private lawsuits. They knew very well that whigs in many colonies, through control of juries, could, and occasionally did, manipulate tort liability as a criminal sanction to "punish" imperial officials for enforcing "unconstitutional" parliamentary statutes.[3]

Once again, the evidence is as indisputable as it is surprising and provides yet another instance of how attention to law can aggrandize our view of the American Revolution. British army officers doing their duty in prerevolutionary North America were concerned about lawsuits, so concerned they acted less

1. The troops found very little positive to do. In one notable instance, their presence saved John Mein, a tory newspaper publisher, from a Boston whig crowd. It is important to emphasize, however, that he fled to them; they were not turned out to rescue him. *In a Defiant Stance*, at 64; Zobel, *Massacre*, at 156–63.

2. Whig control of the criminal jury in Boston, for example, explains what really happened in the case of John Mein (*supra*, note 1). It was not a mob situation as historians have assumed. He accidentally discharged a gun—a criminal offense in Boston. The whig justices of the peace (who imperialists thought should have been reading the riot act and instructing the soldiers on Mein's behalf) issued a warrant for his arrest, which gave the crowd searching for him the color of a *posse comitatus*. When the military hid Mein, they saved him not (as London believed) from physical violence, but from the magistrates of Boston and the judgment of a whig-dominated jury.

3. *In a Defiant Stance*, at 27–64.

boldly than they talked, imposing upon themselves a restraint characteristically unmilitary. An example is Major Arthur Browne, who, it will be recalled, was sent in 1766 by General Gage to assist New York's civil authorities to suppress a tenant uprising. In the vicinity of Fredericksburgh, Browne's troops encountered a party of armed rioters. "[T]hey have fired upon us and wounded three men, two of them badly," he wrote Gage, "we have taken two of the party who fired upon us, and shot one of their Horses."[4] That action converted the rioters, the major concluded, into "Traitors" and freed his men from their orders "not to repel Force by Force unless in case of absolute necessity."[5] Gage agreed. "[W]hilst there is nothing but Mobs & Rioting," he wrote Browne,

> we must take no Steps but at the Requisition of the Civil Power. But if these Sons of Liberty fire upon you, you will not then trouble yourself about Orders, & I am to desire that if they dare fire upon the King's troops, & become Rebels that you will give them a good Dressing, & beat these Sons of Liberty into Loyal Subjects.[6]

Although Gage certainly meant what he said, it should not be assumed he expected his officers to act as decisively as he suggests. Accepting the reality of garrison life in British North America, he did not demand that his officers assume legal risks, even in pursuit of their official duties.[7] The law of trespass was as much justification for military timidity as was constitutional

4. Letter from Major Art. Browne to General Thomas Gage, 30 June 1766, Gage Papers.

5. Kim, *Landlord and Tenant*, at 395.

6. Letter from General Thomas Gage to Major Arthur Browne, 2 July 1766, Gage Papers.

7. For example, Gage did not criticize Dalrymple for not posting a guard at the jail where the officer and men who had taken part in the Boston Massacre were being held. There was some talk they might be lynched. The best explanation why Dalrymple did not act was fear of a lawsuit. See *In a Defiant Stance*, at 43.

law. Browne, after two of his men were "badly" wounded, gave the appearance of acting more decisively than most British soldiers did upon confronting unruly colonists: he returned fire, killing a horse. He was not, however, particularly bold. Considering the circumstances, he had reason to think the owner would not sue him.

The likelihood of not being sued was, even in a case as extreme as Browne's, at best a strong legal possibility, never a legal certainty. For that reason, legal caution was the general rule followed by all military officers. The possibility of tort liability, not constitutional niceties, was what troubled the army officer requested to protect Indians in Philadelphia from a backcountry mob. He asked Governor John Penn "what I should do" in the event a riot took place. Penn "answered that I should defend them with fire &c.," a plan that struck the captain as personally risky. "I proposed [to] him for the Sake of my own security to keep a Magistrate ready to read the Riot Act, and that we then would do what good Soldiers can."[8] The military man was afraid of being sued, and his fear was based on valid legal considerations. The governor acknowledged its substance and so did the assembly when, in response to the officer's demand, it enacted a riot statute.

To appreciate the officer's worry, it is necessary to consider how little he was asking. A riot act provided no immunity from personal liability, it only made a lawsuit less likely. It may be that the officer sought protection from criminal prosecution, but that supposition seems unlikely. Indictment could not have been a serious concern. The governor had asked him not to suppress a mob, but to protect Indians. For injury to have resulted, the rioters would have had to attack, which would provide the officer with a reasonable chance of establishing the privilege of self-defense. Besides, who would have prosecuted? Both the

8. Letter from Captain John Schlosser to General Thomas Gage, 31 January 1764, Gage Papers.

governor and the assembly solicited his help. Yet he refused unless they met his drastic demand and passed a statute. If not prosecution, there are only two other possible explanations. One is that the officer thought he was following orders when refusing to proceed without a riot act. More likely, however, he was worried about a lawsuit. Although the riot act would not protect him absolutely, it diminished his personal risk. Under the riot act, whatever the military did when suppressing a riot, if a magistrate was present directing activities, was, in contemplation of law, done in aid of and under the legal supervision of that magistrate.[9] It was the magistrate, not the army man, who, in law, would be responsible if illegal force, or an unreasonable amount of force, resulted in injury to person, property, or goods.

Gage was not annoyed by his subordinate's forensic timidity. He praised the man's caution: "[Y]ou did very right," he wrote, "to demand that a Civil Magistrate should attend at the Barracks to read the Proclamation and give orders to fire, which Precaution would have brought you out of any Trouble, had this affair come to an Extremity."[10] The reason was that the magistrate, as the responsible official, was the individual who should have been sued for personal injuries.[11] That was what Gage hoped prospective plaintiffs injured by the military would do. That was why he ordered his officers to make themselves as immune as possible from tort liability by shifting all responsibility onto someone else. "[I]f matters should come to an Extremity," he advised, "you will take Care that it shall appear, that any Mischief which shall happen has been thro' the management &

9. Orders from Governor John Penn to Captain John Schlosser, 4 February 1764, enclosed in letter from Captain Schlosser to General Thomas Gage, 9 February 1764, Gage Papers.

10. Letter from General Thomas Gage to Captain John Schlosser, 16 _____ 1764, Gage Papers.

11. And also, as a local official, less likely to be sued, hence lessening the risk of liability.

orders of the *Civil Authority*, and that the Military are in no way concerned, but in obeying the *Civil Magistrates*, and in supporting them in the due Execution of the Laws."[12]

When no magistrate was available, or none would call for military assistance, Gage did not expect his subordinates to police civilians, no matter how provocative the circumstances. In 1765 some frontier rioters in western Pennsylvania invested an army fort and fired muskets at the king's soldiers.[13] The men were restrained by their officer from returning fire, and Gage was satisfied he had acted properly. "I have not heard," he wrote the governor, "that any Man has been killed, and it may therefore be better that the Officer prevented His Men from Firing; but if he had returned the fire of those Ruffians, and killed as many as he was able, I conceive He would have Acted consistent with the Laws of his Own, and of every other Civilized Country."[14]

The lesson is not what Gage thought was law, but that he could not be sure. No one could be certain, especially in times of political and constitutional unrest. Colonial juries were the judges of law as well as fact. It was they, not the court, who determined what conduct was actionable.[15] To make matters even more perilous in Massachusetts, once a question of fact appeared on the record judges could not dismiss a writ, even one contrary to law, and any good pleader could create a question of

12. Letter from General Thomas Gage to Captain John Schlosser, 6 February 1764, Gage Papers. For fear of suits on the part of customs officials, see *In a Rebellious Spirit*, at 30–34.

13. "Extract of a Letter from Philadelphia," 15 March 1765, 34 *London Magazine* (1765), at 264–65.

14. Letter from General Thomas Gage to Lieutenant Governor John Penn, 13 December 1765, Gage Papers.

15. Nelson, *Americanization of the Common Law*, at 26–30; 1 Adams, *Legal Papers*, at 213–30; John Adams's remarks, Quincy, *Reports*, at 556–67; Edith Guild Henderson, "The Background of the Seventh Amendment," 80 *Harvard Law Review* 289, 318–19 (1966).

fact.[16] Moreover, the jury's verdict was final and there was no appeal.[17] Colonel William Dalrymple keenly felt the dilemma once he took command in Boston. Should the mob rise, he admitted, he was not certain how he would respond. "I confess it would be difficult to act with judgement, as on the one hand to abandon those we are in some measure sent to protect might subject me to censure, and to act without the intervention of the Civil Magistrate might on the other be attended with ill & dangerous consequences."[18]

❖ 27 ❖

THE TEMPER OF THE PEOPLE:

THE ROLE OF THE SOLDIERS

It would not do to leave the impression that, because troops could not be employed to police civilians, the military occupation of Boston was a gesture in imperial futility. The army could have an impact in indirect ways. It is possible that by their very presence, the regiments brought a degree of calm to Boston, at least for awhile. Thomas Hutchinson, for one, thought they had. "Short quiet succeeded long disturbance," he concluded. "Troops at first carried terror. There had been no experience of them. The restraint they were under without a civil magistrate was not known to that part of the people most disposed to mobs and riots."[1]

Writing to the earl of Hillsborough the same month that the

16. *In a Defiant Stance*, at 27–40.

17. Nelson, *Americanization of the Common Law*, at 16.

18. Letter from Lieutenant Colonel William Dalrymple to General Thomas Gage, 17 September 1769, Gage Papers.

1. Hutchinson, *History*, at 217–18.

troops landed in Boston, Gage almost agreed with Hutchinson. Although pessimistic about the current state of constitutional law, he expressed cautious hope for the future.

> Your Lordship will naturaly imagine since the Troops are here to support the Dignity of Government, and a due Execution of the Laws, that the Powers of Government are reverted into the hands, where the Constitution has placed them; and that the Civil Officers would immediately avail themselves of so good an opportunity, to restore Affairs to their proper Order, and put the Laws in Execution against those who shall dare to violate them. This is not yet the Case, and it is plainly Seen, even amongst the few Magistrates of whom it is said, that they have a real wish and Desire to support Government, and to do their Duty, that there is a Fear of acting contrary to the general Sentiments of their Fellow Citizens, and a Desire to maintain a certain Degree of Popularity amongst them, which prevents them from being particular, in the Execution of their Offices. All now hoped for is, that things being in a more quiet State than they were, the violent Temper of the People will abate in a little time, and their Minds be more composed, when the Magistrates may do their Duty with less Fear of becoming obnoxious to the People.[2]

Whether because of the presence of the soldiers or a respite in the political quarrels, "the violent Temper of the People" did abate for a season. That is an historical fact from which some irrefutable conclusions could be drawn. It would be wise to resist the temptation. Few aspects of prerevolutionary history are more easily misunderstood. The tendency is to think of the progression from whig violence to the restoration of order by

2. Letter from General Thomas Gage to the earl of Hillsborough, 31 October 1768, 1 Gage, *Correspondence*, at 205.

the British army in Massachusetts, followed by a period of civic calm until about the time of the Boston Massacre, as a result of which the regiments were withdrawn and the mob again ran wild. In truth, the soldiers did not even have such a limited impact upon the course of events. It was after their arrival that nonimportation associations (public, open pressure by whigs to coerce others to obey whig edicts) and the practice of tar and feathering came into vogue.

Soldiers may have been near, but their presence made little difference on those occasions when whig agitators had reasons to raise a crowd. No event better illustrates the impotency of the military as prerevolutionary police in the colonies than one occurring in New York on 14 November 1768. It is especially relevant, for it was staged by local whigs to protest the occupation of Boston, an issue the army might be expected to resent. Troops were in the city, were numerous, had sufficient warning, were held under arms for six hours, yet not only could do nothing to quell the demonstration but also their presence was irrelevant to the whig crowd. Consider the account from the *New-York Gazette*. It is, admittedly, colored by a whiggish hue, and may be exaggerated.[3] Still, it reveals what whigs thought of soldiers, how little they regarded the military presence, and what stories of army activities they thought other Americans would believe.

> On Monday last a Report prevail'd that the Effigies of Governor Bernard and Sheriff Greenleaf of Boston, were to be exhibited that evening: At 4 o'Clock in the Afternoon the Troops in this City appear'd under Arms, at the lower

---

3. The town clerk, at the direction of New York's magistrates, sent the newspapers a rival account, which insisted that the only reason the magistrates had failed to suppress the demonstration was that it had been sparsely attended and was very brief. They had known it would occur and were prepared, but the event was so secret that they could not arrive on time. *Post-Boy*, 28 November 1768, at 1, cols. 2–3.

Barracks, w[h]ere they remained till after 10 o'Clock at Night, during which Time Parties of them, were continually patrolling the Streets, in order it is supposed to intimidate the Inhabitants, and prevent their exposing the Effigies; Notwithstanding which they made their appearance in the Streets, hanging on a Gallows, between 8 and 9 o'Clock, attended by a vast Number of Spectators, who saluted them with loud Huzzas at the Corner of every Street they passed; and after having been exposed some Time at the Coffee-House, they were publickly burnt admidst the Acclamations of the Populace.[4]

The governor of New York offered a reward of £50 "for discovering the Rioters."[5] That was about the strongest action he could have taken had there been no soldiers to assist authorities to police the streets. With soldiers available, it was still the strongest action he could take.

There is no need to prolong the obvious. One fact alone furnishes the measure of the army's effectiveness as a police force: no person was tarred and feathered in Boston until after troops were stationed within the town limits. The process often took several hours, during which the victim[6] was carted through the streets. This provided imperial authorities with opportunities to test the peace-keeping capabilities of the soldiers.[7] They never did. "Last night we had a most outrageous riot," Colonel William Dalrymple wrote his commander in chief from Boston, "the populace laid hole [sic] of a man said to be an informer and mounted him in a Cart besmeared with tar and feathers." Dalrymple was shocked by the affair and had adequate time to

4. *New-York Gazette*, 17 November 1768, reprinted in *Gazette and News-Letter*, 24 November 1768, at 1, col. 2; *Post*, 28 November 1768, at 1, col. 2.

5. *Post*, 5 December 1768, at 3, col. 3.

6. Who was usually a customs informer being "punished" through a method of humiliation. "In a Defensive Rage," at 1070–85.

7. *Boston Gazette*, 21 May 1770, at 3, col. 1; Longley, "Mob," at 121.

act. "I gave the earliest notice to the Lieut[enant] Governor," he wrote, referring to Thomas Hutchinson, then the highest civilian official in the colony, "and he came to my house, but things are got out of the reach of authority."[8] John Alden summed up the times when he wrote, "More than one Boston merchant was forced to sign the nonimportation agreements under the very nose of the British army."[9]

After the Boston Massacre, General Gage admitted the situation was hopeless and the fault lay not with him or his men but with the law. "When the Troops first arrived indeed at Boston," he told his superiors in London, "the People were kept in some awe by them; but they soon discovered, that Troops were bound by Constitutional Laws, and could only Act under the Authority, and by the Orders of the Civil Magistrates; who were all of their Side. And they recommenced their Riots, tho' two or three Regiments were in the Town, with the Same unbridled Licentiousness as before."[10]

8. Letter from Lieutenant Colonel William Dalrymple to General Thomas Gage, 28 October 1769, Gage Papers.

9. Alden, *Gage in America*, at 167.

10. Letter from General Thomas Gage to the earl of Hillsborough, 7 July 1770, 1 Gage, *Correspondence*, at 263.

> It is true in the first Arrival of the troops, the People were kept in some awe by them, but they were bound up by Constitutional Laws, and could not act in quelling Riots & Disturbances but under the authority and orders of the Civil Power than they dispised them, and became as licentious as before their arrival. In the Situation therefore you suppose the troops in, unable to act, I can't foresee they would be of much use, or in any Shape prevent the mob from executing their Designs, unless they shou'd breach the Bonds of Discipline in a Fit of madness and Rage, and attack the People, which I confess upon such an occasion I am of opinion might happen.

Letter from General Thomas Gage to Acting Governor Thomas Hutchinson, 1 July 1770, Gage Papers.

❖ 28 ❖

SOME QUESTIONS UNANSWERED:
THE POLICE ROLE OF THE MILITARY

There are questions remaining to be asked, and answers yet to be suggested. Three questions are now pertinent concerning the constitutional restraints that prevented the British army from playing an active role in the policing of prerevolutionary North America: what could troops have done if constitutionally freed to use force to restrain whig crowds; could the imperial ministry have removed the constitutional impediments inhibiting decisive action; and why were soldiers kept in Boston once London learned they were an irritant to the people and no aid to imperial officials?

The first question was never fully answered, for the troops were not called upon by local officials to confront a mob. One partial answer was provided by the Boston Massacre trials. They revealed that in situations of peril the soldiers could fire upon and even kill civilians if they reasonably believed their lives endangered. They did not need a civil magistrate present, and a riot did not have to be proclaimed.[1]

The second question also was not answered. In an attenuated but very real sense, the British constitution was whatever the ministry, supported by Parliament, said it was, and the men who sent General Gage his orders might have extended his authority. That they did not may be explained by one of three reasons.

1. Such was, of course, the common-law doctrine of self-defense, but it was not the validity of common law that was tested in the Boston Massacre trials. It was the willingness of Suffolk County jurors to apply that law in political cases. Cf. John P. Reid, "A Lawyer Acquitted: John Adams and the Boston Massacre Trials," 18 *American Journal of Legal History* 189 (1974), with Hiller B. Zobel, "Law Under Pressure: Boston, 1769–1771," in *Law and Authority in Colonial America* 187, edited by George Billias (Barre, Mass., 1965).

They may have been unwilling to abandon in North America constitutional values that in Great Britain were still cherished in theory though breached in practice. They may have appreciated the strength of seventeenth-century English constitutionalism in the colonies and realized that American whigs would never accept the British army policing their streets. Or they may have felt that Parliament and the British people were not prepared to jettison a century and a half of constitutional precedent, and revoke the legacy of English constitutional rule in North America by imposing a military constitution resembling the Irish model.

Even the "intolerable acts," Britain's reaction to the Boston Tea Party, and the legislation designed to bring Massachusetts Bay into line with imperial law did little to alter the constitutional impasse. Constitutional timidity was more the rule than constitutional imagination. The military was freed from civilian restraint, not by constitutional independence, but by partial joinder into the civil establishment. Hutchinson was removed as governor and Gage, retaining his post as commander in chief of the army in North America, was appointed in his place. "Your Authority as the first Magistrate, combined with your Command over the King's Troops," Gage was told by Lord Dartmouth, who had replaced Hillsborough as colonial secretary, "will, it is hoped, enable you to meet every opposition and fully to preserve the public peace, by employing those Troops with Effect, should the madness of the People on the one hand, or the timidity or the want of Strength of the peace officers on the other hand, make it necessary to have recourse to their assistance."[2]

The intent of the British ministry had been to solve the colonial constitutional dilemma by merging the military command into the civil government. It was a scheme that might have better met its objectives had it been reversed—had the civil govern-

2. Letter from the earl of Dartmouth to Governor Thomas Gage, 9 April 1774, quoted in Shy, *Toward Lexington*, at 408.

ment been merged into the military command—that is, had the constitution been temporarily suspended or the Irish constitution substituted in its place. Instead of a sweeping reform, Gage was told that the principles of civilian control were not being abandoned. "I do not mean," Dartmouth wrote of the councillors appointed by the crown in place of those previously elected locally, "that any Constitutional power or Authority vested in them, should be set aside by any part of these Instructions."[3]

One major constitutional alteration made Gage's task less complicated. It came from the lawyers, not from Parliament. Justices of the peace were no longer needed to move troops out onto the streets. England's[4] law officers, after much delay caused by doubts concerning statutory as well as constitutional ambiguities, had ruled that the governor "can act in any Case in the capacity of an Ordinary Civil Magistrate."[5] Yet the requirement that the council give its advice and consent still remained to confuse the lines of constitutional authority. When promulgating these reforms, the British cabinet and Parliament were being less than bold. They were putting their trust in a soldier without permitting him to be a soldier.[6] Respect for established constitutional principles, coupled with fear of whig reaction, stood in the way of changes patterned on the Irish model. The structure of Massachusetts government was altered only at the top, and it was made clear to Gage that he was not vested with many of the powers exercised by governors in most of the other royal colo-

3. Ibid., at 409. See also Instructions from the earl of Dartmouth to Governor Thomas Gage, 9 April 1774, 9 Jensen, *Documents*, at 788.

4. It was the English attorney and solicitor generals who were asked for legal opinions on colonial constitutional questions, not British law officers. The advocate general of Scotland was not consulted because the British imperial constitution was based on English principles alone.

5. Letter from the earl of Dartmouth to Governor Thomas Gage, 3 June 1774, 2 Gage, *Correspondence*, at 168 [hereafter cited as Dartmouth Letter].

6. Shy, *Toward Lexington*, at 409.

nies.[7] True, there was now a tory council, for its membership was appointed by writ of mandamus rather than elected by the whig-controlled House of Representatives, but reform had come too late. When American military forces began to gather around his capital, Gage, as commander in chief, could act as a soldier and take the field. As governor he could and did declare martial law,[8] but the very revolution he was combatting scattered his council and made it a useless arm of government.[9] Forced to act without it, Gage found the validity of his decisions again clouded by constitutional ambiguities and open to challenge.

The third question is why troops were kept in Massachusetts Bay after it became evident that the law gave them no role to play. Military men had wanted them removed as soon as they realized the situation,[10] yet they remained until the tragedy of the Boston Massacre forced their removal. There were several reasons,[11] including pressure from the customs commissioners,[12] and the fact that army officers, mixing only with imperial officials and American tories, gained the mistaken impression that a majority of the people wanted them.[13] Perhaps the most

7. Dartmouth Letter, at 164.

8. Proclamation of Governor Thomas Gage, 12 June 1775, 2 *American Archives* at 968–70; Letter from Governor Thomas Gage to the earl of Dartmouth, 12 June 1775, 1 Gage, *Correspondence*, at 405.

9. Letters from Governor Thomas Gage to the earl of Dartmouth, 2 September 1774, 12 September 1774, 15 December 1774, 1 Gage, *Correspondence*, at 370, 374, 387; Letter from the earl of Dartmouth to Governor Thomas Gage, 17 October 1774, 2 Gage, *Correspondence*, at 174; Letter from Samuel Adams to Arthur Lee, 29 January 1775, 3 Adams, *Writings*, at 170.

10. Stout, *Royal Navy*, at 151.

11. It seems unlikely that the revenue the military put into the local economy was a consideration, though some people thought it significant. *Gazette and Post-Boy*, 31 July 1769, at 4, col. 2, and 30 April 1770, at 4, col. 1.

12. *Journal of the Times*, 21 June 1769, at 111, col. 2; Stout, *Royal Navy*, at 151.

13. Thus, on going back to Britain and taking his seat in Parliament, General Alexander Mackay, who had commanded the troops in Massachusetts, told the

persuasive explanation was that the military's continued presence was urged by Governors Bernard and Hutchinson, the imperial officials most responsible for maintaining British authority. Indeed, General Gage placed the blame on Hutchinson. "Experience," he complained to a fellow army officer four years before he was named governor,

> has fully shewn us the inutility of quartering Troops in Boston, either for the support of Government, or the Preservation of the publick Tranquility. And yet the Officers of Government choose to have them near, I believe as a dernier resort, to protect their Persons in a Retreat, if the People should Attempt to drive them away a Circumstance which may happen, & which they appear to have Apprehended. I see no other reason for keeping Troops in the Province unless other Maxims are pursued, than have been Adopted hitherto: And till measures are Changed, neither Law or Government can possibly prevail in Boston.[14]

By "the Officers of Government," who wanted the troops to remain, General Gage meant Hutchinson.

It is true that Hutchinson, even after he became governor, refused to request that the army be removed.[15] His excuse was that he did not have the constitutional authority: the soldiers had been ordered into Massachusetts by the British cabinet and

---

Commons "That three quarters of the Bostonians would be against the combinations, if they could act for themselves.—That not withstanding the cry against the Troops, many prayed for their continuance for the sake of the money they bro't in." *Gazette and Post-Boy*, 30 April 1770, at 4, col. 1.

14. Letter from General Thomas Gage to Lieutenant Colonel William Dalrymple, 9 April 1770, Adams, "New Light," at 301.

15. Hearing that the Fourteenth Regiment was to embark for St. Vincent's and another remain, Hutchinson wrote: "I am glad that one Regiment is not like to leave us until we have another in its place." Letter from Governor Thomas Hutchinson to General Thomas Gage, 6 July 1772, Gage Papers.

only the cabinet or the commander in chief could have them removed.[16] True, he never wrote the earl of Hillsborough recommending withdrawal and, when asked, seems to have opposed their removal,[17] but the explanation is not that he wanted troops for his own safety.

Even more than Gage, Governor Hutchinson appreciated the full extent of the army's "inutility." "A military force was of no sort of use," he later recorded in his history of the times:

> Without the direction of a civil magistrate, it remained perfectly inactive in all times of tumult and riot; and, by this time, it was perfectly despised, seeing that nothing short of actual rebellion and the people's taking up arms, would justify the military, without a civil power, in any offensive acts. In such a case, the small force then in Massachusetts Bay was insignificant.[18]

The "small force" was insignificant for all purposes, including Hutchinson's personal protection. Had the mob been raised against him, either in Boston or at his home in Milton, the troops would have been of no assistance unless he first was warned and had time to flee to the Castle.[19]

The better explanation of why Hutchinson never asked that the military be withdrawn and, in fact, did not want the troops to leave, was that he hoped for a change in constitutional law.[20]

16. Bailyn, *Ordeal*, at 159; Hutchinson, *History*, at 275–76.

17. Shy, *Toward Lexington*, at 312.

18. Hutchinson, *History*, at 263.

19. An island in Boston harbor where, after the massacre, the troops were confined until Gage became governor.

20. Hutchinson also seems to have felt that, even though everyone was aware of the constitutional restrictions making the army impotent as a police force, its very presence served as a restraining force on even wilder crowd activities. After the soldiers were moved from Boston following the massacre, he wrote: "The people of this town are acting a foolish part over again, and are attempting to prevent any Importers from selling their goods. If we had the Naval and Land

It was a reluctant hope, but one he expected would in time be fulfilled. If Massachusetts were to remain part of the British Empire, he wrote as early as 1769, there would sooner or later have to be an "abridgment of what are called English liberties." When that occurred, the army would have a role to play in the policing of Massachusetts Bay.[21]

❖ 29 ❖

A NUMBER TOO MANY:

THE RELEVANCE OF LAW

Although law has often been irrelevant for historians of the American Revolution, it remains relevant for the history they should be writing. Our perception of Thomas Hutchinson provides a case in point. It illustrates how historians' disdain for law furnishes a faulty picture because pertinent questions are not asked. Students of the prerevolutionary era share a vision of a weak, indecisive governor. One reason is that judgments are made about the man without considering his legal options. As a result, Hutchinson's actions—or lack of action—have sometimes been distorted. He could have employed troops to police

---

force which was here this time Twelve month they would not dare to go the length they now go." Letter from Thomas Hutchinson to General Thomas Gage, 22 April 1770, Gage Papers.

21. Letter from Lieutenant Governor Thomas Hutchinson to Thomas Whately, 20 January 1769, Hutchinson, *Letters*, at 16. There is possibly a secondary reason why Hutchinson made no move to initiate the withdrawal of the soldiers: apprehension of the political consequences. If the troops were removed and the mob turned on the customs commissioners, the blame might be his because both the army and the ministry could well make him the scapegoat. Shy, *Toward Lexington*, at 312–13.

the population, it is said, but was too circumspect,[1] not even acting to prevent the Boston Tea Party, when he "felt there were enough soldiers, ships of war and other Crown officers stationed at Boston to suppress any sort of uprising or mob violence."[2]

These judgments about the most important prerevolutionary colonial governor are seldom tested against legal practicalities. Perhaps Thomas Hutchinson "felt" that he had sufficient forces on hand, but that fact is legally irrelevant. He also knew he could not constitutionally employ them.[3] By the same token, Francis Bernard does not deserve his current reputation. He acted decisively, and with a great deal of ingenuity, when persuading London to send troops. That he could not use them does not prove him to be weak or vacillating. It was not Bernard that was tested and found wanting, but the conditions of imperial law.

The major consideration, however, is not that historians are in error, but that they have been repeating the errors of the eighteenth century. Because imperial civilian authorites in the colonies requested troops, London assumed soldiers could serve a purpose. Bernard was only one of several royal governors writing that a military force could "effectually discourage all

1. Bailyn, *Ordeal*, at 134, 163. The same historian says Hutchinson "refused to accede to the customs commissioners' demand that troops be used to put an end to the nonimportation boycotts and to the intimidation of law-abiding merchants." Ibid., at 157. It is not clear how Hutchinson could have legally responded, nor is the important term "law-abiding" defined.

2. Labaree, *Tea Party*, at 104. Statements of this type appear often in general histories and typify the manner in which legal and constitutional practicalities are ignored by historians. See also Hosmer, *Adams*, at 139; and Waters, *Otis Family*, at 168–69.

3. However, the Tea Party is a possible exception. The whigs had placed armed guards on the tea ships, an act Hutchinson might have proclaimed as insurrection, which would authorize him to employ military force without relying on a justice of the peace. For discussion, see John P. Reid, "The Ordeal by Law of Thomas Hutchinson," 49 *New York University Law Review*, 593, 608–12 (1974).

opposition to the Laws"[4] and "bring the people to a sense of their Duty."[5] Reading such words has misled historians, and may have misled the imperial government in London.

True, London should have known better. The ministry frequently was told that troops had no constitutional role to play in North America, that local officials would not cooperate with imperial governors. Had London been only moderately attentive to legal actualities, the ministry would have known that the soldiers ordered to Boston in 1768 were dispatched on a futile mission.[6] "[F]rom the number of these troops," an open letter warned Hillsborough before the first regiments arrived in New England,

> they could not be intended to exterminate the inhabitants, or oppose the civil authority in that country, and if you supposed they would ever be called to its support, you have betrayed a culpable ignorance, since except their governor, and a few of his venal junto, no provincial magistrate will be found so steeled against the sentiments of justice and humanity, as wantonly to order troops to fire on an unarmed populace, and repeat in America the tragic scene exhibited in St. George's Fields.[7]

The problem may have been one of attention rather than knowledge. The ministry knew there were difficulties, but,

4. Letter from Lieutenant Governor Cadwallader Colden to General Thomas Gage, 2 September 1765, 2 *Colden Papers*, at 30.

5. Letter from Governor Henry Moore to Secretary of State Henry Seymour Conway, 20 February 1766, 7 *Documents of Colonial New York*, at 810. See also Letter from Chief Justice Thomas Hutchinson to Richard Jackson, 20 October 1767, quoted in Bailyn, *Ordeal*, at 132n31.

6. Letter from Governor Francis Bernard to the earl of Hillsborough, 23 September 1768, Bernard and Gage, *Letters*, at 83; Letter from Governor Francis Bernard to the earl of Hillsborough, 14 November 1768, 39 *Gentleman's Magazine* (1769), at 84.

7. Anon., *Letter to Hillsborough*, at 34.

assuming they were political in nature, ignored the relevancy of law. "[T]he King is sensible of the weak state of his government in the Massachusetts Bay," Lord Hillsborough wrote Lieutenant Governor Hutchinson, yet he expected his government to act with strength.[8] George III was not alone. Consider the legal illusions guiding the policy of the three men who served as secretary of state for the colonies during the prerevolutionary crisis. They were Henry Seymour Conway, Hillsborough, and the earl of Dartmouth, and each seems to have made the same assumption about law. "It is with the greatest concern," Conway warned Bernard on hearing of the Stamp Act riots, "his Majesty learns of the disturbances which have lately arisen in your province, the general confusion that seems to reign there, and the total languor and want of energy, in your government, to exert itself with any dignity or efficacy, for the suppression of tumults, which seem to strike at the very being of all authority and subordination among you."[9] Despite the weak state of government, Hillsborough told Thomas Hutchinson, "His Majesty nevertheless expects that you should in both your capacities exert the utmost activity supporting the constitution and in giving to all his subjects that protection which the authority of the chief magistrate may be liable to afford them."[10] Even Lord Dartmouth, with the army's experience in Boston to draw on, wrote as if the British military could perform a police function in North America. During the *Gaspee* investigation, he ordered Gage to hold troops in readiness should they be requisitioned "to aid and assist the civil magistrate in the suppression of any

8. Letter from the earl of Hillsborough to Lieutenant Governor Hutchinson, 18 January 1770, 2 *Revolution Documents*, at 33 [hereafter cited as Hillsborough-Hutchinson Letter].

9. Letter from Secretary of State Henry Seymour Conway to Governor Francis Bernard, 24 October 1765, *Prior Documents*, at 40; *Post-Boy*, 27 January 1766, at 3, col. 3.

10. Hillsborough-Hutchinson Letter.

riot or disturbance."[11] He was suggesting the impossible. The colony was Rhode Island, where, even more than in Massachusetts Bay, there was no chance magistrates would call upon British troops to suppress a whig crowd.

If Conway, Hillsborough, and Dartmouth, the officials responsible for maintaining the army in the colonies, could suffer under such legal misconceptions, it is not surprising that some of their contemporaries,[12] as well as later historians, assumed that law and constitutional restraints were irrelevant. As a result, part of the story of the American Revolution has been missed, and some of its more subtle lessons have not been studied. One lesson is that constitutional ambiguities do not always aid the side of government in a confrontation with rebellious citizens. It might be expected they would; when the law is not clear, the government should be able to resolve doubts in its own favor. That was not the case in British-ruled North America during the eighteenth century. Constitutional ambiguities weakened imperial law, for crown officials uncertain of their authority to act often did not act at all. Indeed, considering that rioters in Boston were not even prosecuted let alone confronted by armed troops, it may be concluded that the imperial government was less than inactive; it was immobilized by law or, perhaps more accurately, by the lack of law.

Our historical myths also loom large. There is lurking in the

11. Letter from the earl of Dartmouth to the Governor of Rhode Island, 4 September 1772, *Post*, 4 January 1773, at 2, col. 3.

12. Even some who were close to the scene when passing judgment on others. See, for example, Letter from Commodore Samuel Hood to George Grenville, 8 August 1768, 4 *Grenville Papers*, at 334; Letter from General Thomas Gage to Lieutenant Colonel William Dalrymple, 21 October 1769, Gage Papers; and Letter from Lieutenant Colonel William Dalrymple to General Thomas Gage, 27 March 1770, Gage Papers. See also [Lloyd], *Conduct Examined*, at 109; 1 Adolphus, *History*, at 381ny.

back of the American collective subconscious an image of the prerevolutionary era that makes the British army a more menacing foe than it was in actual fact. The redcoat bully on the streets of Boston, the dread hand of martial law, houses broken into during the dead of night, and civilians arbitrarily arrested by arrogant military men are all scenes that easily come to mind. They are thought to be pictures from American history, but in fact they are borrowings from Irish memories.[13]

There are also general lessons to be drawn, though the most obvious is not that British troops stationed in North America had to await open rebellion before finding a constitutional role to play. By the very fact that the army stood by and did not interfere in local affairs, it was dramatizing the essence of the traditional British imperial constitution and demonstrating why American whigs were resisting Parliament's attempt to change that constitution. The army actually strengthened that resistance because the occupation of Boston united more firmly the bulk of the population behind the whig leadership and added one more grievance dividing the colonies from their mother country.

To be a force in the affairs of a nation, an army must be able to act, and the army commanded by Thomas Gage was not permitted to do so. Too many laws and too many constitutional inhibitions stood in its way. To send troops into a province where there was no government able to employ them was not a decisive action, only an action of provocation. If Francis Bernard and Thomas Hutchinson were expected to rule with the aid of the army, they needed a different constitutional tradition, or else the regiments that landed in Boston during the autumn of 1768 were too few. "If you mean to govern the country by the aid of military force," an American told Thomas Pownall, Bernard's predecessor as governor, "you have not sent a sufficient number

13. *In a Defiant Stance*, at 3–4.

of troops; if you do not mean this, you have already sent too many."[14] More accurately, he should have said that under the eighteenth-century British imperial constitution, any number would have been too many.

❖ 30 ❖

IN THE SAME TRADITION:

CONCLUSION

American whigs of the prerevolutionary era complained about the British army garrisoned in Boston, New York, and Charles Town not because they were thinking of independence or wanted to be free of enforcement of imperial customs laws.[1] They complained for a reason far less complex: they had a constitutional grievance inherited from an ancient constitutional past. The historical point that this book has stressed is that American whigs were adhering to a constitutional tradition still honored in Great Britain, even though breached for at least two generations. Robert Walpole might not have supported the case of the American whigs had he lived during the prerevolutionary era, but he would have understood their arguments. Maintenance of large professional forces obtained permanent constitutional status during the administration of Walpole, yet he did not

14. Speech of Former Governor Thomas Pownall, Commons Debates of 8 February 1769, 16 *Parliamentary History*, at 498.

1. The army and the customs were, however, associated in the constitutional case. For example, a Boston clergyman wrote: "With respect to ourselves, besides the Board of [Customs] Commissioners, there are three grand Grievances to be redres't. The Revenue Laws; the Unconstitutional Pow'rs of the Admiralty Courts, and the Standing Army in Time of Peace." Letter of 30 January 1770, Cooper, "Letters," at 316.

defend the standing army as constitutionally acceptable. It was, he said, a necessary evil—"an Evil we are obliged to submit to, for the Sake of avoiding a greater."[2] Even a resident of Ireland, a country long governed by military force, and in which the state religion was maintained by pikes and bayonets, could say in 1771 that "a standing army is contrary to the spirit of our constitution, and has been often found of prejudice to the subject."[3]

American whigs were the heirs, not the progenitors, of their constitutional world. It was English constitutionalism, not American law, that rendered the British army impotent as a force policing civilians. That same English constitutional tradition provided the language—as well as the motivations—for arguments. It explained what the Massachusetts House of Representatives meant by calling Gage's army "an unlawful assembly, of all others the most dangerous and alarming."[4] Statements such as this deserve closer attention than they have received. The words "unlawful assembly" and "dangerous" were not carelessly chosen and thrown into the debate without meaning. They were generated from a constitutional way of thinking, a pattern of expression shaping legal behavior as well as constitutional attitudes, many aspects of which have not been touched on in this book. There is, for example, a story yet to be told, of why many whigs thought the crowd gathered in front of the Boston customs house on 5 March 1770 was no mob but a constitutional *posse comitatus*. In terms of "whig law," the soldiers of Captain Thomas Preston were the "unlawful assembly." In addition to this inherited constitutional perspective, the legal vocabulary of American whigs depicted the mission of the British army in Boston as an illegal enterprise. It was there,

2. Speech of Robert Walpole in the Commons, 3 February 1738, 7 *London Magazine* (1738), at 263.

3. Anon., *Legality of Putting Soldiers to Death*, at 20.

4. Answer of the House of Representatives to Acting Governor Thomas Hutchinson, 23 April 1770, *Speeches*, at 204.

IN DEFIANCE OF THE LAW

whigs said, "for the Purpose of enforcing unconstitutional Acts of Parliament by Military Execution."[5] As a result, the soldiers of Thomas Gage, both because of their unconstitutional presence and their unconstitutional purpose, were an illicit force that, under certain circumstances, it was not unlawful to oppose. The history of the Boston Massacre will not be understood until it is written in terms of the two constitutions and eighteenth-century definitions of "law."

The British army was removed from the town of Boston after the massacre. Following the Tea Party it was ordered back; Lord North repeated Lord Hillsborough's error and for the same legal reasons. "[I]t was demonstrable," a proministerial pamphleteer explained, "that nothing but force could bring them [Bostonians] to their duty, and troops were sent as preparatory to that end."[6] The military would have no greater effect in 1774 than it had had in 1768. It was restrained by the same constitution as before. What was different was London's awareness of legal consequences. The cabinet knew now that soldiers could not act against civilians, and asked Parliament to alter the governance of Massachusetts Bay. In the ensuing debates, the constitutional tensions surfaced once more, and the question of military power policing civilians in peacetime was placed in the sharpest focus it would receive during the prerevolutionary era. On behalf of the ministry, Lord North spoke for the constitution of coercive force. Opposing the administration's scheme for new modeling the government of Massachusetts Bay, Edmund Burke urged that Parliament resurrect the constitution of opinion and consent.

5. Resolution of Boston, 14 May 1773, *Gazette and Post-Boy*, 17 May 1773, at 3, col. 1.

6. [Shebbeare,] *An Answer*, at 38. "That the rebellious conduct of the Town of Boston, where all the authority of legal government had been long extinguished by the tyranny of a rabble instigated by factious leaders, had rendered a force necessary in that place, to restore order and tranquility, to protect the innocent, and to restrain the excesses of the turbulent and guilty." [Macpherson,] *Rights of Great Britain*, at 70.

❖ 230 ❖

Lord North spoke first. He had much to say, but what he left unsaid is what catches our attention. He did not mention the standing army. The controversy of yesteryear was no longer relevant. Constitutional rules restraining military involvement in civilian affairs, not the constitutionality of regular, professional forces, was what troubled him. But even more telling is the fact that he did not espouse a new constitutionalism. He did not ask for military government, not even to restore imperial law to Massachusetts Bay. The standing army in peacetime was constitutional, and could constitutionally police civilians, but only in a constitutional manner.

> Lord North rose and said . . . that an executive power was wanting in that country, and that it was highly necessary to strengthen the magistracy of it; that the force of the civil power consisted in the *posse comitatus*; and when it is considered, said his lordship, that the *posse* are the very people who have committed all these riots, little obedience to the preservation of the peace is to be expected from them. There appears to be a total defect in the constitutional power throughout. If the democratic part shews that contempt of obedience to the laws, how is the governor to execute any authority vested in him? . . . [T]here is something radically wrong in that constitution, in which no magistrate, for such a number of years, has ever done his duty in such a manner as to force obedience to the laws. . . . I shall always consider that a military power, acting under the authority and controul of a civil magistrate, is part of the constitution; but the military alone ought not, and cannot act without the controul of the civil magistrate. How was it possible for the military to maintain good government when they were not called upon by the civil authority? I propose, in this Bill, to take the executive power from the hands of the democratic part of govern-

ment; I would propose, that the governor should act as a justice of peace, and that he should have the power to appoint the officers throughout the whole civil authority. . . . [U]ntil the executive power is free, it cannot act; our regulations here are of no import, if you have nobody in that country to give them force.[7]

Edmund Burke understood what Lord North was proposing. "If you govern America at all," he told the Commons, "it must be by an army; but the bill before us, carries with it the force of that army; and I am of opinion, they never will consent without force being used."[8] Force was not his way, for he was, at least in colonial affairs, a child of the old constitutionalism of restraint. For a final sampling of that legal school, consider his words as reported in America, with the emphasis indicating what a Boston newspaper editor thought important.

He affirmed, that the evils subsisting in America were of a CIVIL nature, and that, to propose military remedies for the correction of civil abuses, was to act in direct contradiction of every principle of sound policy. . . . Every law process relative to the life, liberty or property of an English subject bespoke a POPULAR origin, from the presentment on the Grand Jury to the final adjudication of a Petty Jury. The principles of Government, therefore, should have respect to the DEMOCRACY OF THE CONSTITUTION, and, as that allowed no appeal to the Sword but in conjunction with the Civil Power, where the Magistracy REFUSED to co-operate, a military force must turn to little account. . . . The introduction of an army would not change the OPINIONS of the Colonists; the men who thought themselves Ill-treated

7. Speech of Lord North, Commons Debates of 28 March 1774, 17 *Parliamentary History*, at 1192–93.

8. Speech of 2 May 1774, 1 *The Speeches of the Right Honourable Edmund Burke in the House of Commons and in Westminster-Hall* (London, 1816), at 242.

now, would not be of different sentiments when the bayonets were pointed to their breasts, and unless, by an alteration of the measures, you effected a change in the OPINIONS of men, you might destroy numbers, without being able to establish any permanent sovereignty over the multitudes who survived the sanguinary policy.[9]

Burke understood why the magistrates of Boston refused to use the standing army when quelling civilian riots, and he believed their refusal constitutional. So did John Wilkes, Isaac Barré, William Beckford, and thousands of other eighteenth-century English and Scots opposed to ministerial power. It is from that constitutional perspective that the coming of the American Revolution must be viewed if we are to comprehend the issues as people of that time comprehended them. Above all, the old English Constitution and what it still meant to people on both sides of the Atlantic must be kept in mind. It might have lost pride of place to the constitution of parliamentary supremacy, but its principles still had validity and still motivated conduct.

In January 1776 the secretary-at-war warned King George III that riots then in progress might continue for some time, "a circumstance much to be apprehended, as the City Magistrates will not call for the assistance of troops."[10] We read these words and recognize that Lord Barrington is writing about Boston, for he had said the same several times before.[11] We would, however, be wrong. He was referring to the magistrates of London, not to the magistrates of Boston. It was the justices of the peace in George III's capital city whom Barrington believed would not

9. *Gazette and Post-Boy*, 9 May 1774, at 2, col. 1.

10. Letter from Lord Barrington to George III, January 1776, Barrington, *Viscount Barrington*, at 164.

11. Letter from Lord Barrington to the earl of Dartmouth, 12 November 1774, ibid., at 148; Speech of Lord Barrington, Commons Debates of 8 May 1770, 16 *Parliamentary History*, at 998.

employ troops to quell civilian riots. For too long, the relevance of those magistrates to the American Revolution has been overlooked. By refusing to have the standing army serve as a police force in London, they were upholding the same constitution for which Massachusetts farmers had already begun to die.

APPENDIX:

THE FUTURE CONSTITUTION

The constitutionalism of governmental command backed by military force, for which Secretary-at-War William Yonge spoke in 1738,[1] had, by a century later, become the constitutional standard. By then, the definition of law had also clearly changed from what it had been for either eighteenth-century British commonwealthmen or prerevolutionary American whigs. In 1833 a British law journal published a statement of legal theory, printed below, that the twentieth century could well study as an indication of where today's law originated. It not only stated the new law, it repudiated every element of the old constitutionalism. Indeed, it is evident that, though the old constitutionalism was still remembered in the 1830s, its former legitimacy had been made irrelevant by changing times. The nineteenth-century concept of law as command not only had become dominant, it had become so in part because power could be entrusted with confidence to military force. Ironically, the standing army had been made reliable as a police agency by the very aspect that previously had made it constitutionally suspect: professionalism. It was now the militia that could not be trusted. Not only had the seventeenth-century constitutional ideal been discarded, but, as if to demonstrate how much that ideal had changed, Ireland was offered as the model for the military's role in civilian government.

At the same time when matters come to extremities, when the civil power is unable to enforce the law, there is no body in this country so effective for the end in view as the regular army. In many instances, soldiers of the militia

---

1. Speech of William Yonge, Commons Debates of 3 February 1738, 10 *Parliamentary History*, at 431.

APPENDIX

are personally acquainted with persons in the mob; they and
their officers, as well as the yeomen and their officers, often
have as individuals a pecuniary or some other interest in the
suppression of disorder. Thus they will be considered as
taking part for their own private advantage, and not for the
mere promotion of peace. The subjects on which riots have
generally occurred,—the amount of wages, the price of
food, or the support of peculiar political opinions, are such
as frequently separate the farmer from the labourer, the
richer from the poorer classes, the yeoman from the multitude against which he is required to act.—The consequence
is that the yeoman is suspected of taking arms, not for the
mere purpose of suppressing riot and protecting himself
and his property, as well as his fellow-subjects and their
property, from the violence of intemperate men, but in
order to promote his own political views, to resist claims
which the multitude believe to be just, and to settle civil
controversies by an appeal to the sword. Can such a motive
widely circulated by some mischievous and artful ring-
leader, fail to raise a general unwillingness to concede? or to
excite amongst the rioters a resolution to imitate the bad
example which they fancy that they perceive in the conduct
of the executive power—i.e., to vindicate by a similar
recourse to arms the opinions and claims which they are
assembled to promote? We might say much of the evil consequences which are felt after peace has been re-established,
of the discordance between the several ranks of society, of
the heart-burnings and anger and indignation with which
the peasantry regard the farmer, and the artizans their
master manufacturer, while they harbour the sorrowful
recollection of some friend or associate who fell a victim in
the struggle, and cherish a determination to take the first
opportunity of vengeance. From these and many other
drawbacks, which attach to the militia and yeomanry, the

regular soldier is wholly exempt. Very probably he marches into the neighborhood of the scene of action but a few days before the event occurs, and he leaves it immediately afterwards. He has no friends amongst the multitude, no interest in the circumstances out of which the disorder arises—he is the mere agent of the law, and cannot be suspected of any other desire or intention than to perform his duty as a soldier and in obedience to the commands which he receives to overcome the enemies of disorder. His interference is humane, because the multitude know the impossibility of resistance, and retire from the struggle: it is effective, because his discipline, confidence in his comrades, and acquaintance with the use of arms, insure him an easy victory. Thus it generally happens that life is saved, while the law is enforced.

It is obviously desirable that the people should learn to regard the executors of the law as altogether distinct from the law itself, to consider their actions as altogether mechanical and independent of the merits or demerits of the law, and in times of riot to regard them as solely endeavouring to reestablish order, without any reference to the cause from which the disturbance arose. How this notion can gain ground, if yeomanry, or militia, or any persons principally interested in the causes of disturbance, are themselves to repress it, we are at a loss to conceive.

The superiority of the regular army over yeomanry and militia for the suppression of riot, has been long experienced in Ireland. In that country party spirit is inflamed to the highest pitch, and its bitter fruits are too plainly perceived in the distrust and personal hostility which divide all ranks of society. The yeomanry are accused (whether justly or unjustly is little to our present purpose) of partiality, violent party feelings, and a fanatical opposition to the religion of the vast bulk of the people. They constantly encounter a vigorous resistance, and their conduct is invariably mis-represented. On the other hand, the soldiers, although per-forming the same duties and enforcing the same laws, are generally respected, are even popular, are seldom obliged to draw the sword, but compel the restoration of order by the mere apprehension of their force.

Having explained the law as to the employment of sol-diers in maintaining the public peace, we cannot help touch-ing upon the idle complaints which have been not unfre-quently made, that such an employment of them is uncon-stitutional, or contrary to the liberties and privileges of the subject. As we have shown that the law under which they act is consistent with the other laws by which the whole community are bound, and that in reality they are author-ised to act by precisely the same law which authorises all private individuals, we need not detain our readers by proving the complaints to be unfounded, but will merely allude to some of the causes to which the mistakes may be attributed. In almost all nations, and at different periods of our history in England, the soldiers have been the agents of despotic power,—it is therefore assumed that they will again act in the same capacity: they have sometimes been employed to restrain the constitutional privilege of meeting and petitioning,—a recurrence of the same conduct is there-fore anticipated. Again, they have been required to enforce obnoxious laws, laws perhaps in themselves of an oppres-sive character,—and the nature of the law has been confused with the character of those who carry it into execution. But the badness of a law supplies no charge against the agent who brings it faithfully into operation; and acts of tyranny are not now to be anticipated, merely because they were committed in ancient times, when the checks and restraints upon government were adjusted less favourably to the maintenance of public liberties. If it were carefully borne in mind that the law military conforms to the civil law; that, if an arbitrary minister endeavours to employ the army for illegal purposes, there is a remedy in the civil courts; that the refusal to re-enact the military law would at once annihilate this engine of his power; that the number of the army depends entirely upon the legislature, and most especially upon that part of it which represents the people and has the exclusive authority over the soldiers' pay—it would at once be acknowledged that very little danger is to be apprehended from the mere employment of the military force, whilst it would be by no means difficult to prove that we should run the greatest risk by unduly diminishing it.[2]

By the decade that these paragraphs were written, the old constitution of restraint had also been replaced in the United States. What had become "law" in Great Britain and always been "law" in Ireland was now "law" in North America.

2. Anonymous, "On the Suppression of Riots by Military Interference," 9 *The Law Magazine; or Quarterly Review of Jurisprudence* 66, 79–82 (1833).

KEY TO SHORT TITLES

Abercromby, "Examination of the Acts"
James Abercromby. "An Examination of the Acts of Parliament
Relative To the Trade and the Government of our American Colo-
nies." May 1752. AB 976, Huntington Library, San Marino, Calif.
Acherley, *Britannic Constitution*
Roger Acherley. *The Britannic Constitution: or, the Fundamental Form
of Government in Britain*. London, 1727.
[Adair,] *Dismission of Officers*
[James Adair.] *Thoughts on the Dismission of Officers, Civil or Mili-
tary for their Conduct in Parliament*. London, 1765.
Adams, *Legal Papers*
Legal Papers of John Adams. Edited by L. Kinvin Wroth and Hiller B.
Zobel. 3 vols. Cambridge, Mass., 1965.
Adams, "New Light"
Randolph G. Adams. "New Light on the Boston Massacre." 47
Proceedings of the American Antiquarian Society 259 (1936).
Adams, *Writings*
The Writings of Samuel Adams. Edited by Harry Alonzo Cushing. 3
vols. New York, 1904–7.
Adolphus, *History*
John Adolphus. *The History of England From the Accession of King
George The Third, to the Conclusion of Peace in the Year One Thousand
Seven Hundred and Eighty-three*. 3 vols. London, 1802.
Alden, *Gage in America*
John Richard Alden. *General Gage in America*. Baton Rouge, 1948.
[Allen,] *The American Alarm*
[John Allen.] *The American Alarm, or the Bostonian Plea, For the
Rights and Liberties of the People. Humbly Addressed to the King and
Council, and to the Constitutional Sons of Liberty, in America*. Boston,
1773.
American Archives
*American Archives, Fourth Series. Containing a Documentary History of
the English Colonies in North America From the King's Message to Par-
liament, of March 7, 1774, to the Declaration of Independence by the
United States*. Vols. 1 and 2. Washington, 1837.

Annual Register, 1764
  The Annual Register, or a *View of the History, Politics, and Literature,*
  For the Year 1764. 3d ed. London, 1783.
Annual Register, 1768
  The Annual Register, or a *View of the History, Politics, and Literature,*
  For the Year 1768. 4th ed. London, 1786.
Annual Register, 1769
  The Annual Register, or a *View of the History, Politics, and Literature,*
  For the Year 1769. 4th ed. London, 1786.
Annual Register, 1770
  The Annual Register, or a *View of the History, Politics, and Literature,*
  For the Year 1770. 7th ed. London, 1816.
Annual Register, 1771
  The Annual Register, or a *View of the History, Politics, and Literature,*
  For the Year 1771. 7th ed. London, 1817.
Anon., *A Complaint against a Pamphlet*
  Anonymous. *A Complaint to the [Bishop] of [St. Asaph] Against a
  Pamphlet Intitled, A Speech Intended to have been Spoken on the Bill for
  Altering the Charters of the Colony of Massachuset's Bay.* London,
  1775.
Anon., *A Speech Never Intended*
  Anonymous. *A Speech Never Intended to be Spoken in Answer to a
  Speech Intended to have been Spoken on the Bill for Altering the Charter
  of the Colony of Massachusetts Bay.* London, 1774.
Anon., *An Argument*
  Anonymous. *An Argument Proving that a Small Number of Regulated
  Forces Established during the Pleasure of Parliament, cannot damage our
  Present Happy Establishment.* London, 1698.
Anon., *Apology for Smugglers*
  Anonymous. *A Free Apology In Behalf of the Smugglers, So far as their
  Case affects the Constitution. By an Enemy to all Oppression, whether by
  Tyranny, or Law.* London, 1749.
Anon., *Budget Inscribed*
  Anonymous. *The Budget. Inscribed to the Man, Who Thinks Himself
  Minister.* 9th ed. London, 1764.
Anon., *Conduct of the Minister*
  Anonymous. *Considerations on the American Stamp Act, and on the
  Conduct of the Minister Who planned it.* London, 1766.
Anon., *Constitutional Considerations*
  Anonymous. *Constitutional Considerations on the Power of Parliament*

to *Levy Taxes on the North American Colonies*. London, 1766.

Anon., *Four Letters*
Anonymous. *Four Letters on Interesting Subjects*. Philadelphia, 1776.

Anon., *Fundamentall Lawes*
Anonymous. *Touching the Fundamentall Lawes, or Politique Constitution of this Kingdome, the Kings Negative Voice, and the Power of Parliaments*. London, 1643.

Anon., *General Opposition*
Anonymous. *The General Opposition of the Colonies to the Payment of the Stamp Duty; and the Consequence of Enforcing Obedience by Military Measures; Impartially Considered. Also A Plan for uniting them to this Kingdom, in such a manner as to make their Interest inseparable from ours, for the future. In a Letter to a Member of Parliament*. London, 1766.

Anon., *History of George III*
Anonymous. *The History of the Reign of George the Third, King of Great-Britain, &c. to the Conclusion of the Session of Parliament Ending in May, 1770*. London, 1770.

Anon., *Independency of Military Officers*
Anonymous. *The Question of the Independency of Military Officers Serving in Parliament, Stated and Considered; With some Remarks upon the present Constitution of the Militia in England*. London, 1764.

Anon., *Justice and Necessity of Taxing*
Anonymous. *The Justice and Necessity of Taxing the American Colonies Demonstrated. Together with a Vindication of the Authority of Parliament*. London, 1766.

Anon., *Late Occurrences in North America*
Anonymous. *The Late Occurrences in North America, and Policy of Great Britain Considered*. London, 1766.

Anon., *Legality of Putting Soldiers to Death*
Anonymous. *An Enquiry into the Legality of Putting Soldiers to Death By Sentence of a Court-Martial in Time of Peace*. Dublin, 1771.

Anon., *Letter Relating to Mutiny*
Anonymous. *A Letter to a Member of Parliament: In Relation to the Bill for punishing Mutiny and Desertion, &c*. London, [177?].

Anon., *Letter to Charles Townshend*
Anonymous. *A Letter to the Right Honourable Ch_____s T_____nd, Esq*; 2d ed. London, 1763.

Anon., *Letter to Granby*
Anonymous. *A Letter to the Right Honourable the Marquis of Granby, Commander in Chief of the Army. Concerning the Regulations lately*

established, Relative to the Sale of Military Commissions. London, 1767.

Anon., *Letter to Hillsborough*
Anonymous. *A Letter to the Right Honourable the Earl of Hillsborough on the Present Situation of Affairs in America.* Boston, 1769.

Anon., *Necessity of Repealing the Stamp Act*
Anonymous *The Necessity of Repealing the American Stamp-Act Demonstrated: Or, A Proof that Great-Britain must be injured by that Act.* London, 1766.

Anon., *Peaceable Militia*
Anonymous. *The Peaceable Militia: or the Cause and Cure of this late and Present Warre. Shewing The Manifest safety and Freedome of the People of England, both in their Persons and Estates, under a Militia prudently limited by expresse and plaine Lawes; With a Proposall of a Peaceable and Reasonable setling of the Militia, to a just and lasting Reconciliation of all Parties.* London, 1648.

Anon., *Power and Grandeur*
Anonymous. *The Power and Grandeur of Great-Britain, Founded on the Liberty of the Colonies, and The Mischiefs attending the Taxing them by Act of Parliament Demonstrated.* New York, 1768.

Anon., *Private Letters*
Anonymous. *Private Letters from an American in England to his Friends in America.* London, 1769.

Anon., *Reasons for an Augmentation*
Anonymous. *Reasons for an Augmentation of the Army on the Irish Establishment, Offered to the Consideration of the Public.* Dublin, 1768.

Anon., *Reflections on the Short History*
Anonymous. *Reflections on the Short History of Standing Armies in England in Vindication of His Majesty and Government.* London, 1699.

Anon., *Some Late Dismissions*
Anonymous. *The Question on Some late Dismissions Truly Stated. By a friend to the Army and the Constitution. In answer to An Address to the Public, &c.* London, 1764.

Anon., *Some Thoughts on the Land Forces*
Anonymous. *Some Thoughts on the Land Forces, Kept up in this Kingdom.* London, 1739.

Anon., *Thoughts English and Irish*
Anonymous. *Thoughts, English and Irish, on the Pension-List of Ireland.* London, 1770.

Anon., *To Committee of the London Merchants*
Anonymous. *A Letter to the Gentlemen of the Committee of London Merchants, Trading to North America: Shewing In what Manner, it is apprehended, that the Trade and Manufactures of Britain may be affected by some late Restrictions on the American Commerce, and by the Operation of the Act for the Stamp Duty in America; as also how far the Freedom and Liberty of the Subjects residing in Britain, are supposed to be interested in the Preservation of the Rights of the Provinces, and in what Manner those Rights appear to be abridged by the Statute.* London, 1766.

Anon., *Two Papers*
Anonymous. *Two Papers, On the Subject of Taxing the British Colonies in America.* London, 1767.

Appeal to the World
An Appeal to the World: Or, a Vindication of the Town of Boston, From Many False and Malicious Aspersions Contained in Certain Letters and Memorials, Written by Governor Bernard, General Gage, Commodore Hood, the Commissioners of the American Board of Customs, and Others; And by them respectively transmitted to the British Ministry. London, 1769.

Bailyn, *Ordeal*
Bernard Bailyn. *The Ordeal of Thomas Hutchinson.* Cambridge, Mass., 1974.

Bailyn, *Pamphlets*
Pamphlets of the American Revolution, 1750–1776. Edited by Bernard Bailyn. Cambridge, Mass., 1965.

Baird, "Drummond"
William Baird. "George Drummond: An Eighteenth Century Lord Provost." 4 *The Book of the Old Edinburgh Club* 1–54. Edinburgh, 1911.

Barrington, *Viscount Barrington*
Shute Barrington. *The Political Life of William Wildman Viscount Barrington, Compiled from Original Papers by his Brother, Shute, Bishop of Durham.* London, 1815.

[Barton,] *Conduct of the Paxton-Men*
[Thomas Barton.] *The Conduct of the Paxton-Men, Impartially Represented: With Some Remarks on the Narrative.* Philadelphia, 1764.

Bernard and Barrington, *Correspondence*
The Barrington-Bernard Correspondence. Edited by Edward Channing and Archibald Cary Collidge. Cambridge, Mass., 1912.

Bernard and Gage, *Letters*
*Letters to the Ministry From Governor Bernard, General Gage, and
Commodore Hood. And Also, Memorials to the Lords of the Treasury
From the Commisioner of the Customs, With Sundry Letters and Papers
Annexed to the said Memorials.* Boston, 1769.
[Bingham,] *Essay on Militia in Ireland*
[Sir Charles Bingham.] *An Essay on the Use and Necessity of
Establishing a Militia in Ireland, And some Hints towards a Plan For that
Purpose.* Dublin, 1767.
Blackstone, *Commentaries*
William Blackstone. *Commentaries on the Laws of England.* 4 vols.
Oxford, Eng., 1765–69.
Bland, *An Inquiry*
Richard Bland. *An Inquiry into the Rights of the British Colonies,
Intended as an Answer to the Regulations lately made concerning the
Colonies, and the Taxes imposed upon them considered.* Williamsburg,
Va., 1766.
[Bolingbroke,] *Freeholder's Catechism*
[Bolingbroke, H. St. John, 1st Viscount.] *The Freeholder's Political
Catechism. Very Necessary to be Studied by every Freeman in America.*
New-London, Conn., 1769.
[Bollan,] *Continued Corruption*
[William Bollan.] *Continued Corruption, Standing Armies, and Popu-
lar Discontents Considered; And the Establishment of the English
Colonies in America, with Various subsequent Proceedings, and the
Present Contests, examined; with Intent to promote their cordial and
perpetual Union with their Mother-Country, for their Mutual Honour,
Comfort, Strength, and Safety.* London, 1768.
[Bollan,] *Free Britons Memorial*
[William Bollan.] *The Free Britons Memorial, to all the Freeholders,
Citizens and Burgesses, who Elect the Members of the British Parliament
Presented in Order to the Effectual Defence of their Injured Right of
Election.* London, 1769.
[Bollan,] *Mutual Interest Considered*
[William Bollan.] *The Mutual Interest of Great Britain and the
American Colonies Considered, With respect to an Act passed last Sessions
of Parliament for laying a Duty on Merchandise, &c. With Some Remarks
on a Pamphlet, intitled, "Objections to the Taxation of the American
Colonies &c. considered." In a letter to a Member of Parliament.* London,
1765.

Boston Gazette
> The Boston Gazette and Country Journal. 1766–71.

Boston Merchants, *Observations*
> *Observations on Several Acts of Parliament Passed In the 4th, 6th and 7th*
> *Years of his present Majesty's Reign: and also on The Conduct of the*
> *Officers of the Customs, since Those Acts were passed, and The Board of*
> *Commissions appointed to Reside in America. Published by the Merchants*
> *of Boston*. Boston, 1769.

Bowdoin Papers
> *The Bowdoin and Temple Papers: Collections of the Massachusetts*
> *Historical Society*. 6th series, vol. 9. Boston, 1897.

Breen, *Good Ruler*
> T. H. Breen. *The Character of the Good Ruler: A Study of Puritan*
> *Political Ideas in New England, 1630–1730*. New Haven, Conn.,
> 1970.

Bridges, *Smuglers Defeated*
> George Bridges. *The Smuglers Defeated: Or the Golden Fleece*
> *Reviv'd. In a familiar Method for the Restoration of Trade. By the*
> *Experience, Travels and Imprisonments of the Sufferer, by the Clandestine*
> *Exporters of Combed Wool, Raw Wool, and Woollen Yarn from Ireland to*
> *France*. London, 1739.

British Liberties
> *British Liberties, or the Free-born Subject's Inheritance; Containing the*
> *Laws that form the Basis of those Liberties, with Observations thereon;*
> *also an Introductory Essay on Political Liberty and a Comprehensive*
> *View of the Constitution of Great Britain*. London, 1766.

Britton, *Authorship of Junius*
> John Britton. *The Authorship of the Letters of Junius Elucidated:*
> *Including a Biographical Memoir of Lieutenant-Colonel Issac Barré,*
> *M.P.* London, 1848.

[Burnet,] *Coronation Sermon*
> [Gilbert Burnet.] *A Sermon Preached at the Coronation of William III.*
> *and Mary II. King and Queen of England, —France, and Ireland,*
> *Defenders of the Faith; in the Abby-Church of Westminster, April 11,*
> *1689*. London, 1689.

[Butler,] *Standing Army*
> [John Butler.] *A Consultation On the Subject of a Standing Army, Held*
> *at the Kings-Arms Tavern, on the Twenty-eighth of February 1763*
> London, 1763.

Carter, "Commander in Chief"
  Clarence E. Carter. "The Office of Commander in Chief: A Phase
  of Imperial Unity on the Eve of the Revolution." In *The Era of the
  American Revolution*, edited by Richard B. Morris, pp. 170–213.
  New York, 1965.
Cary, *Warren*
  John Cary. *Joseph Warren: Physician, Politician, Patriot*. Urbana, Ill.,
  1961.
"Cato," *Discourse of Standing Armies*
  "Cato" [John Trenchard]. *A Discourse of Standing Armies; Shewing
  the Folly, Uselessness, and Danger of Standing Armies in Great Britain*.
  2d ed. London, 1722.
"Cato's Letters"
  John Trenchard and Thomas Gordon. "Cato's Letters." Reprinted
  in *The English Libertarian Heritage From the Writings of John Trenchard
  and Thomas Gordon in The Independent Whig and Cato's Letters*, edited
  by David L. Jacobson. Indianapolis, 1965.
[Chandler,] *What Think Ye of Congress?*
  [Thomas B. Chandler.] *What think Ye of the Congress Now? or, An
  Enquiry, How far the Americans are Bound to Abide by, and Execute the
  Decisions of, the Late Congress*. New York, 1775.
Chauncy, *A Discourse on "the good News"*
  Charles Chauncy. *A Discourse on "the good News from a far Country."
  Deliver'd July 24th. A Day of Thanks-giving to Almighty God,
  throughout the Province of the Massachusetts-Bay in New England, on
  Occasion of the Repeal of the* STAMP-ACT. Boston, 1766.
Christie and Labaree, *Empire*
  Ian R. Christie and Benjamin W. Labaree. *Empire or Independence,
  1760–1776: A British-American Dialogue on the Coming of the Ameri-
  can Revolution*. New York, 1977.
Chronicle
  The Boston Chronicle.
"Citizen," *Observations on Livingston's Address*
  "A Citizen." *Observations on Mr. Justice Livingston's Address to the
  House of Assembly, In Support of his Right to a Seat*. New York, 6
  December 1769.
[Clarendon,] *An Answer to a Pamphlet*
  [Edward Hyde, Earl of Clarendon.] *An Answer to a Pamphlet,
  Entitled, A Declaration of the Commons of England in Parliament
  assembled, expressing their Reasons and Grounds of passing the late*

Resolutions touching no further Addresses or Application to be made to the King. [London, 1648].

[Clement,] *Faults on Both Sides*
> [Simon Clement.] *Faults on Both Sides: Or, an Essay Upon the Original Cause, Progress, and Mischievous Consequences of the Factions in this Nation.* London, 1710.

Clode, *Military Forces*
> Charles M. Clode. *The Military Forces of the Crown: Their Administration and Government.* 2 vols. London, 1869.

[Colden,] *Conduct*
> [Cadwallader Colden.] *The Conduct of Cadwallader Colden, Esquire, Late Lieutenant Governor of New York Relating to the Judges Commissions, Appeals to the King, and the Stamp Duty.* 1767. Reprinted in *The Colden Letter Books, Vol. II, 1765–1775,* pp. 433–67 (Collections of the New-York Historical Society for the Year 1877, vol. 10, New York, 1878).

Colden Papers
> *The Colden Letter Books, Vol. II, 1765–1775.* Collections of the New-York Historical Society for the Year 1877. Vol. 10. New York, 1878.

Commons Debates, 1628
> *Commons Debates, 1628.* Edited by Robert C. Johnson . . . [et al.]. 4 vols. New Haven, Conn., 1977–78.

Common Sense
> *Common Sense: or, the Englishman's Journal. Being A Collection of Letters, Political, Humorous, and Moral: Publish'd Weekly under that Title for the First Year.* London, 1737–39.

Cooper, "Letters"
> Frederick Tuckerman. "Letters of Samuel Cooper to Thomas Pownall, 1769–1777." 8 *American Historical Review* 301–30 (1903).

Costin and Watson, *Documents*
> W. C. Costin and J. Steven Watson, *The Law and Working of the Constitution: Documents, 1660–1914.* 2 vols. London, 1952.

[Crowley,] *Letters*
> [Thomas Crowley.] *Letters and Dissertations, by the Author of the Letter Analysis A.P. On the Disputes between Great Britain and America.* London, 1782.

Dalrymple, *Military Essay*
> Campbell Dalrymple. *A Military Essay: Containing Reflections on the Raising, Arming, and Cloathing, and the Discipline of the British*

Infantry and Cavalry; with Proposals for the Improvement of the Same.
London, 1761.
"Declaration of the Gentlemen"
"The Declaration of the Gentlemen, Merchants and Inhabitants of
Boston, and the Country Adjacent. April 18, 1689." Reprinted in
Narratives of the Insurrections, 1675–1690, edited by Charles M.
Andrews, pp. 175–82. New York, 1915.
[Defoe,] *A Brief Reply to the History*
[Daniel Defoe.] *A Brief Reply to the History of Standing Armies in
England*. London, 1698.
De Lolme, *Constitution*
J. L. De Lolme. *The Constitution of England, or an Account of the
English Government*. Dublin, 1775.
"Demophilus," *Genuine Principles*
"Demophilus." *The Genuine Principles of the Ancient Saxon, or
English Constitution*. Philadelphia, 1776.
Dickerson, *Acts*
Oliver M. Dickerson. *The Navigation Acts and the American Revolu-
tion*. Philadelphia, 1951.
Documents of Colonial New York
Documents Relative to the Colonial History of the State of New-York.
Vol. 7. Edited by E. B. O'Callaghan. Albany, N.Y., 1856.
[Dowdeswell,] *Address to Electors*
[William Dowdeswell.] *An Address to such of the Electors of Great-
Britain as are not Makers of Cyder and Perry. By the Representative of a
Cyder-County*. London, 1763.
[Downer,] *Discourse in Providence*
[Silas Downer.] *A Discourse Delivered in Providence, in the Colony of
Rhode-Island, upon the 25th Day of July 1768. At the Dedication of the
Tree of Liberty, From the Summer House in the Tree*. Providence, R. I.,
1768.
[Drayton, et al.,] *The Letters*
[William Henry Drayton, William Wragg, Christopher Gadsden,
and John Mackenzie.] *The Letters of Freeman, &c*. London, 1771.
Eliot, "Letters"
"Letters from Andrew Eliot to Thomas Hollis." 4 *Collections of the
Massachusetts Historical Society* 398–461 (1858).
Emerson, *Sermon of Thanksgiving*
Joseph Emerson. *A Thanksgiving-Sermon Preach'd at Pepperell, July
24th 1766. A Day set apart by public Authority As a Day of*

Thanksgiving on the Account of the Repeal of the Stamp-Act. Boston, 1766.

[Erskine,] *Shall I Go to War?*
> [John Erskine.] *Shall I go to War with my American Brethren? A Discourse from Judges the xxth and 28th. Addressed to all Concerned in Determining that Important Question*. London, 1769.

Everard, *The 29th Foot*
> H. Everard. *History of Tho.ˢ. Farrington's Regiment Subsequently Designated the 29th (Worcestershire) Foot 1694 to 1891*. Worcester, Eng., 1891.

Ewing, "The Constitution"
> J. Ewing. "The Constitution and the Empire—From Bacon to Blackstone." In *The Cambridge History of the British Empire: Volume I, The Old Empire From the Beginnings to 1783*, edited by J. Holland Rose, A. P. Newton, and E. A. Benians, pp. 603–33. Cambridge, Eng., 1929.

Extract of Letter to De Berdt
> *Extract of a Letter From the House of Representatives of the Massachusetts-Bay to their Agent Dennys De Berdt, Esq; with some Remarks*. London, 1770.

Finlason, *Riot or Rebellion*
> W. F. Finlason. *A Review of the Authorities as to the Repression of Riot or Rebellion, with Special Reference to Criminal or Civil Liability*. London, 1868.

[Fletcher,] *Discourse of Government*
> [Andrew Fletcher.] *A Discourse of Government with Relation to Militia's*. Edinburgh, 1698.

[Fletcher,] *Militias and Standing Armies*
> [Andrew Fletcher.] *A Discourse Concerning Militia's and Standing Armies. With relation to the Past and Present Governments of Europe, and of England in particular*. London, 1697.

Foner, *Labor and Revolution*
> Philip S. Foner, *Labor and the American Revolution*. Westport, Conn., 1976.

Franklin, *Writings*
> *The Writings of Benjamin Franklin, 1767–1772*. Vol. 5. Edited by Albert Henry Smyth. New York, 1906.

Franklin and Jackson, *Letters*
> *Letters and Papers of Benjamin Franklin and Richard Jackson, 1753–1785*. Edited by Carl Van Doren. Philadelphia, 1947.

Franklin's Letters to the Press
  Benjamin Franklin's Letters to the Press, 1758–1775. Edited by Verner
  W. Crane. Chapel Hill, N.C., 1950.
Gage, *Correspondence*
  *The Correspondence of General Thomas Gage With the Secretaries of
  State 1763–1775.* Vol. 1. Edited by Clarence Edwin Carter. New
  Haven, Conn., 1931. *The Correspondence of General Thomas Gage
  with the Secretaries of State, and with the War Office and the Treasury
  1763–1775.* Vol. 2. Edited by Clarence Edwin Carter. New Haven,
  Conn., 1933.
Gage Papers
  Military Papers of General Gage. Ann Arbor, Mich. Clements
  Library, University of Michigan.
Gardiner, *Two Stuarts*
  Samuel Rawson Gardiner. *The First Two Stuarts and the Puritan
  Revolution, 1603–1660.* Appolo ed. New York, 1970.
Gazette and News-Letter
  The Massachusetts Gazette and Boston News-Letter. 1764–68.
Gazette and Post-Boy
  The Massachusetts Gazette and Boston Post-Boy and the Advertiser.
  1764–74.
Gentleman's Magazine
  The Gentleman's Magazine and Historical Chronicle.
Gipson, "Revolution as Aftermath"
  Lawrence Henry Gipson. "The American Revolution as an After-
  math of the Great War for the Empire, 1754–1763." 65 *Political
  Science Quarterly* 86–104 (1950).
Glasgow Extracts
  *Extracts from the Records of the Burgh of Glasgow A.D. 1718–38. With
  Charters and Other Documents.* Edited by Robert Renwick. Glasgow,
  Scotland, 1909.
Greene, "Paine and Modernization"
  Jack P. Greene. "Paine, America, and the 'Modernization of
  Political Consciousness.'" 93 *Political Science Quarterly* 73–92
  (1978).
[Grenville,] *Letter to Grafton*
  [George Grenville.] *A Letter to His Grace the Duke of Grafton, on the
  present Situation of Public Affairs.* London, [1768].
Grenville Papers

The Grenville Papers: Being the Correspondence of Richard Grenville Earl Temple, K.G., and The Hon: George Grenville their Friends and Contemporaries. 4 vols. Edited by William James Smith. London, 1852–53.

[Grenville,] *The Regulations*
[George Grenville.] *The Regulations Lately Made Concerning the Colonies, and the Taxes Imposed Upon Them, Considered.* London, 1765.

Grey's Debates
Debates of the House of Commons From the Year 1667 to the Year 1694. Collected by the Hon. Anchitell Grey, Esq; Who Was Thirty Years Member for the Town of Derby: Chairman of Several Committees; and Decyphered Coleman's Letters for Use of the House. London, 1763.

[Guthrie,] *Dismission of a General Officer*
[William Guthrie.] *An Address to the Public, On the late Dismission of a General Officer.* London, 1764.

Hamilton, *Farmer*
Alexander Hamilton. *The Farmer Refuted: or A more impartial and comprehensive View of the Dispute between Great-Britain and the Colonies, Intended as a Further Vindication of the Congress* (1775). Reprinted in *The Papers of Alexander Hamilton,* edited by Harold C. Syrett, vol. 1, pp. 81–165. New York, 1961.

[Hardwicke,] *Two Speeches*
[Philip Yorke, Earl of Hardwicke.] *Two Speeches of a Late Lord Chancellor.* London, 1770.

Harris, *Eighteenth-Century England*
R. W. Harris. *England in the Eighteenth Century: A Balanced Constitution and New Horizons.* New York, 1963.

Headlam, "Imperial Reconstruction"
Cecil Headlam. "Imperial Reconstruction, 1763–1765." In *The Cambridge History of the British Empire.* Volume I, *The Old Empire from the Beginnings to 1783,* edited by J. Holland Rose, A. P. Newton, and E. A. Benians, pp. 634–46. Cambridge, Eng., 1929.

[Herle,] *An Answer*
[C. Herle.] *An Answer to Mis-led Doctor Ferne According to his own Method.* London, 1642.

Higgins, *Bernard*
Mrs. Napier Higgins. *The Bernards of Abington and Nether Winchendon: A Family History.* Vol. 2. New York, 1903.

Hill, *Century of Revolution*
  Christopher Hill. *The Century of Revolution, 1603–1714*. New York, 1961.
Hinkhouse, *Preliminaries*
  Fred Junkin Hinkhouse. *The Preliminaries of the American Revolution as Seen in the English Press, 1763–1775*. New York, 1926.
Holmes and Speck, *Divided Society*
  The Divided Society: Party Conflict in England, 1694–1716. Edited by Geoffrey Holmes and W. A. Speck. London, 1967.
Hosmer, *Adams*
  James K. Hosmer. *Samuel Adams*. Boston, 1899.
Howard, *Artillery-Election Sermon*
  Simeon Howard. *A Sermon Preached to the Ancient and Honorable Artillery-Company, in Boston, New-England, June 7th, 1773. Being the Anniversary of their Election of Officers*. Boston, 1773.
Humphries, "Lord Shelburne"
  R. A. Humphries. "Lord Shelburne and British Colonial Policy, 1766–1768." 50 *English Historical Review* 257–77 (1935).
Hutchinson, *Diary*
  The Diary and Letters of His Excellency Thomas Hutchinson, Esq. 2 vols. London, 1883.
Hutchinson, *History*
  Thomas Hutchinson. *The History of the Province of Massachusetts Bay, From 1749 to 1774, Comprising a Detailed Narrative of the Origin and Early Stages of the American Revolution*. London, 1828.
Hutchinson, *Letters*
  Copy of Letters Sent to Great-Britain, By his Excellency Thomas Hutchinson, The Hon. Andrew Oliver, and Several Other Persons, Born and Educated Among Us. Boston, 1773.
"Ignotus," *Thoughts on Trade*
  "Ignotus." *Thoughts on Trade in General, our West-Indian in Particular, our Continental Colonies, Canada, Guadaloupe, and the Preliminary Articles of Peace. Addressed to the Community*. London, 1763.
"In Accordance with Usage"
  John Phillip Reid. "In Accordance with Usage: The Authority of Custom, the Stamp Act Debate, and the Coming of the American Revolution." 45 *Fordham Law Review* 335–68 (1976).
"In a Constitutional Void"
  John Phillip Reid. "In a Constitutional Void: The Enforcement of

Imperial Law, the Role of the British Army, and the Coming of the American Revolution." 22 *Wayne Law Review* 1–37 (1975).

"In a Defensive Rage"

John Phillip Reid. "In a Defensive Rage: The Uses of the Mob, the Justification in Law, and the Coming of the American Revolution." 49 *New York University Law Review* 1043–91 (1974).

In a Defiant Stance

John Phillip Reid. *In a Defiant Stance: The Conditions of Law in Massachusetts Bay, the Irish Comparison, and the Coming of the American Revolution.* University Park, Pa., 1977.

"In an Inherited Way"

John Phillip Reid. "In an Inherited Way: English Constitutional Rights, the Stamp Act Debates, and the Coming of the American Revolution." 49 *Southern California Law Review* 1109–29 (1976).

In a Rebellious Spirit

John Phillip Reid. *In a Rebellious Spirit: The Argument of Facts, the Liberty Riot, and the Coming of the American Revolution.* University Park, Pa., 1979.

"In Legitimate Stirps"

John Phillip Reid. "In Legitimate Stirps: The Concept of 'Arbitrary,' the Supremacy of Parliament, and the Coming of the American Revolution." 5 *Hofstra Law Review* 459–99 (1977).

Jefferson, "A Summary View"

Thomas Jefferson, "A Summary View." In *The American Revolution: The Anglo-American Relation, 1763–1794,* edited by Charles R. Ritcheson, pp. 75–80. Reading, Mass., 1969.

Jefferson, *Summary View*

Thomas Jefferson. *A Summary View of the Rights of British America Set Forth in Some Resolutions Intended For the Inspection of the Present Delegates of the People of Virginia Now in Convention* (1774). Reprinted in *The Papers of Thomas Jefferson, 1760–1776,* edited by Julian Boyd, vol. 1, pp. 121–35. Princeton, N.J., 1950.

Jensen, *Documents*

English Historical Documents: American Colonial Documents to 1776. Edited by Merrill Jensen. Vol. 9. New York, 1955.

[Johnson,] *A Confutation of a Late Pamphlet*

[Samuel Johnson.] *A Confutation of a Late Pamphlet Intituled a Letter Ballancing the Necessity of Keeping a Land-Force in Times of Peace; with the Dangers that may follow on it.* London, 1698.

Johnson, "Standing Army"
 Samuel Johnson. "Several Reasons for the Establishment of a
 Standing Army, and the Dissolving the Militia." In *The Works of the
 Late Reverend Mr. Samuel Johnson, Sometime Chaplain to the Right
 Honourable William Lord Russel*, pp. 149–54. 2d ed. London, 1713.
Johnson, *Works*
 *The Works of the Late Reverend Mr. Samuel Johnson, Sometime
 Chaplain to the Right Honourable William Lord Russel.* 2d ed. London,
 1713.
Jones, *Suppressing Riots*
 William Jones. *An Inquiry into the Legal Mode of Suppressing Riots
 with a Constitutional Plan of a Future Defence.* 2d ed. London, 1782.
Journal of the Times
 *Boston Under Military Rule 1768–1769 as Revealed in a Journal of the
 Times.* Compiled by Oliver Morton Dickerson. Reprint. New
 York, 1970.
"Junius," *Junius*
 ["Junius."] *Junius.* 2 vols. London, [1772].
Kim, *Landlord and Tenant*
 Sung Bok Kim. *Landlord and Tenant in Colonial New York Manorial
 Society, 1664–1775.* Chapel Hill, N.C., 1978.
Knollenberg, *Origin*
 Bernard Knollenberg, *Origin of the American Revolution, 1759–1766.*
 Rev. ed. New York, 1965.
"L.," *Letter to G[renville]*
 "L." *A Letter to G. G. Stiff in Opinions, always in the wrong.* London,
 1767.
Labaree, *Patriots and Partisans*
 Benjamin W. Labaree. *Patriots and Partisans: The Merchants of
 Newburyport, 1764–1815.* New York, 1975.
Labaree, *Tea Party*
 Benjamin Woods Labaree. *The Boston Tea Party.* New York, 1968.
Lathrop, *Innocent Blood*
 John Lathrop. *Innocent Blood Crying to God From the Streets of Boston:
 A Sermon Occasioned by the Horrid Murder of Messieurs Samuel Gray,
 Samuel Maverick, James Caldwell, and Crispus Attucks, with Patrick
 Carr, since dead, and Christopher Monk, judged irrecoverable, and several
 others badly wounded, by a Party of Troops under the Command of
 Captain Preston: On the Fifth of March, 1770, and Preached the Lord's
 Day Following.* London, 1770.

KEY TO SHORT TITLES

Leder, *Liberty*
  Lawrence H. Leder. *Liberty and Authority: Early American Ideology, 1689–1763.* Chicago, 1968.
[Lee,] *Junius Americanus*
  [Arthur Lee.] *The Political Detection; or, the Treachery and Tyranny of Administration, both at Home and Abroad; Displayed in a Series of Letters signed Junius Americanus.* London, 1770.
Letters of Walpole
  The Letters of Horace Walpole, Fourth Earl of Oxford. Edited by Peter Cunningham. Vol. 5. Edinburgh, 1906.
Letters to Hillsborough
  Letters to the Right Honourable The Earl of Hillsborough, from Governor Bernard, General Gage, and The Honourable His Majesty's Council for the Province of Massachusetts Bay. Boston, 1769.
Linebaugh, "Tyburn Riot"
  Peter Linebaugh. "The Tyburn Riot against the Surgeons." In *Albion's Fatal Tree: Crime and Society in Eighteenth-Century England,* pp. 65–117. New York, 1975.
Livingston, *Address to the House*
  The Address to Mr. Justice Livingston, to the House of Assembly, In Support of his Right to a Seat. New York, [1769].
[Lloyd,] *Conduct Examined*
  [Charles Lloyd.] *The Conduct of the Late Ministry Examined: From July, 1765, to March, 1766.* London, 1767.
London Magazine
  The London Magazine or Gentleman's Monthly Intelligencer
Longley, "Mob"
  R. S. Longley. "Mob Activities in Revolutionary Massachusetts." 6 *New England Quarterly* 98–130 (1933).
Lords' Protests
  A Complete Collection of the Lords' Protests, From the First Upon Record in the Reign of Henry the Third, to the Present Time; With a Copious Index. 2 vols. London, 1767.
Lovell, *An Oration*
  James Lovell. *An Oration Delivered April 2d, 1771. At the Request of the Inhabitants of the Town of Boston; to Commemorate the bloody Tragedy of the Fifth of March, 1770.* Boston, 1771.
Lucas, *An Address to Dublin*
  Charles Lucas. *An Address to the Right Honorable the Lord Mayor, the Worshipful the Board of Aldermen, the Sheriffs, Commons, Citizens and*

Freeholders of Dublin, Relating to the Intended Augmentation of the Military Force in the Kingdom of Ireland. London, 1768.

McAulay, *Legality of Pensions*
Alexander McAulay. *An Inquiry into the Legality of Pensions on the Irish Establishment.* London, 1763.

McIlwain, *Revolution*
Charles Howard McIlwain. *The American Revolution: A Constitutional Interpretation.* Ithaca, N.Y., 1958.

[Macpherson,] *Rights of Great Britain*
[James Macpherson.] *The Rights of Great Britain Asserted against the Claims of America: Being an Answer to the Declaration of the General Congress.* 10th ed., London, 1776.

Maier, *Resistance*
Pauline Maier. *From Resistance to Revolution: Colonial Radicals and the Development of American Opposition to Britain, 1765–1776.* New York, 1972.

Massacre Orations
Orations Delivered at the Request of the Town of Boston to Commemorate the Evening of the Fifth of March, 1770; When a Number of Citizens were Killed by a Party of British Troops, Quartered Among them, in a Time of Peace. Boston, 1785.

Mather, *Vindication*
Increase Mather. *A Vindication of New-England.* 1690. Reprinted in 2 *The Andros Tracts* 21–81 (Prince Society Publications, vol. 6, 1869).

[Mildway,] *Laws and Policy*
[William Mildway.] *The Laws and Policy of England, Relating to Trade, Examined By the Maxims and Principles of Trade in general; and By the Laws and Policy of Other Trading Nations.* London, 1765.

Military Massacre
An account of a late Military Massacre at Boston, or the Consequences of Quartering Troops in a populous well-regulated Town, taken from the Boston Gazette, of March 12, 1770 (1770). Reprinted as *The Bloody Massacre Perpetrated in King-Street Boston, on March 5th 1770 by a Party of the 29th Regiment.* Barre, Mass., 1970.

Miller, *Origins*
John Chester Miller. *Origins of the American Revolution.* Boston, 1943.

[Molesworth,] *Denmark*
[Robert Molesworth.] *An Account of Denmark as It was in the Year 1692.* 3d ed. London, 1694.

Montesquieu, *The Spirit of Laws*
  Baron de Montesquieu, *The Spirit of Laws*. 2 vols. 2d. ed. London, 1752.
Monthly Review
  The Monthly Review; or, Literary Journal: by Several Hands (London).
Morgan, *Birth*
  Edmund S. Morgan. *The Birth of the Republic, 1763–89*. Chicago, 1956.
Morgan, *Prologue*
  Prologue to Revolution: Sources and Documents on the Stamp Act Crisis, 1764–1766. Edited by Edmund S. Morgan. Chapel Hill, N.C., 1959.
Namier, *Age of Revolution*
  L. B. Namier. *England in the Age of the American Revolution*. London, 1930.
Narratives of the Insurrections, 1675–1690
  Narratives of the Insurrections, 1675–1690. Edited by Charles M. Andrews. New York, 1915.
Nelson, *Americanization of the Common Law*
  William E. Nelson. *Americanization of the Common Law: The Impact of Legal Change on Massachusetts Society, 1760–1830*. Cambridge, Mass., 1975.
Nenner, *Colour of Law*
  Howard Nenner. *By Colour of Law: Legal Culture and Constitutional Politics in England, 1660–1689*. Chicago, 1977.
Neville, *New-Jersey Acts*
  Samuel Neville. *The Acts of the General Assembly of the Province of New-Jersey*. Vol. 2. Woodbridge, N.J., 1761.
Noble, *Some Strictures*
  Oliver Noble. *Some Strictures upon the Sacred Story Recorded in the Book of Esther, Shewing the Power and Oppression of State Ministers tending to the Ruin and Destruction of God's People:—And the Remarkable Interpositions of Divine Providence, in Favour of the Oppressed; in a discourse Delivered at Newbury-Port, North Meeting House, March 8th, 1775. in Commemoration of the Massacre at Boston, March the Fifth, 1770*. Newburyport, Mass., 1775.
North Briton
  The North Briton. To Which is added, By Way of Appendix, The Letters which passed between The Rt. Hon. Earl Talbot, &c. and John Wilkes, Esq; Previous to their Duel. Together with all the Papers relative to the

Confinement and Enlargement of Mr. Wilkes. With many other Curious Particulars. Vol. 2. Dublin, 1763.

Omond, *The Army*
> J. S. Omond. *Parliament and the Army, 1642–1904*. Cambridge, Eng., 1933.

Otis, *Rights*
> James Otis, *The Rights of the British Colonies Asserted and Proved*. 1764. Reprinted in *Pamphlets of the American Revolution, 1750–1776*, edited by Bernard Bailyn, vol. 1, pp. 419–82. Cambridge, Mass., 1965.

[Otis,] "Substance"
> [James Otis.] "Substance of a Memorial Presented [by] the Assembly in Pursuance of the Above Instructions; and by the House Voted to be Transmitted to JASPER MAUDUIT, Esq., Agent for this Province, to be Improved As He may Judge Proper." Appendix to Otis, *Rights*, pp. 474–82.

[Parker,] *Observations upon Some Answers*
> [Henry Parker.] *Observations upon some of his Majesties late Answers and Expressions*. London, [1642].

Parliamentary History
> Series variously titled as *Cobbetts Parliamentary History of England From the Norman Conquest, in 1066 to the Year 1803*, or *The Parliamentary History of England From the Earliest Period to the Year 1803*. 36 vols. London, 1806–20.

"Philonomos," *Liberty of the Subject*
> Anonymous. *The Liberty of the Subject, and Dignity of the Crown, Maintained and Secured Without the Application of a Military, Unconstitutional Force, or the Tyranny of any inconsiderable Minister. Supported By the Opinion of a Lord High Chancellor of England. Inscribed to Sir Richard Perrot, Bart*. London, [1768].

Pocock, *Ancient Constitution*
> J. G. A. Pocock. *The Ancient Constitution and the Feudal Law: A Study of English Historical Thought in the Seventeenth Century*. Cambridge, Eng., 1957.

Post
> *The Boston Evening-Post*. 1765–74.

Post-Boy
> *The Boston Post-Boy and Advertiser*. 1764–74.

Pownall, *Administration*
> Thomas Pownall. *The Administration of the Colonies. Wherein their*

Rights and Constitution are Discussed and Stated. 4th ed. London, 1768.

[Prescott,] *Calm Consideration*

> [Benjamin Prescott.] *A Free and Calm Consideration of the Unhappy Misunderstandings and Debates, which have of late Years arisen, and yet subsist, Between the Parliament of Great-Britain, and these American Colonies. Contained in Eight Letters, Six whereof, Directed to a Gentleman of Distinction in England, Formerly printed in the Essex Gazette. The other two, directed to a Friend.* Salem, Mass., 1774.

Prior Documents

> [John Almon.] *A Collection of Interesting, Authentic Papers, Relative to the Dispute Between Great Britain and America; Shewing the Causes and Progress of that Misunderstanding From 1764–1775.* London, 1777.

Protests of the Lords

> *A Complete Collection of the Protests of the Lords with Historical Introductions.* Edited by James E. Thorold Rogers. 3 vols. Oxford, Eng., 1875.

Quincy, *Observations with Thoughts*

> Josiah Quincy, Jun'r. *Observations on the Act of Parliament Commonly Called the Boston Port-Bill; with Thoughts on Civil Society and Standing Armies.* 1774. Reprinted in *Memoir of the Life of Josiah Quincy Jun. of Massachusetts: By his Son Josiah Quincy*, pp. 355–469. Boston, 1825.

Quincy, *Reports*

> *Reports of Cases Argued and Adjudged in the Superior Court of Judicature of the Province of Massachusetts Bay, Between 1761 and 1772.* Edited by Josiah Quincy, Jr. Boston, 1865.

Ray, *Importance of the Colonies*

> Nicholas Ray. *The Importance of the Colonies of North America, and the Interest of Great Britain with regard to them, Considered. Together with Remarks on the Stamp-Duty.* London, 1766.

"Report of October 1769"

> "Report of the Committee appointed to vindicate the Town of Boston from the many false and malicious Aspersions contained in certain Letters and Memorials, written by Governor Bernard, General Gage, Commodore Hood, the Commissioners of the American Board of Customs, and others. . . . ," 18 October 1769. In *Town Records*, pp. 303–25.

Revolution Documents

> *Documents of the American Revolution, 1770–1783.* Edited by K. G. Davies. Vols. 1, 3, and 6. Dublin, 1972–74.

Ritcheson, "Introduction"
Charles R. Ritcheson. "Introduction." In *The American Revolution: The Anglo-American Relation, 1763–1794*, edited by Charles R. Ritcheson. Reading, Mass., 1969.

Robbins, *Commonwealthman*
Caroline Robbins. *The Eighteenth-Century Commonwealthman: Studies in the Transmission, Development, and Circumstance of English Liberal Thought from the Restoration of Charles II until the War with the Thirteen Colonies*. Cambridge, Mass., 1959.

Robson, *American Revolution*
Eric Robson. *The American Revolution in its Political and Military Aspects, 1763–1783*. New York, 1966.

Rossiter, *Six Characters*
Clinton Rossiter. *Six Characters in Search of a Republic: Studies in the Political Thought of the American Colonies*. New York, 1964.

Rowe, "Diary"
"Diary of John Rowe." 10 *Proceedings of the Massachusetts Historical Society* 11–108 (1895).

[Ruffhead,] *Considerations*
[Owen Ruffhead.] *Considerations on the Present Dangerous Crisis*. Edinburgh, 1763.

Sainsbury, "Pro-Americans"
John Sainsbury. "The Pro-Americans of London, 1769 to 1782." 35 *William and Mary Quarterly* 423–54 (1978).

St. Amand, *Historical Essay*
George St. Amand. *An Historical Essay on the Legislative Power of England. Wherein the Origin of Both Houses of Parliament*, presented with 2 *A Complete Collection of the Lords' Protests, From the First Upon Record, in the Reign of Henry the Third, to the Present Time; With a Copious Index*. London, 1767.

Saint-John, *Argument of Law*
Oliver Saint-John. *An Argument of Law concerning the Bill of Attainder of High-Treason of Thomas Earle of Strafford: At a Conference in a Committee of both Houses of Parliament*. London, 1641.

Samuel, *British Army*
E. Samuel. *An Historical Account of the British Army, and of the Law Military, as Declared by the Ancient and Modern Statutes, and Articles of War for its Government with a Free Commentary on the Mutiny Act, and the Rules and Articles of War*. London, 1816.

Schwoerer, *No Standing Armies*

Lois G. Schwoerer. *"No Standing Armies!" The Antimilitary Ideology in Seventeenth-Century England.* Baltimore, 1974.

Schwoerer, "The Fittest Subject"
Lois G. Schwoerer. " 'The Fittest Subject for A King's Quarrell': An Essay on the Militia Controversy, 1641–1642." 11 *Journal of British Studies* 45–76 (1971).

[Serle,] *Liberty*
[Ambrose Serle.] *Americans Against Liberty: or, an Essay on the Nature and Principles of True Freedom, Shewing that the Design and Conduct of the Americans Tend Only to Tyranny and Slavery.* 3d ed. London, 1776.

[Shaftesbury,] *Parliamentman*
Anthony Ashley Cooper, Earl of Shaftesbury. *A Letter from a Parliamentman to his Friend, Concerning the Proceedings of the House of Commons this last Sessions, begun the 13th of October, 1675.* N.p., 1675.

[Shaftesbury,] *Person of Quality*
[Anthony Ashley Cooper, Earl of Shaftesbury.] *A Letter from a Person of Quality, to his Friend in the Country,* N.p. 1675.

Shaftesbury and Buckingham, *Two Speeches*
Two Speeches. I. The Earl of Shaftesbury's Speech in the House of Lords the 20th. of October, 1675. II. The D. of Buckinghams Speech in the House of Lords the 16th. of November 1675. Amsterdam, 1675.

[Shebbeare,] *An Answer*
[John Shebbeare.] *An Answer to the Printed Speech of Edmund Burke, Esq; Spoken in the House of Commons, April 19, 1774. In which his Knowledge in Polity, Legislation, Humankind, History, Commerce and Finance is candidly examined.* London, 1775.

[Sheridan,] *Observations on the Doctrine*
[Charles Francis Sheridan.] *Observations on the Doctrine laid down by Sir William Blackstone, Respecting the extent of the Power of the British Parliament, Particularly with relation to Ireland. In a Letter to Sir William Blackstone, with a Postscript Addressed to Lord North.* London, 1779.

Short Narrative
A Short Narrative of the horrid Massacre in Boston, Perpetrated in the Evening of the Fifth Day of March, 1770, By Soldiers of the XXIXth Regiment, Which with the XIVth Regiment Were then Quartered there: With some Observations on the State of Things Prior to that Catastrophe. Boston, 1770.

Shy, *Toward Lexington*
    John Shy. *Toward Lexington: The Role of the British Army in the Coming of the American Revolution.* Princeton, N.J., 1965.
Somers' Tracts
    A Collection of Scarce and Valuable Tracts, on the Most Interesting and Entertaining Subjects: But Chiefly such as Relate to the History and Constitution of these Kingdoms. Selected from an Infinite Number in Print and Manuscript, in the Royal, Cotton, Sion, and other Public, as well as Private, Libraries; Particularly that of the Late Lord Somers. Edited by Walter Scott. Vols. 4 and 5. London, 1809–15.
Speeches
    Speeches of the Governors of Massachusetts From 1765 to 1775; And the Answers of the House of Representatives to the Same; with their Resolutions and Addresses for that Period. Boston, 1818.
Statutes of the Realm
    The Statutes of the Realm Printed By Command of His Majesty King George the Third in Pursuance of an Address of the House of Commons of Great Britain. N.p., 1819.
Stout, *Royal Navy*
    Neil R. Stout. *The Royal Navy in America, 1760, 1775: A Study of Enforcement of British Colonial Policy in the Era of the American Revolution.* Annapolis, Md., 1973.
Thomas, *British Politics*
    P. D. G. Thomas. *British Politics and the Stamp Act Crisis: The First Phase of the American Revolution, 1763–1767.* Oxford, Eng., 1975.
[Tindal,] *Present Disaffection*
    Matthew Tindal. *An Enquiry into the Causes of the Present Disaffection.* London, 1723.
Toland, *Anglia Libera*
    Jo[hn] Toland. *Anglia Libera: or The Limitation and Succession of the Crown of England explain'd and asserted; As grounded on His Majesty's Speech; The Proceedings in Parliament; The Desires of the People; The Safety of our Religion; The Nature of our Constitution; The Balance of Europe; and the Rights of all Mankind.* London, 1701.
[Toland,] *Militia Reform'd*
    [John Toland.] *The Militia Reform'd; or an Easy Scheme of Furnishing England with a Constant Land-Force, capable to prevent or to subdue any Forein [sic] Power; and to maintain perpetual Quiet at Home, without endangering the Publick Liberty.* London, 1698.
Town Records

A Report of the Record Commissioners of the City of Boston Containing the Boston Town Records, 1758 to 1769 (Report #16, Boston, 1886; Report #18, Boston, 1887).

[Trenchard,] *A Letter from the Author*
 [John Trenchard.] *A Letter from the Author of the Argument against a Standing Army, to the Author of the Balancing Letter.* London, 1697.

[Trenchard,] *An Argument Shewing*
 [John Trenchard.] *An Argument Shewing, that a Standing Army is inconsistent with a Free Government, and absolutely destructive to the Constitution of the English Monarchy.* London, 1697.

[Trenchard,] *Short History*
 [John Trenchard.] *A Short History of Standing Armies in England.* London, 1698.

Trevelyan, *English Revolution*
 G. M. Trevelyan. *The English Revolution, 1688–89.* London, 1938.

Tudor, *Otis*
 William Tudor. *The Life of James Otis of Massachusetts.* Boston, 1823.

Wade, *Junius*
 John Wade. *Junius: Including Letters by the Same Writer Under Other Signatures; to Which are Added his Confidential Correspondence with Mr. Wilkes, and his Private Letters to Mr. H. S. Woodfall.* 2 vols. London, 1850.

Walett, "Bowdoin"
 Francis G. Walett. "James Bowdoin, Patriot Propagandist." 23 *New England Quarterly* 320–38 (1950).

[Walpole,] *Dismission of a General Officer*
 [Horace Walpole.] *A Counter-Address to the Public, on the Late Dismission of a General Officer.* 3d ed. London, 1764.

Walpole Letters
 The Letters of Horace Walpole, Earl of Orford: Including Numerous Letters Now First Published From the Original Manuscripts. Vol. 3 (1759–69). Philadelphia, 1842.

Warren, *American Revolution*
 Mercy Warren. *History of the Rise, Progress, and Termination of the American Revolution.* 3 vols. Boston, 1805.

Waters, *Otis Family*
 John J. Waters, Jr. *The Otis Family in Provincial and Revolutionary Massachusetts.* Chapel Hill, N.C., 1975.

Webb, *Military Treatise*
 T. Webb. *A Military Treatise on the Appointments of the Army.*

Containing Many useful Hints, not touched upon before by any Author: And Proposing some new Regulations in the Army, which will be particularly useful in carrying on the War in North-America. Philadelphia, 1759.

Webb, "Trials of Andros"
Stephen Saunders Webb. "The Trials of Sir Edmund Andros." In *The Human Dimensions of Nation Making: Essays on Colonial and Revolutionary America*, edited by James Kirby Martin, pp. 23–53. Madison, Wis., 1976.

Wedgewood, *Trial*
C. V. Wedgewood. *The Trial of Charles I.* London, 1964.

[Whately,] *Considerations on Trade*
[Thomas Whately.] *Considerations on the Trade and Finances of this Kingdom, and on the Measures of Administration, with Respect to those great National Objects Since the Conclusion of the Peace.* London, 1766.

Wickwire, *Subministers*
Franklin B. Wickwire. *British Subministers and Colonial America, 1763–1783.* Princeton, N.J., 1966.

Wood, *Creation*
Gordon S. Wood. *The Creation of the American Republic, 1776–1787.* Chapel Hill, N.C., 1969.

Wright, *Freedom*
Esmond Wright. *Fabric of Freedom, 1763–1800.* New York, 1961.

Zobel, *Massacre*
Hiller B. Zobel. *The Boston Massacre.* New York, 1970.

ACKNOWLEDGMENTS

Research on this book was conducted at the Huntington Library, aided by a three-month Huntington Library Fellowship. A debt of gratitude is owed to the many individuals who make the library the nation's outstanding center for historical scholarship: James Thorpe, first among equals, Daniel Woodward, collector of the materials, Virginia Renner, succorer of the readers, Mary Wright, keeper of the rare books, Ray Billington, leader of the good talks, and Honorable Martin Ridge, drover of the coyotes. At New York University the manuscript benefited from the dedicated work of Mary Smith and Martha Webb. Responsibility for checking the accuracy of quotations used and materials cited was undertaken by Peter Anglum and Alan Kaufmann, each of whom pledges that all errors have been corrected. Some of the arguments and materials in Chapter 21 to Chapter 28 first appeared in an article published in the November 1975 issue of *Wayne Law Review*. Permission of the editors of *Wayne Law Review* is appreciated, as is the generous permission of John Dann, director of the Clements Library, to quote from the papers of General Thomas Gage. Thanks are also due to Professor Hendrik Hartog of the School of Law, University of Indiana-Bloomington, who pointed out that the archaic is not necessarily anachronistic, and who was the first to call my attention to the original research conducted by Franklin Pierce on the standing-army debates that occurred in New Hampshire during 1771.

Huntington Library   JOHN PHILLIP REID
San Marino, California
17 March 1980

INDEX

Abercromby, Gen. Ralph, 176n
Accountability, principle of: and
  government-by-ministry,
  26–31, 101, 131–32, 133,
  135–36, 169, 170
Act for the better securing the
  Constitution, An (1734), 140
Act of Settlement, 139, 163
"Acts, intolerable," 217
Adair, James, 142
Adams, John, 3, 45
Adams, Samuel, 99; on the evolu-
  tion of the English constitution,
  41; and standing-army con-
  troversy, 49, 149–50; and
  American military establish-
  ment, 50, 53, 136–37, 174,
  184–85
Admiralty Courts, constitution-
  ality of, 228n
"Advices": and presence of British
  troops in Boston, 16, 17, 19,
  21–22
Advocate General of Scotland,
  218n
Albemarle, 1st Duke of. See
  Monk, Gen. George
Amherst, Jeffrey, Baron Amherst,
  175–76, 196
Andros, Gov. Edmund: garrison
  government of, 74–75; Boston
  revolt against, 151–52, 165
Anglicanism: and the American
  military establishment, 76
Anne, Queen of Great Britain,
  139
Antigua: and military enforcement of the Stamp Act, 76, 77

Argyle, Archibald Campbell, 3rd
  Duke of, 102
Army, British imperial, in Boston, 10–11, 12–15; reasons for
  presence of, 13–20, 22–23,
  29–30, 174, 178–82; and arbitrary power of ministers, 30,
  31–32; and revolt against Andros, 152, 165; constitutional
  restrictions on, 177–88 passim,
  197–205, 223n, 229–30; role of,
  179n, 180, 182, 185–86, 198–
  205, 211–13, 215; number of
  troops, 180–81, 182, 184, 200;
  impotency of, 186–88, 211–13,
  215, 224–25; removal of to Castle Island, 219, 221; and Boston
  Massacre, 219, 221, 230
Army, British imperial, in Ireland. See Ireland; Military establishment, Irish
Army, British imperial, in Massachusetts: reasons for presence
  of, 22–24, 219–22; revenue
  brought in by, 219n, 220n; as
  colonial police force, 222–23
Army, British imperial, in North
  America: role of, 4–5, 42–43,
  49–50, 148, 149, 174–75, 186,
  187, 211–15, 228; colonial control of, 32, 147, 217–19,
  220–21; and New York tenant
  farmers riot (1766), 120, 153,
  193–94, 203, 207; use of foreign
  mercenaries by, 148, 150–51;
  constitutional restraints upon,
  186–87, 202–3, 220, 221,
  226–27, 230–34; and protection

167, 169; evolution of, 34–35,
43, 44, 47–48, 112, 148–49; and
20th-century American constitution, 135; applicability of to
the colonies, 160, 163–66, 169,
175, 206
Constitution, 19th-century
British: evolution of, 42, 44;
and use of military as police in
peacetime, 235–39
Constitution, 20th-century
American: and 18th-century
British constitution, 135
Constitutional ambiguities: effect
of on imperial law, 226
Constitutional custom: and
standing-army controversy,
160, 161, 164–65, 167; tests for,
161–62; and colonial governments, 164, 169, 217
Constitutional dilemma: and legal
restrictions on the military,
189–98 passim; and merger of
military with colonial civil government, 217–19
Constitutional grievances: redress
of, 128; and American whigs,
228–30
Constitutional innovation: fears of
and standing-army con-
troversy, 160–61; and colonial
rights, 162n
Constitutional methods: and colonial riots, 177–88
Constitutional principles and
theory: and governance of the
American colonies, 24; and accountability of crown and
ministers, 25–28; 17th-century

vs. 18th-century, 37–38, 172;
and standing-army con-
troversy, 156–71 passim; and
doctrine of consent, 168; parliamentary respect for, 218
Constitutional restraint: and
17th-century English vs. 18th-
century British constitution,
173–75; and British troops as
colonial police, 216–22, 226,
230–31
Constitutional rule: and control of
military by civil authority in
peacetime, 176–98 passim
Constitutional traditions: and opposition to arbitrary power,
28–31; and British military presence in North America,
148–56, 177–78, 179; and role
of military in Stamp Act crisis,
185–86. See also Standing-army
controversy: 17th-century English vs. 18th-century British
constitution
Constitutional values: theory vs.
practice, 217
Constitution of coercive force:
Lord North on, 230–32
Constitution of opinion and consent: Edmund Burke on, 230,
232–33
Continental Congress, First: and
opposition to standing army,
157, 158, 159, 160
Conway, Gen. Henry Seymour,
226; and Stamp Act crisis, 77,
185–86, 225; dismissal of,
141–42, 143n, 144–45, 147, 148
Cooper, Anthony Ashley. See

40, 43–44, 163–64, 166
Gordon, Lord George, 176n
Gordon, Thomas, 9, 125n, 126
Governors, colonial: authority of,
189, 193, 194–98, 203–5,
218–19, 220–21, 223–24,
231–32, commissions of, 203,
204; as magistrates, 203, 205,
232; rewards by to informers,
214. *See also* Customs commissioners, colonial: protection of
by British troops
Great Britain, government of. *See*
Crown, British; Ministry,
British; Lords, House of; Parliament, British
Greenleaf, Stephan, sheriff of Boston, 213
Grenada, West Indies: and military
enforcement of the Stamp Act,
76
Grenville, George, 142; and
standing-army controversy, 11;
and American military establishment, 51, 55, 56; ministry
of, 72; and Conway dismissal,
144–47
Guilford, Earl of. *See* North, Frederick
Gun laws, Boston, 206n
Guthrie, William, 143; quoted,
141

Habeas corpus: nonapplicability of
in the colonies, 164
Half pay: officers in British military establishment on, 58–59,
134
Halifax, Nova Scotia: British

troops sent to Boston from,
182, 200
Hamilton, Alexander, 99, 137n
Hampden, John, 3, 107
Hancock, John, 29, 79, 104
Hardwicke, 1st Earl of. *See*
Yorke, Philip
Hertford, Francis Seymour Conway, Earl of, and later Marquis
of, 142–43
Hicks, ——: arrested as spy on
Pennsylvania frontier, 188n
Hicks, William, 149
Hillsborough, Wills Hill, Earl of,
and later Marquis of Down-
shire, 182, 195, 211, 217, 221,
230; and British military presence in Boston, 14–15, 22, 36,
49, 114, 130–31, 165, 170–71,
174, 177–81, 199, 225–26; and
ministerial misrepresentations,
130; and customs commissioners, 200, 202n
Hinton, John Poulett, Viscount,
and later 2nd Earl Poulett, 86n,
91, 121
House of Commons. *See* Parliament, British
House of Lords. *See* Lords, House
of; Parliament, British
Howard, Rev. Simeon: quoted,
80, 106, 128, 134
Hume, David, 95
Hutchinson, Gov. Thomas, 215,
217, 225; charges against,
15–16; and taxation, 125; and
customs commissioners, 201,
202; authority of, 203–4, 205,
222–23; and use of military

and standing-army con-
troversy, 30, 110, 119; and John
Wilkes, 131
Military, British: half pay for
officers, 58–59, 134; as arm of
civil government, 128–29,
231–32, 235–39; as ministerial
servants, 134, 135–37
—as police in peacetime, 124, 130,
200, 230; opposition to, 28,
126–27; and arbitrary power of
ministry, 130–37; constitutionality of, 163, 172, 176–78,
231–32, 238–39; in civilian
riots, 173, 175, 235–38; restrictions on, 175–77, 202–5; inef-
fectiveness of, 232–33. See also
Army, British imperial, in
North America; Officers,
British military
Military Act. See Mutiny Act
Military establishment, American:
creation of, 10, 49–50, 68, 156,
157; size of, 49–50, 68–69,
152n; constitutional objections
to, 50, 52–54, 55–56, 68–71,
78–79; need for, 50–53, 56–57,
59, 66, 69, 73–76, 105, 178–82;
financing of by colonial taxation, 51, 54, 55–56, 66–70, 72;
and Indians, 52–53, 152n; and
violation of local autonomy,
54–55; as police force, 54, 57,
72–79, 107; and colonial officers
in, 56–57; composition of, 67;
cost of, 68–69; and Stamp Act
crisis, 69, 71; and religious freedom, 76; legal restrictions on,
189–98 passim. See also Army,

British imperial, in North
America
Military establishment, British:
enlisted veterans of, 57–58; size
of, 57, 60, 66, 86; cost of, 57,
61, 86; officers of on half pay,
58–59, 134; compared with
Irish military establishment, 60;
role of in North America
(1690), 74–75; foreign troops
in, 150–51
Military establishment, Irish:
officers of, 59–61, 62, 64;
British manipulation of, 59–62;
size of, 59–62, 86; compared
with British military establishment, 60; Irish enlisted men in,
61–62; as source of troops for
the colonies, 65, 66, 68, 78; as
model for American military establishment, 65, 70–71, 75; protection of Protestants by, 75
Militia: control of by crown, 30,
70, 81–82, 83–84; vs. standing
army, 101–6, 108, 126–27; opposition to, 108–9; and control
of smuggling, 111; colonial
legislatures' right to form, 162;
control of by parliament,
169–70; 19th-century distrust
of, 235–36
Militia laws, 114
Ministry, British: misrepresentations of and British military
presence in North America,
21–24, 26, 29–30, 130–32,
136–37; accountability of,
26–31, 101, 130–32, 133,
135–36, 169, 170, 189, 192; and

213–14; Council of, 196–97
Nobletown, New York: tenant
riot at (1766), 153
Nonimportation associations,
213, 215; and boycotts, 223n
Nonuse, doctrine of, 165. *See also*
Constitutional custom
North, Frederick, Lord North,
and later Earl of Guilford, 230–
32
Nova Scotia: and American mili-
tary establishment, 52, 76, 77

Officers, British military: on half
pay, 58–59, 134; commissions
of controlled by parliament,
139, 140–47; colonial lawsuits
against, 206–11; and American
tories, 219
Officials, civilian, in the colonies:
role of in riot control, 193–95,
199, 201, 203, 208–10, 215, 216,
220, 223–24. *See also* Magistrates, civil: colonial
Orford, 1st Earl of. *See* Walpole,
Sir Robert
Orford, 4th Earl of. *See* Walpole,
Horace
Otis, James, 14, 41, 70–71

Pacificus, 136
Paine, Thomas, 125n
Pardons of criminals: by the
crown, 115
Parliament, British: and
standing-army controversy, 4,
48–49, 82–83, 86, 88–89, 93,
137–47, 158–59; and creation of
American military establishment, 10, 49–50, 68, 156, 157,

179; elections for, 109; and use
of military as police in
peacetime, 118–19, 216–18,
230–33; and military commissions, 139–47
—supremacy of, 25n, 70, 116,
132, 175, 205; as constitutional
creator, 3, 8, 32–38, 88–89,
109, 216–18; and the colonies,
16–17, 25n, 29, 36–37, 124–25,
164, 166–69, 217, 230–34;
limitations on, 26, 36, 39,
40–42, 45; and control of the
military, 55, 82–83, 88, 91, 93,
140, 216–18; and control of the
militia, 81–82, 169–70, 239; and
control of finances and taxation,
88, 89, 91, 92, 124–25; and control of elections, 109; and government by ministry, 131,
148–49; and the crown, 132
Paxton Boys, 190
Penn, Gov. John, 208–9
Pennsylvania, Province of: and
American military establishment, 67; and civil control of
British troops, 188; frontiersmen of, 190–91, 210
Pennsylvania Assembly: and riot
statute, 190–91, 208–9
Pensacola: British troops in supported by colonial taxes, 68
Pensions, British: on the Irish establishment, 63, 64
Perceval, John, 2nd Earl of Eg-
mont, 43–44
Philadelphia: British troops at, 65;
riots in, 176; and protection of
Indians, 190–91, 208–9
Phillips, Capt.-Lt. Ralph, 195n

Right vs. power: and taxation of
the colonies by parliament,
124–25
Riot Act: and military as police in
peacetime, 118, 132; reading of,
189, 202–3, 206n; function of,
189–91, 208–9; and protection
of Pennsylvania Indians by
British troops, 190–91, 208–9;
as protection against lawsuits
for British military officers,
208–9
Riots, civilian: in the colonies, 20,
29–30, 120, 153, 176, 193–94,
195n, 199n, 203, 207, 226, 229;
in London, 23, 118–19, 173,
175, 233–34; provocation for
and suppression of, 112–19,
121–22, 130, 186–96 passim,
209, 213–15; class aspects of,
113–16; 19th-century attitudes
toward, 235–39. *See also* Mobs,
Boston; Mobs, British; Mobs,
colonial
Rising of '45: and standing-army
controversy, 9–10
Roman Catholics, Irish: and attacks on Irish Protestants, 75
Ruffhead, Owen: quoted, 57–58,
132

Sackville, Lord George, later Lord
Germain and 1st Viscount Sack-
ville of Drayton, 181
Saint-John, Oliver, 8
Schlosser, Capt. John, 208–9,
208n; quoted, 190
Schyler, Hermanus, 153
Scotland: and Rising of '45, 9–10;
and rights of under British con-

stitution, 55, 136; and
standing-army controversy, 84
Scott, Rev. James, 77–78
Search warrants, general, 141, 145
Self-defense, right of: and British
military presence in North
America, 207, 210, 216
Serle, Ambrose, 158–60
Sewall, Jonathan, 179n
Shaftesbury, Anthony Ashley
Cooper, 1st Earl of, 48–49, 84,
102
Shebbeare, John: quoted, 230
Shelburne, William Petty, 2nd
Earl of, and later 1st Marquis of
Lansdowne, 66, 173–74
Sheriffs, colonial: authority of in
suppressing riots, 120, 193n,
194, 202–3
Shipmoney tax, 46–47, 69
Shippen, William, 95, 98; quoted,
45
Smuggling: British compared
with colonial, 111
Solicitor generals, English: opin-
ions of on colonial constitu-
tional questions, 218n
Somers, John, Baron Somers of
Evesham, 87–88
Somerset, Charles Noel, 4th
Duke of Beaufort, 133, 139
Southwark, Borough of: and 1769
riots, 173. *See also* London:
riots in
Spanish colonies: as British pos-
sessions, 51
Spies, British: in colonies, 20,
188n
Stalker, Andrew, 153
Stamp Act, 3, 51, 67, 68; colonial